EMBEDDED SYSTEMS

AUTHOR (S)

Deepa M,
Susithra N,
Dr. G. Santhanamari

Department of Electronics and Communication,
PSG Institute of Technology and Applied Research,
Avinashi Road, Neelambur, Coimbatore,
Tamil Nadu, India.

REVIEWER

Dr. V. J. K. Kishore Sonti

Professor, School of Electrical and Electronics Engineering
Sathyabama Institute of Science and Technology,
Jeppiaar Nagar, Rajiv Gandhi Salai,
Chennai, Tamil Nadu, India

KHANNA BOOK PUBLISHING CO. (P) Ltd.
4C/4344, Ansari Road, Darya Ganj,
New Delhi, India

All India Council for Technical Education
Nelson Mandela Marg, Vasant Kunj,
New Delhi, India

Dear Readers,

To prevent the piracy, this book is secured with HIGH SECURITY HOLOGRAM on the front title cover. In case you don't find the hologram on the front cover title, please write us to at contact@khannabooks.com or whatsapp us at +91-99109 09320 and avail special gift voucher for yourself.

Specimen of Hologram on front Cover title:

Moreover, there is a SPECIAL DISCOUNT COUPON for you with EVERY HOLOGRAM.

How to avail this SPECIAL DISCOUNT:

Step 1: Scratch the hologram
Step 2: Under the scratch area, your "coupon code" is available
Step 3: Logon to www.khannabooks.com
Step 4: Use your "coupon code" in the shopping cart and get your copy at a special discount
Step 5: Enjoy your reading!

ISBN: 978-93-5538-469-0
Book Code: DIP494EN

Embedded Systems
by Deepa M, Susithra N and Dr. G. Santhanamari

First Edition: 2026

Originally Published by:
All India Council for Technical Education, Ministry of Education, GOI

Exclusively Published & Distributed by:
Khanna Book Publishing Co. (P) Ltd.
4C/4344, Ansari Road, Daryaganj,
New Delhi (INDIA)

Visit us at: **www.khannabooks.com**
Write us at: **contact@khannabooks.com**

To view complete list of books, Please scan the QR Code: KPH

Printed in Bharat.

प्रो. टी. जी. सीताराम
अध्यक्ष
Prof. T. G. Sitharam
Chairman

सत्यमेव जयते

आज़ादी का अमृत महोत्सव

अखिल भारतीय तकनीकी शिक्षा परिषद्
(भारत सरकार का एक सांविधिक निकाय)
(शिक्षा मंत्रालय, भारत सरकार)
नेल्सन मंडेला मार्ग, वसंत कुंज, नई दिल्ली–110070
दूरभाष : 011–26131498
ई–मेल : chairman@aicte-india.org

ALL INDIA COUNCIL FOR TECHNICAL EDUCATION
(A STATUTORY BODY OF THE GOVT. OF INDIA)
(Ministry of Education, Govt. of India)
Nelson Mandela Marg, Vasant Kunj, New Delhi-110070
Phone : 011-26131498
E-mail : chairman@aicte-india.org

FOREWORD

Engineers are the backbone of any modern society. They are the ones responsible for the marvels as well as the improved quality of life across the world. Engineers have driven humanity towards greater heights in a more evolved and unprecedented manner.

The All India Council for Technical Education (AICTE), have spared no efforts towards the strengthening of the technical education in the country. AICTE is always committed towards promoting quality Technical Education to make India a modern developed nation emphasizing on the overall welfare of mankind.

An array of initiatives has been taken by AICTE in last decade which have been accelerated now by the National Education Policy (NEP) 2020. The implementation of NEP under the visionary leadership of Hon'ble Prime Minister of India envisages the provision for education in regional languages to all, thereby ensuring that every graduate becomes competent enough and is in a position to contribute towards the national growth and development through innovation & entrepreneurship.

One of the spheres where AICTE had been relentlessly working since past couple of years is providing high quality original technical contents at Under Graduate & Diploma level prepared and translated by eminent educators in various Indian languages to its aspirants. For students pursuing 2nd year of their Engineering education, AICTE has identified 87 books, which shall be translated into 12 Indian languages - Hindi, Tamil, Gujarati, Odia, Bengali, Kannada, Urdu, Punjabi, Telugu, Marathi, Assamese & Malayalam. In addition to the English medium, books in different Indian Languages are going to support the students to understand the concepts in their respective mother tongue.

On behalf of AICTE, I express sincere gratitude to all distinguished authors, reviewers and translators from the renowned institutions of high repute for their admirable contribution in a record span of time.

AICTE is confident that these outcomes based original contents shall help aspirants to master the subject with comprehension and greater ease.

T. G. Sitharam

(Prof. T. G. Sitharam)

Acknowledgement

The authors are grateful to the authorities of AICTE, particularly Prof (Dr.) T G Sitharam, Chairman; Dr Abhay Jere, Vice-Chairman, Prof. Rajive Kumar, Member-Secretary, Dr Sunil Luthra, Director and Reena Sharma, Hindi Officer Training and Learning Bureau for their planning to publish the books on Embedded Systems.

Writing this book has been a dream come true, brought to life through a fortunate happenstance. Despite our many attempts over the years, it was a serendipitous series of events that finally made it possible. Our journey began with a shared passion for technology and a vision to demystify the complexities of embedded systems for students, enthusiasts, and professionals alike.

We express our profound gratitude to the Almighty for the wisdom, strength, and guidance. We thank our families, spouses and children for their unwavering support and patience. We would like to extend our sincere thanks to the reviewer Dr V J K Kishore Sonti, Professor Sathyabama Institute of Science and Technology, whose constructive criticism and insightfu suggestions helped refine and shape the units and the sub modules. His thorough reviews and thoughtful feedback were invaluable in enhancing the quality of this book.

We are indebted to the Management of PSG Institute of Technology and Applied Research Secretary Dr P V Mohanram, Principal Dr N Saravanakumar and Dr P Vijayakumar, Head o the Department of ECE for providing the resources and conducive environment needed fo conducting experiments and working on the book. We express our gratitude to our well-wishe and friend Dr P Reba for her immense encouragement, support and help in writing the book Finally, we want to express our deep appreciation to our readers. Your enthusiasm and engagement are what makes writing worthwhile. We hope this book resonates with you and sparks the same passion in you that it did in us while working on it.

This book is as much yours as it is ours. May this book inspire you to explore, learn, and innovate.

Deepa M
Susithra M
Dr. G. Santhanaman

Preface

Welcome to the fascinating realm of Embedded Systems! This book serves as an introduction to the fundamental concepts and practical applications of Embedded Systems programming, with a specific focus on utilizing the Arduino platform.

Embedded Systems are at the heart of countless modern technologies, from smart devices to industrial automation. This book aims to provide a structured approach to learning Embedded C programming for Arduino, along with essential knowledge of Arduino boards and communication interfaces.

We begin with an exploration of the basics of Embedded C programming in Unit I, tailored for Arduino. This unit covers foundational topics such as operators, sketch design in the Arduino IDE, serial communication interface, and essential operations for coding. The second unit focuses on control structures essential for programming embedded systems. Readers will learn looping mechanisms (for, do, while) and branching operations based on conditional expressions, enabling them to control the flow of code execution effectively. In unit III, we delve deeper into the capabilities of the Arduino Mega board, a versatile microcontroller board with expanded capabilities. Topics include Arduino Mega specifications, differences between standard C language and Embedded C, and an exploration of ports, pins, and digital/analog peripherals unique to the Arduino Mega platform. In the final unit, we explore various communication modules compatible with Arduino for real-life applications. Readers will gain insights into different communication modules and I/O devices, enabling them to establish reliable connections with Arduino for data exchange.

This book is specifically designed to suit the different maturity levels of students by emphasizing ‘learning by doing’. Each unit is structured with clear explanations, practical examples, and hands-on exercises to reinforce application-based experiential learning. Readers are encouraged to write and experiment with code independently before referring to provided solutions. Additional functionalities can be added to enhance the programs, fostering creativity and deeper understanding. With a blend of theoretical insights and hands-on practical exercises, readers will emerge equipped to tackle diverse embedded systems challenges with confidence and proficiency.

The structured approach aims to provide a foundational understanding of Embedded Systems programming with Arduino, catering to the educational needs and skill development of aspiring electronics and engineering professionals at the diploma level. The contents are prepared as per the latest model curriculum of All India Council for Technical Education (AICTE) for the students pursuing Diploma. The inclusion of concepts and analogies from the Indian Knowledge System (IKS) offers a unique perspective with traditional wisdom and innovative approaches that resonate with our cultural heritage.

We hope this book sparks your interest in Embedded Systems and inspires you to explore further in this exciting field. Embedded Systems Programming with Arduino opens doors to endless possibilities, and we trust that you will find joy and satisfaction in developing practical applications through the carefully-crafted examples and illustrations presented in this book.

Happy learning, and may you embark on an exhilarating journey together into the realm of Embedded Systems!

If you have any feedback to improve the book, feel free to write to the authors directly.

Best regards,

Deepa M
Susithra N
Dr. G. Santhanamar

Outcome Based Education

For the implementation of an outcome based education the first requirement is to develop an outcome based curriculum and incorporate an outcome based assessment in the education system. By going through outcome based assessments, evaluators will be able to evaluate whether the students have achieved the outlined standard, specific and measurable outcomes. With the proper incorporation of outcome based education there will be a definite commitment to achieve a minimum standard for all learners without giving up at any level. At the end of the programme running with the aid of outcome based education, a student will be able to arrive at the following outcomes:

Programme Outcomes (POs) are statements that describe what students are expected to know and be able to do upon graduating from the program. These relate to the skills, knowledge, analytical ability, attitude and behavior that students acquire through the program. The POs essentially indicate what the students can do from subject-wise knowledge acquired by them during the program. As such, POs define the professional profile of an engineering diploma graduate.

National Board of Accreditation (NBA) has defined the following seven POs for an Engineering diploma graduate:

PO1. Basic and Discipline specific knowledge: Apply knowledge of basic mathematics, science and engineering fundamentals and engineering specialization to solve the engineering problems.

PO2. Problem analysis: Identify and analyses well-defined engineering problems using codified standard methods.

PO3. Design/ development of solutions: Design solutions for well-defined technical problems and assist with the design of systems components or processes to meet specified needs.

PO4. Engineering Tools, Experimentation and Testing: Apply modern engineering tools and appropriate technique to conduct standard tests and measurements.

PO5. Engineering practices for society, sustainability and environment: Apply appropriate technology in context of society, sustainability, environment and ethical practices.

PO6. Project Management: Use engineering management principles individually, as a team member or a leader to manage projects and effectively communicate about well- defined engineering activities.

PO7. Life-long learning: Ability to analyse individual needs and engage in updating in the context of technological changes.

Course Outcomes

By the end of the course, the students will be able to:

CO-1: Understand the fundamentals of Embedded C for Arduino programming

CO-2: Familiarize with the Arduino IDE and establish communication with the Arduino board

CO-3: Utilize control structures and looping mechanisms in Embedded C programming for control applications based on specified conditions.

CO-4: Demonstrate an understanding of Arduino Mega's specifications and its peripherals

CO-5: Interface I/O devices and integrate appropriate communication modules for real-world applications

Mapping of Course Outcomes with Programme Outcomes to be done according to the matrix is given below:

Course Outcomes	Expected Mapping with Programme Outcomes *(1- Weak Correlation; 2- Medium correlation; 3- Strong Correlation)*						
	PO-1	PO-2	PO-3	PO-4	PO-5	PO-6	PO-7
CO-1	3	1	1	2	-	-	-
CO-2	3	1	1	3	-	-	-
CO-3	3	2	2	3	-	-	-
CO-4	3	1	1	2	-	-	-
CO-5	3	3	3	3	2	1	-

Guidelines for Teachers

To implement Outcome Based Education (OBE) the knowledge level and skill set of the students should be enhanced. Teachers should take a major responsibility for the proper implementation of OBE. Some of the responsibilities (not limited to) for the teachers in OBE system may be as follows:

- Within reasonable constraints, they should manipulate time to the best advantage of all students.
- They should assess the students only upon certain defined criterion without considering any other potential ineligibility to discriminate against them.
- They should try to grow the learning abilities of the students to a certain level before they leave the institute.
- They should try to ensure that all the students are equipped with quality knowledge as well as competence after they finish their education.
- They should always encourage the students to develop their ultimate performance capabilities.
- They should facilitate and encourage group work and team work to consolidate newer approaches.
- They should follow Bloom's taxonomy in every part of the assessment.

Bloom's Taxonomy

Level	Teacher should Check	Student should be able to	Possible Mode of Assessment
Create	Students ability to create	Design or Create	Mini project
Evaluate	Students ability to justify	Argue or Defend	Assignment
Analyse	Students ability to distinguish	Differentiate or Distinguish	Project/Lab Methodology
Apply	Students ability to use information	Operate or Demonstrate	Technical Presentation/ Demonstration
Understand	Students ability to explain the ideas	Explain or Classify	Presentation/Seminar
Remember	Students ability to recall (or remember)	Define or Recall	Quiz

Guidelines for Students

Students should take equal responsibility for implementing the OBE. Some of the responsibilities (not limited to) for the students in OBE system are as follows:

- Students should be well aware of each UO before the start of a unit in each and every course.
- Students should be well aware of each CO before the start of the course.
- Students should be well aware of each PO before the start of the programme.
- Students should think critically and reasonably with proper reflection and action.
- Learning of the students should be connected and integrated with practical and real life consequences.
- Students should be well aware of their competency at every level of OBE.

Abbreviations

List of Abbreviations

Abbreviations	Full form
IDE	Integrated Development Environment
GUI	Graphic User Interface
IKS	Indian Knowledge System
RTOS	Real-Time Operating System
USB	Universal Serial Bus
SPI	Serial Peripheral Interface
I2C	Inter-Integrated Circuit
UART	Universal Asynchronous Receiver-Transmitter
ROM	Read Only Memory
RAM	Random Access Memory
EEPROM	Electrically Erasable Programmable Read-Only Memory
OS	Operating system
COM port	Communication port
PWM	Pulse Width Modulation
MIPS	Million Instructions Per Second
RTS	Ready to Send
CTS	Clear to Send
SMCR	Sleep Mode Control Register
SE	Sleep Enable
ADC	Analog-to-Digital Converter
I/O	Input/Output
RX	Receive
TX	Transmit
MISO	Master In Slave Out
SCK	Serial Clock
MOSI	Master Out Slave In

Abbreviations	Full form
SS	Slave Select
SDA	Serial Data Line
SCL	Serial Clock Line
ICSP	In-Circuit Serial Programming
LED	Light Emitting Diodes
LCD	Liquid Crystal Display
IR	Infrared
MSB	Most Significant Bit
LSB	Least Significant Bit
OLED	Organic Light-Emitting Diode

List of Figures

List of Tables

Table of Contents

1 Embedded C Basics and Operators for Arduino

Unit Specifics

This Unit emphasizes the following aspects:

- Features of Arduino IDE.
- Sketch designing for Arduino
- Communication interface using serial port
- Basic understanding of the code with Boolean operations, pointer access operations, bitwise operations, and compounded operations.

IKS Insights

This section explores how concepts from Indian Knowledge Systems (IKS) align with and enrich contemporary practices and technologies.

Vasudhaiva Kutumbakam - Cohesive Integration

The beauty of Indian Philosophy, particularly its teachings on societal living, has served as a vital inspiration to the world. Central to this is the concept of "Vasudhaiva Kutumbakam". It originates from the Maha Upanishad and translates to "The World is One Family". This philosophy was also the theme of India's G20 Presidency in 2023. An analogy can be drawn to the Integrated Development Environment (IDE) of Arduino Embedded Systems. The characteristics of a typical embedded unit—such as oneness, coherence, and proper interfacing—reflect the spirit of unity and collaboration needed to achieve desired outcomes.

Rationale

This Unit delves into the essential aspects of Arduino programming, providing readers with a comprehensive understanding of foundational concepts. The primary goal is to equip beginners with the skills and knowledge required to confidently create and understand Arduino sketches. Starting from the introduction to Arduino Integrated Development Environment (IDE), by the end of this Section, readers will feel comfortable navigating the IDE and utilizing its features for sketch development. Next, the focus is on the process of sketch design. This includes understanding the structure of an Arduino sketch, the use of setup() and loop() functions, and best practices for organizing code. The readers are guided through writing their first sketch, emphasizing clarity and simplicity in programming. Further, Communication with the Arduino via a serial port is fundamental for interacting with sensors, displays, or other devices. In this Unit, readers learn to establish serial communication between their Arduino board and a computer system. The procedure for sending and receiving data are covered, which is crucial for debugging and interfacing with external systems. The various operations are explored with practical examples and exercises. Through this comprehensive Unit, readers will gain a solid foundation in Arduino programming. By the end of this Unit, students will have acquired the skills required to write and comprehend Arduino sketches, establish communication with external devices, and utilize fundamental programming techniques to develop projects. This Unit lays the groundwork for further exploration into the exciting world of Arduino development.

Prerequisites

- Basic programming knowledge (preferably C)
- Foundation of Digital Principles
- Understanding the architecture of microprocessors

Unit Outcomes

At the end of this Unit, students will be able to

U1-O1: Navigate and utilize the features of Arduino IDE.

U1-O2: Understand the structure of sketch and write simple programs using different operators

U1-O3: Establish serial communication between the Arduino board and the computer

UO - CO Mapping

Course Outcomes	Expected Mapping with Programme Outcomes (1- Weak Correlation; 2- Medium correlation; 3- Strong Correlation)				
	CO-1	CO-2	CO-3	CO-4	CO-5
U1-O1	2	3	2	1	1
U1-O2	2	3	1	1	1
U1-O3	1	3	1	2	2

1.1 Introduction to Embedded Systems

A system is a collection of physical components connected together to perform a specific task or function. A system processes the input provided by the user to provide a meaningful output as depicted in Fig. 1.1. The mapping function (system) transforms (processes) the input from the user into another useful form, output. Systems are everywhere around us, from the human body (with its organs working together) to a car (with its engine, wheels, and other parts).

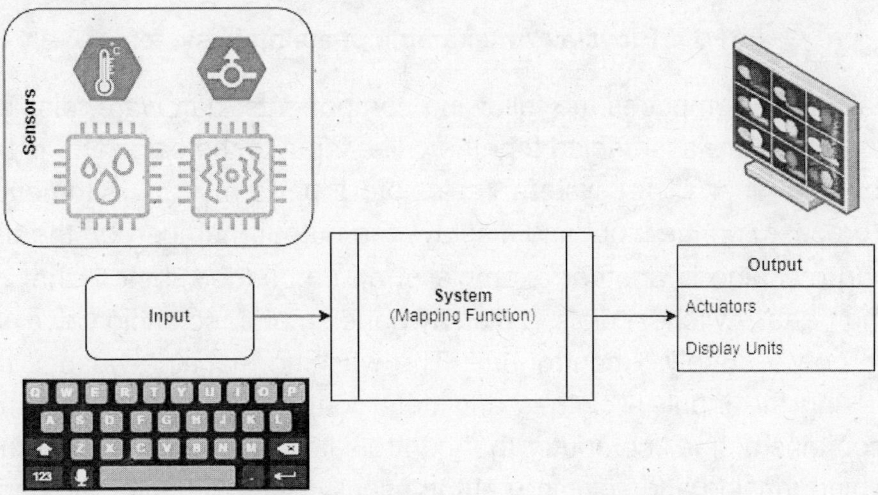

Fig. 1.1 System - A typical structure

A bicycle is a great example of a system because it is made up of several interconnected parts (such as frame, wheels, tyres, pedals, chain, handlebar and brakes) that work together to perform a specific task, i.e., transportation. Each component plays a specific function within the bicycle system. However, if any part of the system malfunctions or is used incorrectly, it can affect performance and safety while cycling.

What is an Embedded System? What makes an embedded system unique is that they are designed for a specific purpose and often have limited resources like memory and processing power. It has computer hardware with integrated software. Examples of an embedded system include as simple as a calculator (as shown in Fig. 1.3 (a)) to complex systems like industrial robots.

Fig. 1.2 Bicycle - An example of a simple system

A typical calculator comprises the following components: hardware, display, battery, and chassis, which are assembled together. The input to the calculator is the number provided by the user. The system (calculator) performs an arithmetic/algebraic operation (process) on the input and displays the output (number) on the display unit. The washing machine is another example of an embedded system that consists of the following parts: switches, dials, a display panel, motor, solenoid valve, water level sensor and power supply & control unit. The washing machine washes the clothes (process) using the inputs - clothes and detergent and produces clean clothes as output. It contains a small computer that controls its operation and performs specific tasks (washing, rinsing and spinning) automatically. The computer (tiny brain) inside the machine manages everything from water intake to spinning. Nowadays, fuzzy logic allows washing machines to make intelligent and adaptive decisions to optimally use the water and detergent, based on the weight of the laundry, fabric type and stain level.

(a) (b)

Fig. 1.3 Examples of embedded system (a) Calculator (b) Washing machine

Embedded systems are specialized computers integrated into devices to perform dedicated functions within real-time constraints, crucial in domains like automotive safety, medical devices, and industrial control. They range from simple task-specific devices like calculators to complex systems with Graphic User Interfaces (GUI) like the modern car infotainment system. Embedded systems utilize Real-Time Operating Systems (RTOS) and communicate with hardware through ports (like Serial Port, Universal Serial Bus (USB) Port, Ethernet Port, and SPI (Serial Peripheral Interface) Port, often transmitting data to other embedded systems via protocols (like SPI, Inter-Integrated Circuit (I2C), Universal Asynchronous Receiver-Transmitter (UART for serial ports) and Ethernet (TCP/IP)).

1.1.1 Embedded System - Characteristics

Typically, embedded systems are low-cost, low-power, and compact, consisting of a processor, memory, and communication ports, executing highly specific software tailored to their function. Fig. 1.4 outlines the major characteristics of an embedded system.

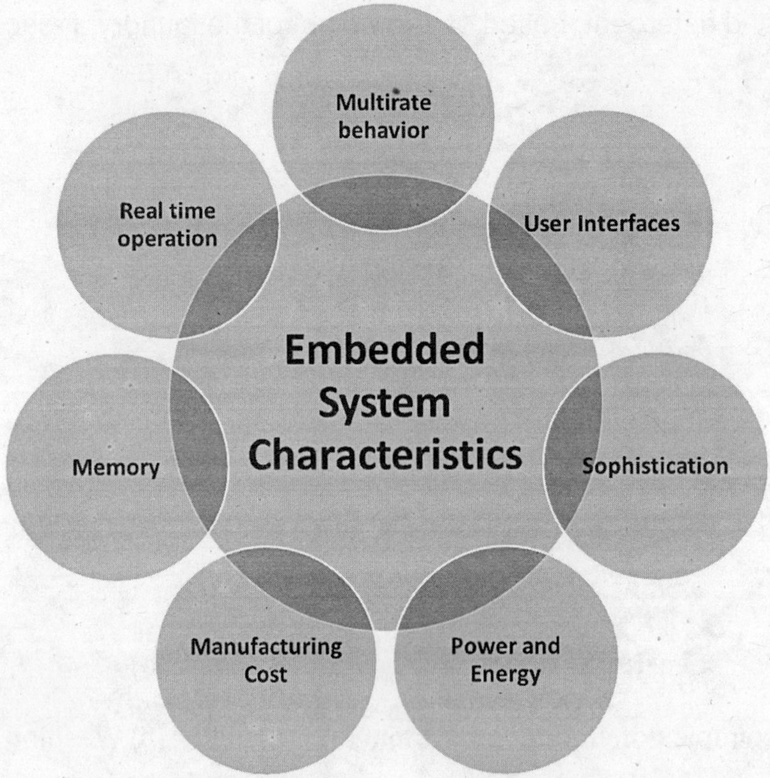

Fig. 1.4 Characteristics of an Embedded System

1. **Real time operation:** Most systems perform in real-time in domestic and industrial environments. For instance, the microwave oven is a widely used kitchen appliance. Similarly, an embedded system that controls robotic arms in an assembly line of a manufacturing plant is a real time example.
2. **Multirate behaviour:** They can simultaneously manage operations running at different speeds. Multimedia applications exemplify this multirate behaviour. In a multimedia stream, audio and video components operate at varying rates, but they must remain perfectly synchronized. If either the audio or video lags behind, it ruins the whole experience for the viewer.
3. **User Interfaces:** Embedded systems are capable of controlling complex user interfaces, which may feature numerous options and multiple menus. A prime example is the dynamic maps used in GPS (Global Positioning System) navigation systems in mobile phones and automobiles.

4. **Sophistication:** An embedded system is capable of performing even sophisticated applications involving complex algorithms. For example, the microprocessor, also known as the engine control unit in this context, performs complex filtering functions that optimize the car's performance. This is done by making real-time decisions to adjust various engine parameters including the amount of fuel to inject into the engine cylinders for efficient combustion, ignition timing, and air-fuel ratio. This helps in optimizing automobile performance to minimize fuel consumption and pollution.
5. **Power and Energy:** Power consumption directly impacts hardware costs, while energy consumption influences battery life, which is important, especially in IoT-based real-time applications. Smartwatches are designed to carry out specific tasks efficiently, thereby resulting in longer battery life compared to smartphones, which have more features and higher power consumption. So, while both devices may require batteries, smartwatches can often last longer on a single charge due to their optimized functionality and lower power consumption for their intended tasks.
6. **Manufacturing Cost:** The manufacturing cost depends on various factors such as the type of microcontroller used, the amount of memory required, and the types of I/O (Input/Output) devices interfaced.
7. **Memory:** In an embedded system, memory determines the ability of a system to store and access instructions and data. For example, in a digital camera, the operating system, camera settings and built-in features are saved in ROM (Read only memory), Random Access Memory (RAM) is a temporary image storage and working space, EEPROM ((Electrically Erasable Programmable Read-Only Memory) stores user preferences and settings and Flash memory is the external memory card where photos and videos are stored. These also determine speed and power requirements.

1.2 Familiarizing with the Arduino IDE

An Integrated Development Environment (IDE) is a comprehensive software platform or code editing, building, testing, and packaging for different hardware boards. Fig. .5 shows a typical structure of an Arduino IDE.

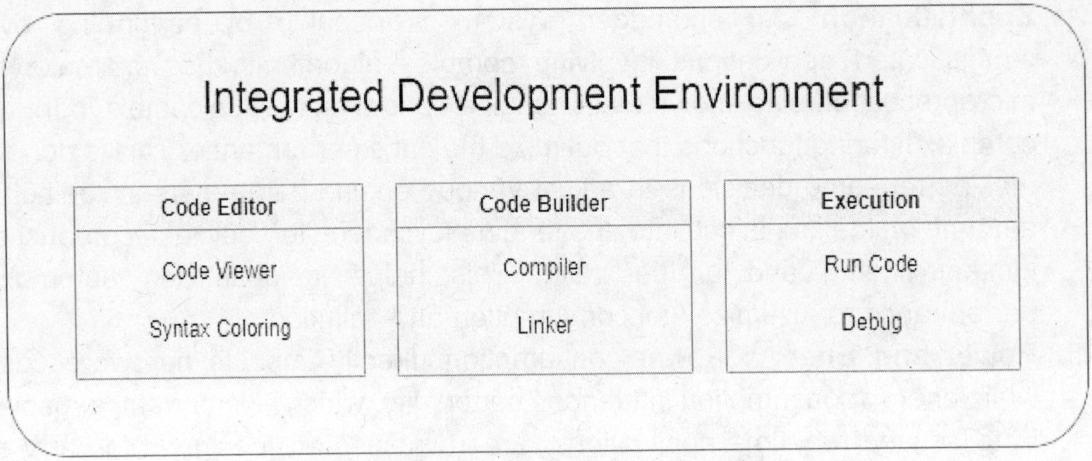

Fig. 1.5 Structure of Arduino IDE

The Arduino IDE is an open-source software application designed to program and upload code to Arduino microcontroller boards. The IDE offers a user-friendly interface to write, edit, and debug code, as well as to manage libraries and upload codes onto various Arduino boards. This IDE primarily supports programming in a dialect of C and C++, making it easy for both entry-level and expert developers.

The Arduino IDE typically combines several essential tools such as editor, compiler, and basic debugging tools into a unified environment to facilitate software and hardware project development in one cohesive platform. The steps involved in the use of Arduino IDE are shown in Fig. 1.6.

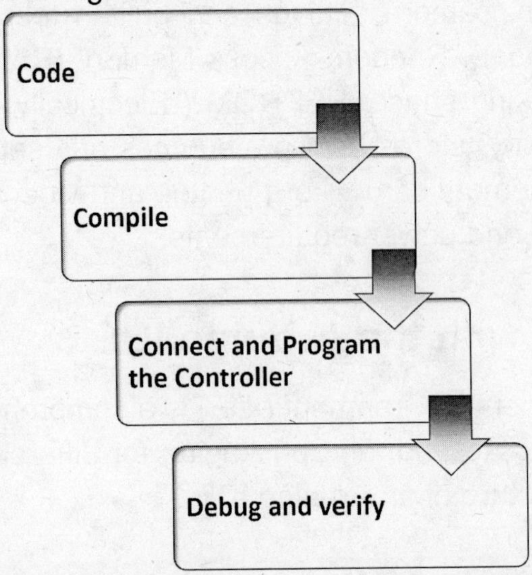

Fig. 1.6 Steps in the use of Arduino IDE

The various steps involved in the use of the Arduino IDE, or any IDE are:

a. **Writing the Code:** Developers write the Arduino program in the code editor which provides features like automatic indentation and syntax highlighting, which simplify the process of writing code.
b. **Compiling the Code:** The compiler converts the high-level Arduino code written by developers into machine-readable code that the microcontroller can execute. The compilation process checks for syntax errors and generates the necessary machine code in the form of binary files (.hex or .bin) for uploading to the Arduino board.
c. **Connecting the Controller:** The connection between the Arduino board and the computer is established through a USB interface.
d. **Programming the Controller:** Load the compiled code (in .hex or .bin format) onto the controller - "burning" or "dumping" the code into the memory.
e. **Debugging and verification:** It is essential to test the code for its functionality. The Arduino IDE offers basic debugging functionalities. Developers can use a serial monitor for printing debug messages to the serial console, which helps in tracking program flow and identifying issues during runtime. This is explained with an example in Section 1.5.

Know More

Embedded C is an upgraded version of the C programming language customized for developing embedded systems including Arduino based applications.

1.2.1 Arduino IDE - Installation Procedure

In order to install Arduino IDE, download the typical version of Arduino IDE from https://www.arduino.cc/en/software (Arduino IDE 2.2.1).

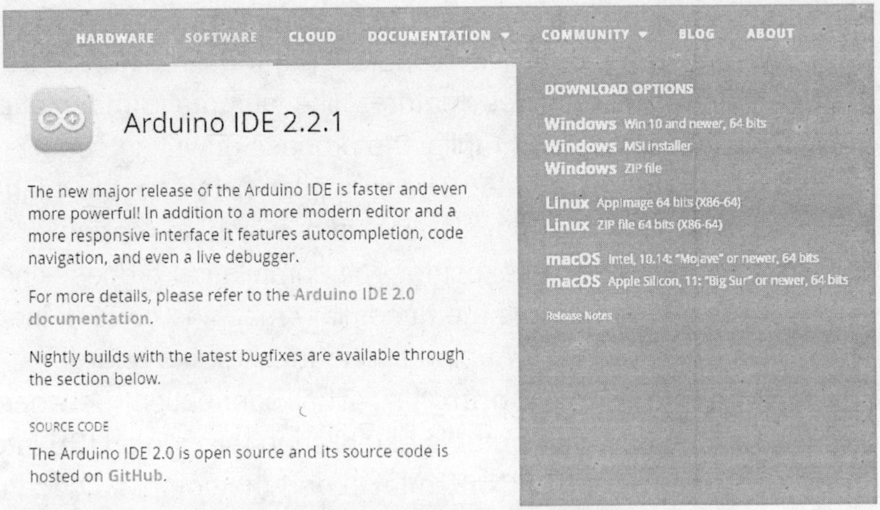

Fig. 1.7 Download the typical version of Arduino from the website

Select the download option based on the Operating system (OS) of your computer and download the IDE (Windows Win 10 and newer, 64 bits). Click on the Just Download button as shown in Fig. 1.8.

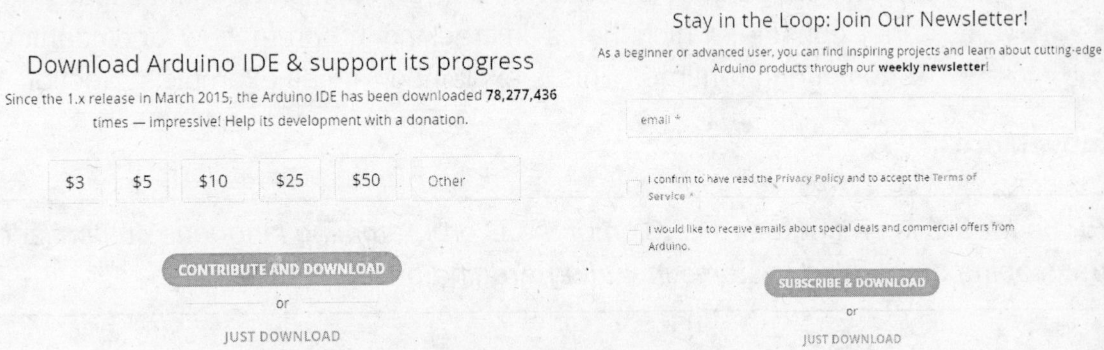

Fig. 1.8 Click Just Download

In this book, Windows Operating System (OS) is considered for installation and projec development. Once the executable file is downloaded (arduino ide_2.2.1_Windows_64bit.exe), double click on the executable file and the Arduinc IDE Setup window will appear as shown in Fig. 1.9. Click on the button 'I Agree situated at the bottom of the window.

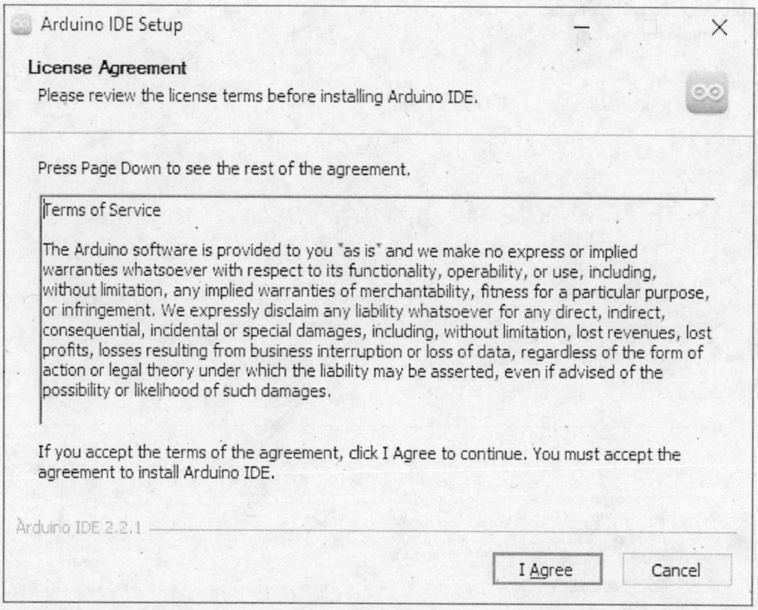

Fig. 1.9 Installation pop-up after running the downloaded executable file

Click on the Next button and leave the Install location as provided and click on the Install button at the bottom of the window as shown in Fig. 1.10.

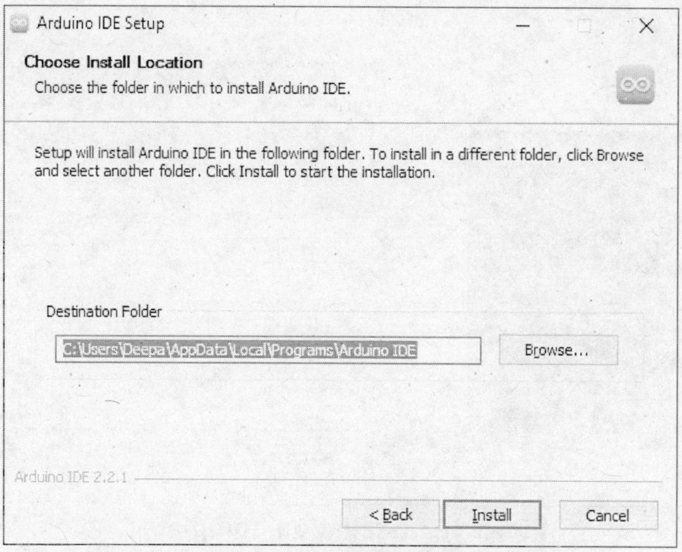

Fig. 1.10 Choose Installation Location

The progress of the installation will appear as shown in Fig. 1.11. Wait until the Arduino IDE is successfully installed as shown in Fig. 1.12.

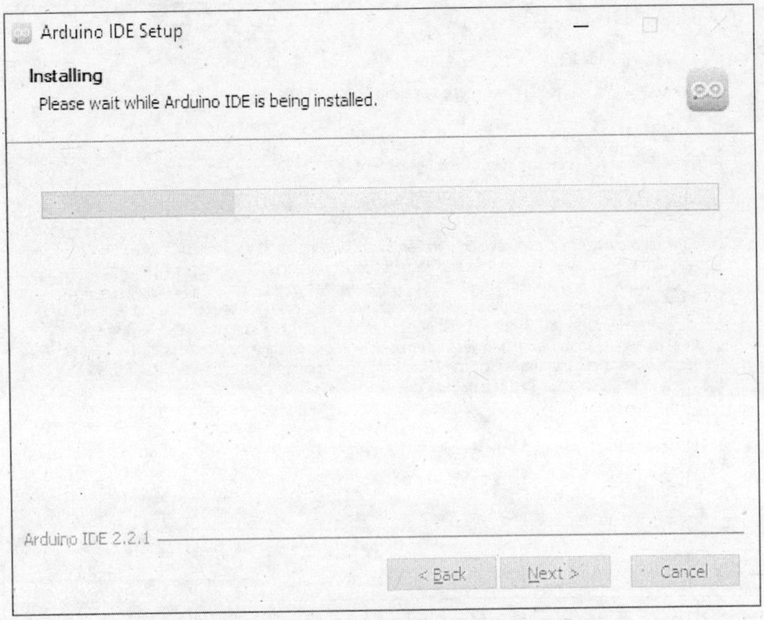

Fig. 1.11 Installation in progress

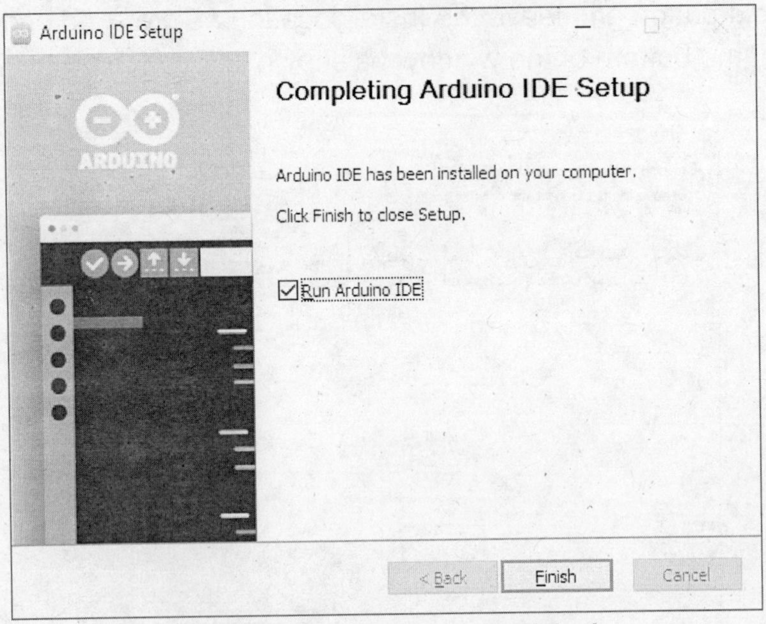

Fig. 1.12 Installation completed

Click the Finish button to complete the installation and launch the Arduino IDE. Now you are all set to explore the features of Arduino IDE.

1.2.2 Exploring the Arduino IDE

When the Arduino IDE is run, a Graphic User Interface (GUI) window appears as shown in Fig. 1.13.

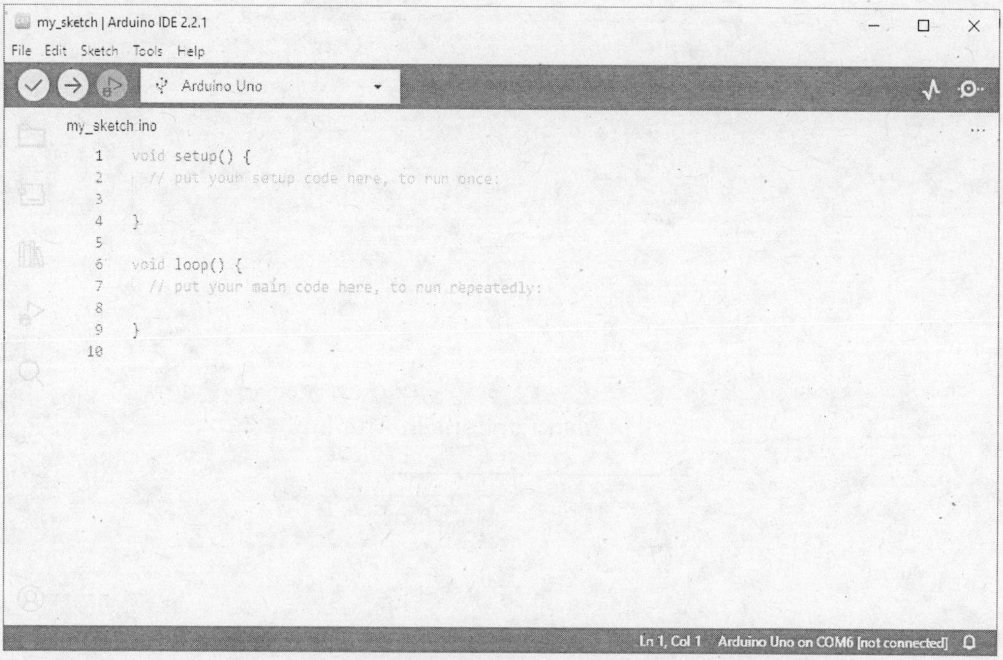

Fig. 1.13 Landing Window in Arduino IDE

The window that appears is the code editor window used to create an Arduino sketch file with the extension '.ino'. The programs written in Arduino IDE are saved in sketch files. By default, the sketch usually consists of two functions namely setup and loop and it is saved as an 'ino' file.

Note: A main function is mandatory in all C/C++ codes. An Arduino program must possess setup() and loop() functions as default functions.

Let us explore some of the menu options available in Arduino IDE.

1.2.2.1 File Menu

This menu provides the options listed as shown in Fig. 1.14. Click on File Menu -> New Sketch to write a new program. Similarly, there are options to open existing sketch files/ recent sketch files. Save and save as options are also available in the

File menu to save the sketch at a preferred location in the drive. Example codes have also been provided under the File Menu as shown in Fig. 1.15.

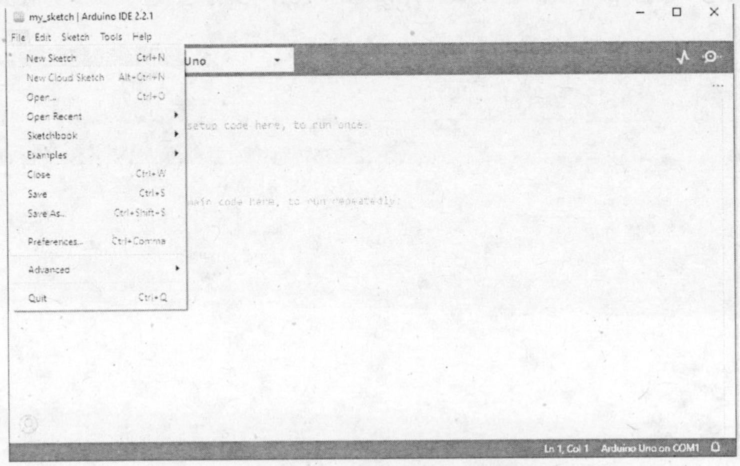

Fig. 1.14 Menu options in Arduino

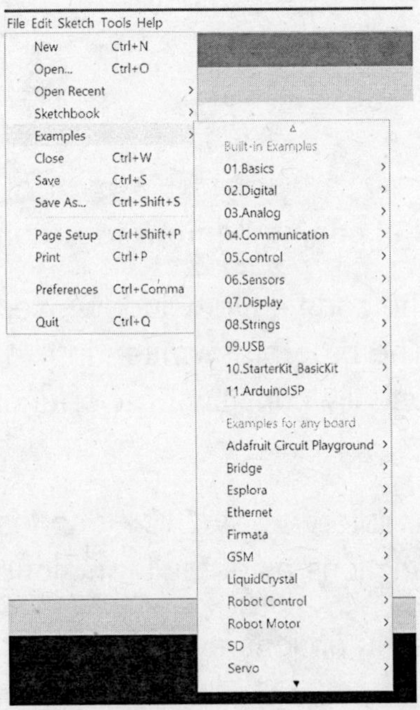

Fig. 1.15 Arduino Examples in File Menu

1.2.2.2 Sketch Menu

Once the program is written, it can be compiled using the 'Verify/Compile' option available under the Sketch Menu as shown in Fig. 1.16. This option checks the syntax of the code and compiles it into machine-readable instructions which can be comprehended by the microcontroller embedded on the Arduino board. 'Ctrl + R' is a shortcut key combination to perform compiling. During the compilation, the IDE window appears as shown in Fig. 1.17.

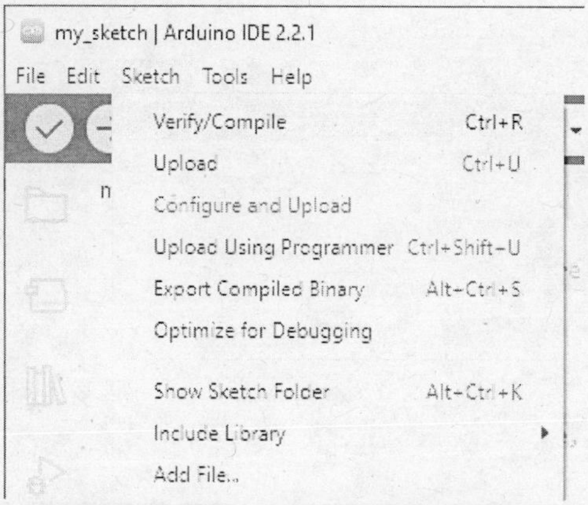

Fig. 1.16 Compiling the sketch

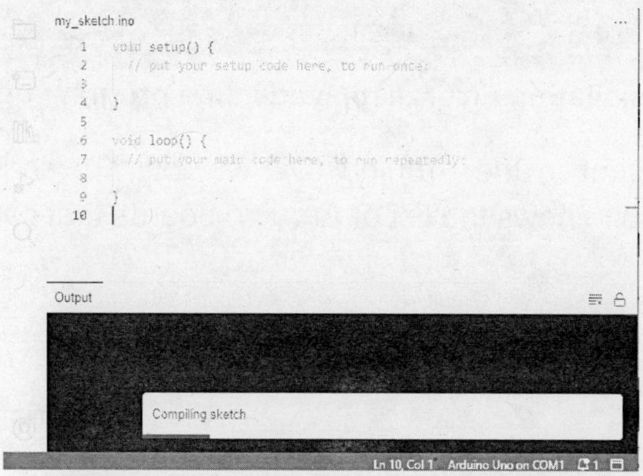

Fig. 1.17 Compilation in progress

Once the compilation is completed successfully without any error, the output screen will be displayed as shown in Fig. 1.18. The output screen will display the errors if any during the compilation process as shown in Fig. 1.19.

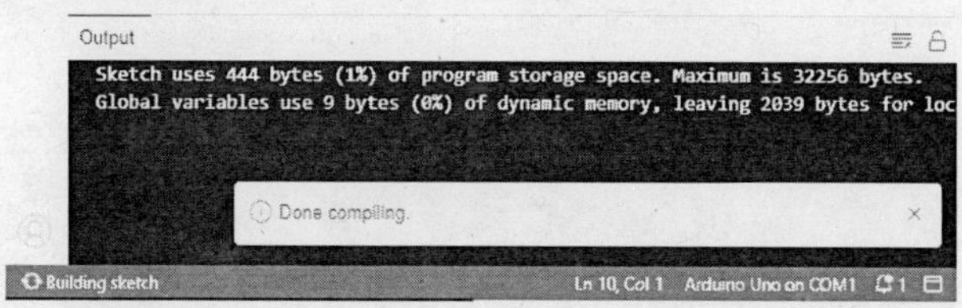

Fig. 1.18 Compilation successful without errors

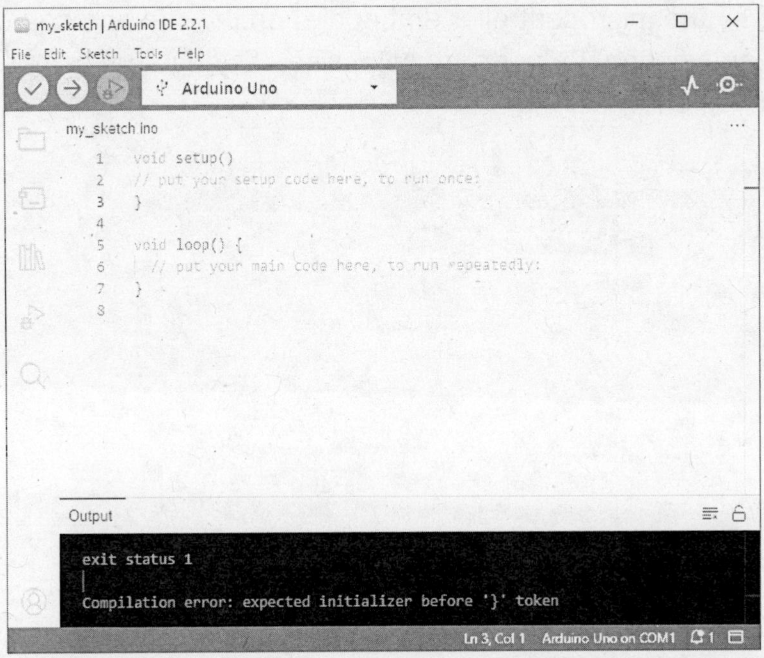

Fig. 1.19 Compilation Error displayed in the program output window

The basic icons present in the Arduino IDE window are shown in Fig. 1.20. The Arduino board selection shows the list of Arduino boards that can be connected to the IDE.

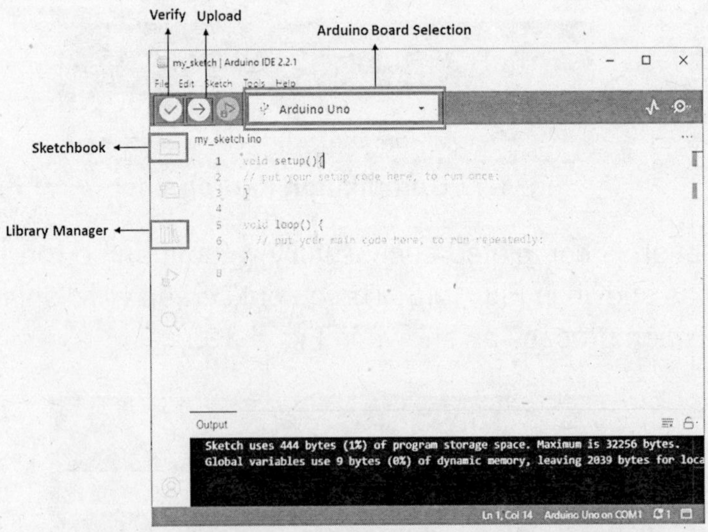

Fig. 1.20 Major Icons in the Arduino IDE

1.3 Sketch Designing for Arduino

Let us start writing our first program in C language for Arduino.

1.3.1 C Programming for Arduino

The Arduino IDE employs a customized version of the C language for programming Arduino boards. Additionally, the IDE provides libraries and features specifically designed to support Arduino boards and other compatible devices.

1.3.1.1 Parts of the Sketch

A function is a self-contained segment of code created to perform a particular task or operation. Functions help organize code into reusable modules, enhancing the manageability and maintainability of large programs. Arduino processes instructions sequentially, one at a time, and can execute only one task at a time. When Arduino encounters a function call in the program, it executes the function's code line by line before returning to the main program (calling function).

In the context of Arduino programming, functions play a crucial role in structuring code and separating different tasks. There are two main types of functions commonly used in Arduino sketches:

a. **Built-in Functions:** These are functions provided by the Arduino environment or libraries that perform specific tasks. For example, *digitalRead(), digitalWrite(), analogRead(),* and *analogWrite()* are built-in functions used to read from and write to digital and analog pins on the Arduino board. These functions will be explored in detail in Unit 3.
b. **Default functions:** In Arduino, by default, the setup() function is executed first and then the Loop() function will be executed.

   Setup() - This function is executed only once when a sketch starts after powering the Arduino board. It is used to initialize and set initial values to variables.

   Loop() - The loop function executes repeatedly until the Arduino board is powered OFF. The code inside the loop() runs continuously.
c. **User-defined Functions:** These functions are created by the user to encapsulate specific operations or tasks. User-defined functions allow programmers to

modularize their code and improve readability. They can be called from within the default functions or other user defined functions.

1.4 Board and Port Selection

The connection between the Arduino board and the computer is established through the COM port. COM port is otherwise called the Communication port or the serial port. It acts as an interface between the computer and other peripherals like printers, modems and other boards.

The following sections and the forthcoming units will use the Arduino Mega board for demonstration purposes. However, the procedure and code snippets are applicable to any Arduino board like the Uno board which is also popularly used for prototyping. It is to be noted that the pin configurations change with respect to the development board of choice, and the same can be obtained from the respective component datasheets.

1.4.1 Connecting the Arduino Board to the USB Port

The Arduino Mega board (shown in Fig. 1.21 a) is connected to the computer using the USB cable (shown in Fig. 1.21 b).

a) b)

Fig. 1.21 a) Arduino Mega Board b) Connector for Arduino board

Once the connection is made, the COM port where the board is connected can be identified from the Device Manager as shown in Figure 1.22.

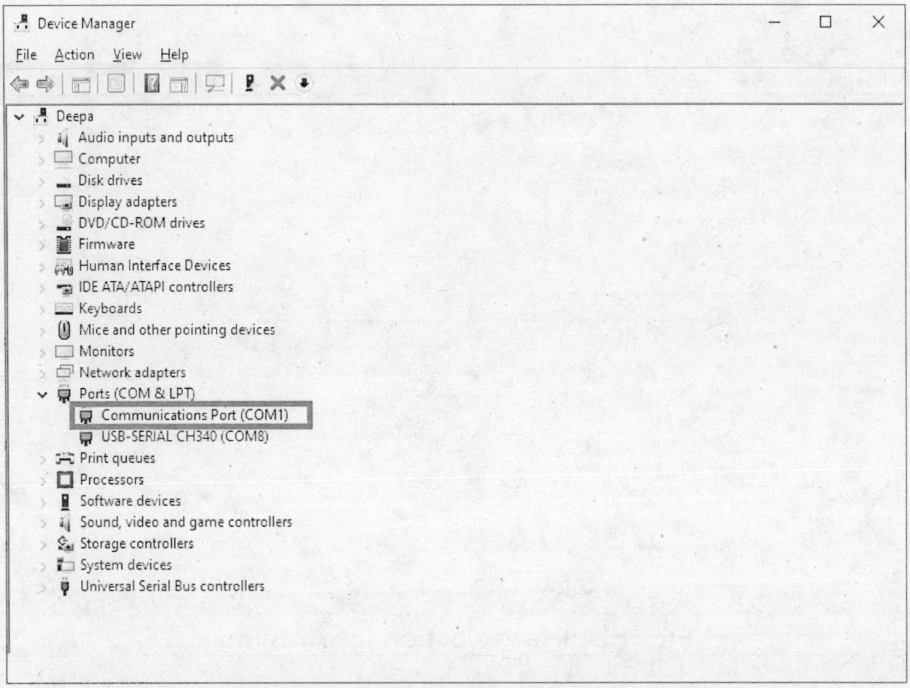

Fig. 1.22 Device Manager displaying the name of the COM port

The COM Port and the Board selection can be done from the Tools menu as shown in Fig. 1.24 and Fig. 1.23 respectively.

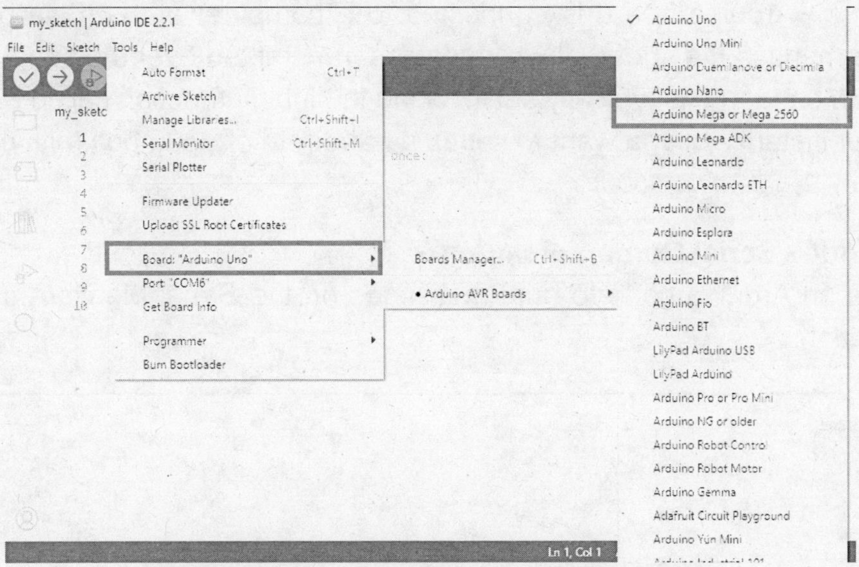

Fig. 1.23 Board Selection for Arduino Mega

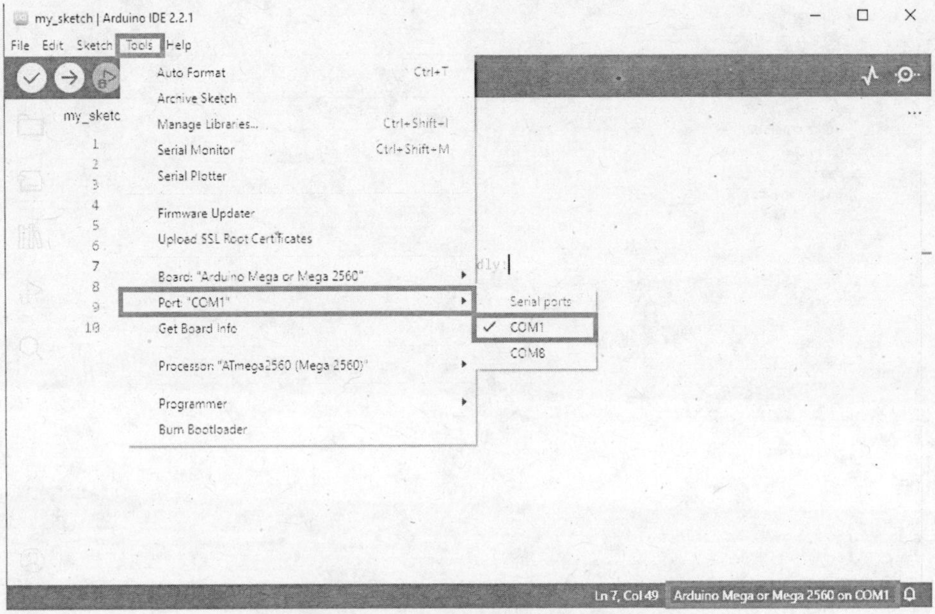

Fig. 1.24 Port selection for Arduino

1.5 Communication Interface using Serial Port

Let us perform a simple communication with an Arduino board through Serial Monitor. The serial communication is initialized in the setup function by setting up the baud rate. When an Arduino board is connected to a computer via USB, a baud rate is specified to mention the speed at which data is transmitted over the serial connection channel. The baud rate is typically set invoking the inbuilt function called *Serial.begin()* function. For instance, if you want to set up a baud rate of 9600 bps (bits per second), you can use: *Serial.begin(9600).*

Arduino Code - Serial Communication

Let us write an Arduino code to print messages on the Serial Monitor through serial communication.

```
void setup() {
  // Start serial communication at 9600 baud rate
  Serial.begin(9600);

  // Wait for the serial port to open
```

```
  while (!Serial) {
    ;
  // Waiting for the serial port connection.
  }
  // Send a welcome message to the Serial Monitor
  Serial.print("Hello ");
  Serial.println("Welcome to Arduino Serial Communication!");
  }
void loop() {
  // Print a message asking the user to type the text
  Serial.println("Enter a message:");

  // Wait until the user enters data in the Serial Monitor
  while (Serial.available() == 0) {
  // Do nothing, wait for input data
  }

  // Read the user input from Serial Monitor
  String usr_Input = Serial.readStringUntil('\n');

  // Print the received message back to Serial Monitor
  Serial.print("You entered: ");
  Serial.println(usr_Input);

  // Provide a time delay to avoid the Serial Monitor being flooded
  delay(1000);
}
```

The output of the program can be viewed using the Serial Monitor option available at the top right corner of the Arduino IDE. Fig. 1.25 illustrates the Serial Monitor being opened and the space provided to send messages to the Arduino Mega board connected to the COM Port.

Know More

Comment lines in Embedded C

Comments are written in the codes to make it more understandable and maintainable.

Single-line comments are written using two forward slashes (//). Everything written after two slashes in the same line is treated as a comment and the compiler ignores it.

Multi-line comments commence with / and end with */. They can be spread across multiple lines.*

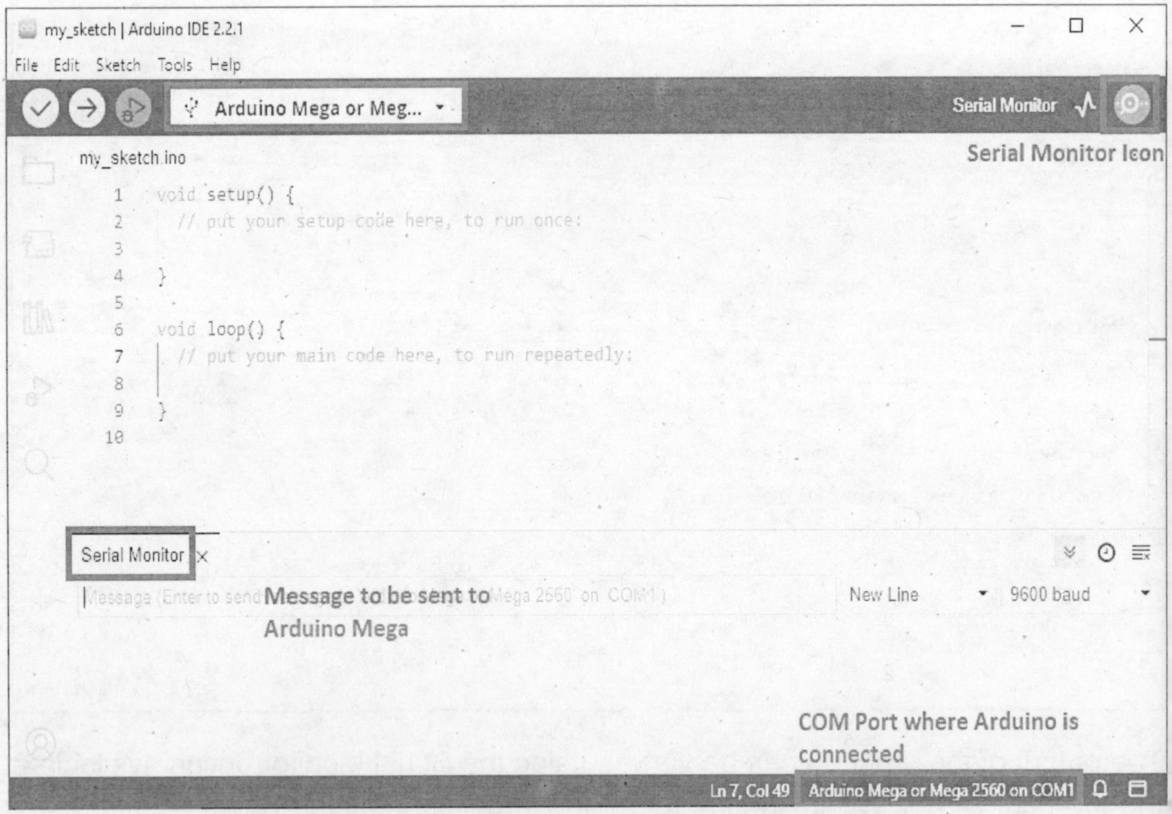

Fig. 1.25 Arduino Mega board connected to COM port

The connection between the Arduino board and the Arduino IDE is established through a USB connection. The code written in the Arduino IDE can be uploaded to the processor on the board via USB connection.

1.5.1 Verifying the Arduino C Code

The program code has to be verified and compiled for any errors before dumping the code onto the Arduino board. The Verify/Compile option is available under the Sketch Menu option as shown in Fig. 1.26a. The Verify icon can also be used to Verify/Compile the program code.

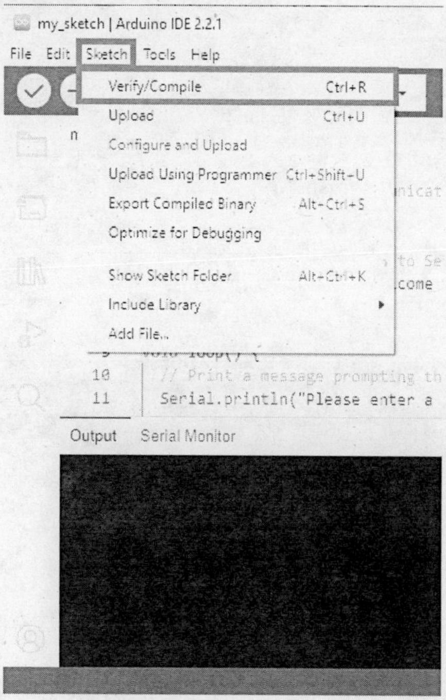

a)

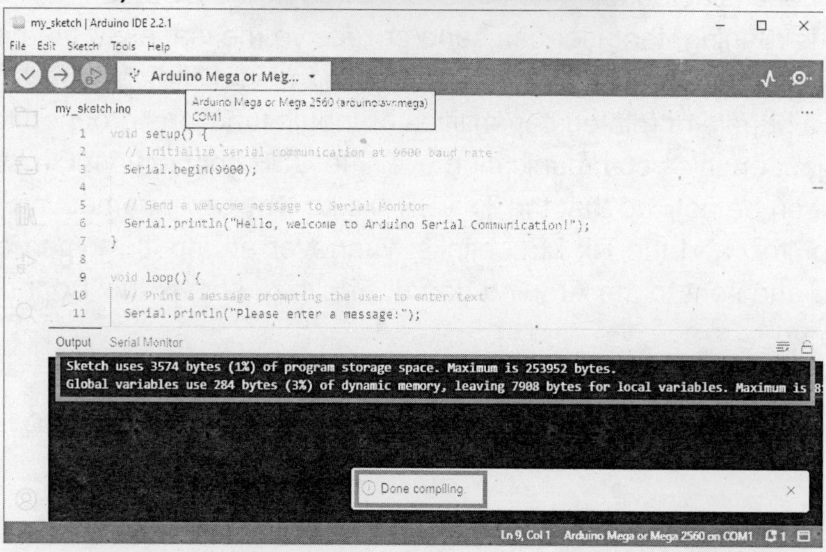

b)

Fig. 1.26 Verifying the code in Arduino IDE a) Before Compilation b) After Compilation

1.5.2 Upload the Sketch/Code to Arduino

The code (also called the Arduino sketch) is uploaded onto the Arduino board using the Sketch menu as shown in Fig. 1.27.

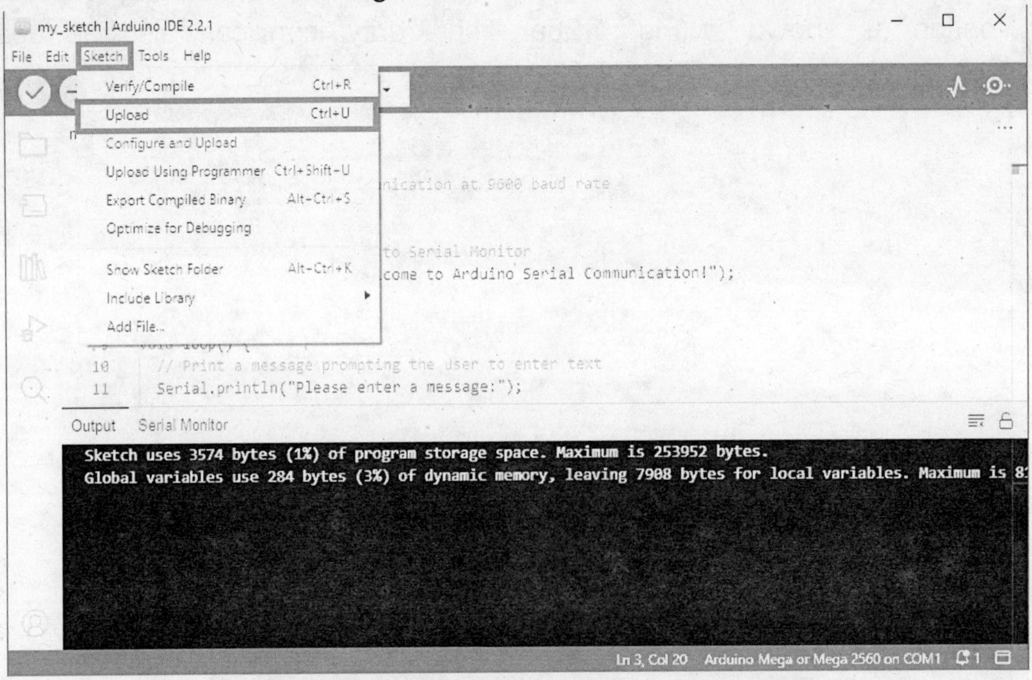

Fig. 1.27 Uploading the code in Arduino IDE

After the code is uploaded onto the board through the USB connection, and when the program is running, the user can send or receive messages to the board through the Serial Monitor as shown in Fig. 1.29. This is done in a sketch using a serial object. An object is a bundle of related capabilities or inbuilt functions grouped together, and the serial object enables communication over the USB connection. On the Arduino Mega board, it can be noticed that the Tx LED blinks whenever something is printed on the serial monitor, and the Rx LED blinks whenever an input is typed on the computer keyboard and sent to the Arduino board. Fig. 1.28 shows the Tx and Rx LEDs in the Mega board.

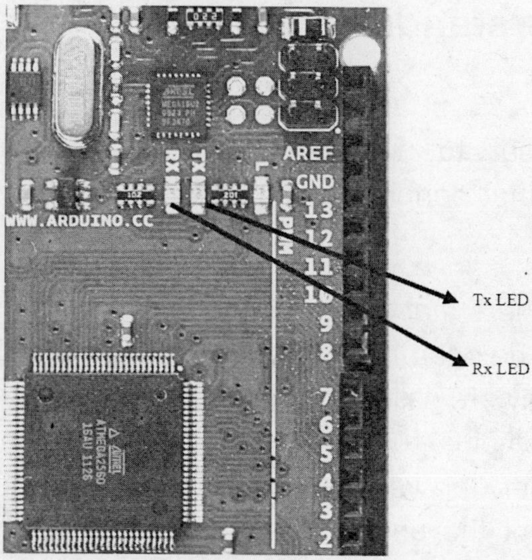

Fig. 1.28 Serial Tx and Rx indicator LEDs

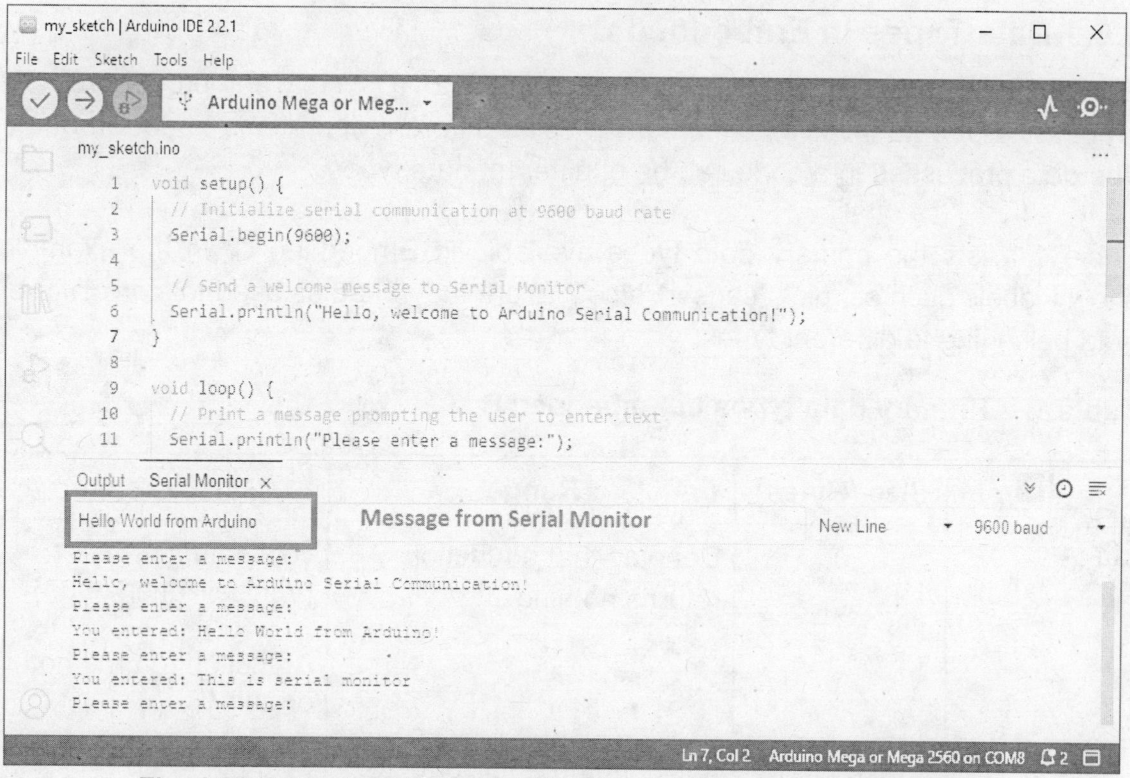

Fig. 1.29 Output in the Serial Monitor, waiting for the user input

1.6 Basic Understanding of the Code with Different Operations

To write code, it is necessary to know about declaring and defining variables that store data and the operators that perform various operations upon the data stored in the variables.

Variables are like containers that store information. They can be imagined as boxes with labels, where each box can hold a value. The value inside the box can vary or change, which is why they are called 'variables'. For example, var1_a=10. 'Var1_a' is a variable that stores the value 10. Variables can be reassigned with any other value or expression. Remember, the variable name is case sensitive, and it cannot have special characters except the underscore '_'. Also, variable names begin with an alphabet only (upper or lower case) and cannot begin with a number.

1.6.1 Data Types in Embedded C

Given a task, numeric or verbal data are input to a system for processing. The processing of data involves computation using different operations to get an output. The data processed in a code can be of different data types.

Table 1.1 lists the primary data types available in Embedded C. In the examples shown labels such as 'pin', 'sensorValue', 'a' are the variables used to store different data belonging to different types.

Table 1.1: Primary data types in Embedded C

Data Type	Size (Bytes)	Range	Example
Void	0	Denotes that a function returns nothing	void setup() {// Initialization code} /*function returns nothing or null*/
Byte	1 (8 bits)	unsigned number (0 to 255) byte pin = 13	byte pin = 13;

Integer	2	–32,768 to 32,767 (Signed) 0 to 65,535 (Unsigned)	int sensorValue = 1023; unsigned int a=100;
Floating point	4	–3.4028235E+38 to 3.4028235E+38	float temp = 36.5;
Boolean	1	True/False	bool ledState = true;
Character	1	-128 to +127	char letter = 'A';

1.6.1.1 Custom Data Types: String, Array, Structure and Pointer

Data structures like string, array, structure and pointers are Custom Data Types, where the size and components are determined by their definition. Given below are some examples.

String is an array of characters.

```
char message[] = "Hello, Arduino!";
```

Array is a homogeneous list of values. Arrays can be of any data type, e.g., int, char, etc.

```
int numbers[] = {11, 12, 13, 14, 15};
char sample[] = {'S', 'y', 's', 't', 'e', 'm', 's', '\0'};
```

Structures are used to create a composite data type. For example,

```
struct Sensor {
  int id;
  float value;
};
Sensor tempSensor = {1, 36.7};
```

Pointer is a data type that points to various other data types. Further the operations using pointers will be explained in Section 1.6.2.

```
int value = 10;
int *ptr = &value;
```

1.6.2 Types of Operators

Different operators in Embedded C serve different purposes and can be utilized depending on the specific needs of the system. Table 1.2 lists the different types of operators in Embedded C.

Table 1.2: Different types of Operators

Type of Operator	Operator
Arithmetic Operators	Addition (+), Subtraction (-), Multiplication (*), Division (/), Modulo (%)
Boolean Operators	AND (&&), OR (||), NOT (!)
Bitwise Operators	AND (&), OR (|), XOR (^), Complement (~), Left shift (<<), Right shift (>>)
Compounded Operators	Increment (++), Decrement (--), Compound Addition (+=), Compound Subtraction (-=), Compound Multiplication (*=), Compound Division (/=),

	Compound Modulo (%=), Compound AND (&=), Compound OR (|=)
Comparison Operators	Equality (==), Greater than (>), Greater than or equal to (>=), Inequality (!=), Less than (<), Less than or equal to (<=)
Pointer access operators	Pointer Initialisation (&) Pointer Dereferencing (*)

1.6.2.1 Arithmetic Operations

Embedded systems use mathematical calculations for processing input data and producing a meaningful output. Arithmetic operators like addition (+), subtraction (-), multiplication (*), division (/), and modulus (%) are used for these purposes.

Code	**Output**
int k=20; int m=10;	
C = k+m	30
D = k-m	10

Arduino Code - Temperature Conversion:

The temperature given in Celsius can be converted into Fahrenheit using the formula Fahrenheit = (Celsius * 9.0 / 5.0) + 32.0

```
// Program to convert Celsius to Fahrenheit
void setup() {
    Serial.begin(9600); // Start serial communication at 9600 bits per
second
```

```
    float Celsius = 25.0; // Example temperature in Celsius
    float Fahrenheit = (Celsius * 9.0 / 5.0) + 32.0; // Convert from
Celsius to Fahrenheit
    // Output the result to the Serial Monitor
    Serial.print("Enter the temperature (Celsius): ");
    Serial.print(Celsius);
    Serial.print(" °C, ");
    Serial.print("Temperature converted to Fahrenheit: ");
    Serial.print(Fahrenheit);
    Serial.println(" °F");
}
// Loop function executes continuously after setup function completes
void loop() {
    // Nothing to do here in this example
}
```

This program will convert the specified temperature from Celsius to Fahrenheit and display the results on the Serial Monitor once.

Output - Temperature Conversion:

```
Enter the temperature (Celsius): 35.00 °C, Temperature converted to
Fahrenheit: 95.00 °F
```

Know More

> ***Print with new line***
> *Serial.print("Message") prints the message and remains in the same line after printing, Serial.println("Message") prints the message and returns to the next line after printing.*

Know More

> ***Operator precedence***
> *Operators within parentheses are evaluated first. Unary operators (++ and --) have higher precedence than other arithmetic operators. Multiplication, division, and*

modulus operators have higher precedence than addition and subtraction operators. Remember it is similar to the famous BODMAS (B – Brackets, O – Order of powers or roots, D – Division, M – Multiplication A – Addition, and S – Subtraction) rule.

1.6.2.2 Boolean Operations

Boolean Operators are used for implementing control logic in an embedded system. The Boolean operators include AND (&&), OR (||), and NOT (!). The code example to simulate a two-way doorbell example using the Serial Monitor for input and output is shown. The same application will be revisited in Unit 3 using real buttons and buzzer interfacing. In the example, Serial.available(), Serial.begin(), and Serial.read() are inbuilt functions. Serial.begin() initializes the serial communication. Serial.available() enables the serial monitor to wait for an input from the user. Serial.read() function reads the serial input and stores it in the variable on the left side. Here, the input is read and stored in 'incomingByte'.

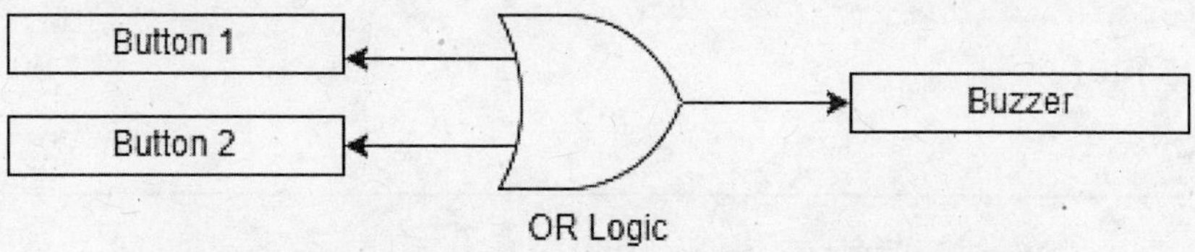

Fig. 1.30 Application example of an OR gate

Arduino code - Simulation of two-way doorbell

```
void setup() {
  Serial.begin(9600);    // Start serial communication
  Serial.println("Two-Way Doorbell Simulation");
  Serial.println("Type '1' to press Button 1");
  Serial.println("Type '2' to press Button 2");
}
void loop() {
  // Check if data is available in the Serial Monitor
  if (Serial.available() > 0) {
    // Read the incoming byte
    char incomingByte = Serial.read();
```

```
    // Simulate button states
    bool button1= (incomingByte == '1');
    bool button2= (incomingByte == '2');
       // Implement OR logic: if either button is "pressed", turn on
the buzzer
    bool buzzer = button1 || button2;
    //Print states in the Serial Monitor
    Serial.println("*~~~****~~~*");
    Serial.print("Buzzer status:");
    Serial.println(buzzer);
    Serial.print("Status of Button 1:");
    Serial.println(button1);
    Serial.print("Status of Button 2:");
    Serial.println(button2);
    Serial.println("*~~~****~~~*");
    delay(5000);
  }
```

Output - Two-way doorbell simulation

The output of the Two-way doorbell simulation is shown below. The buzzer goes to high "1" state even if any one of the buttons is pressed.

```
Two-Way Doorbell Simulation
Type '1' to press Button 1
Type '2' to press Button 2
*~~~****~~~*
Buzzer status:1
Status of Button 1:1
Status of Button 2:0
*~~~****~~~*
```

1.6.2.3 Bitwise Operations

Bitwise operations are used to manipulate individual bits to control hardware peripherals like motors and actuators. The basic bitwise operators available in Arduino

C programming are AND (&), OR (|), XOR (^), Complement (~), Left shift (<<) and Right shift (>>).

Arduino Code - Bitwise XOR Operation of two bytes

```
void setup() {
Serial.begin(9600); // Start serial communication at 9600 bits per second
    // Define two values
    byte Byte1 = B10101010; // Decimal number = 170
    byte Byte2 = B10011000; // Decimal number = 152
    // Output the result on the serial port
    Serial.print("First Byte: ");
    Serial.println(Byte1);
    Serial.print("Second Byte: ");
    Serial.println(Byte2);
    // Calculating the result of the two input bytes
    byte Out = Byte1 ^ Byte2;
    Serial.print("XOR operation of two bytes: ");
    Serial.print(Out);
}
void loop() {
    // Nothing to do here, since we're demonstrating a one-time operation
in setup()
}
```

The output of the above XOR operation will perform bitwise XOR of the two given inputs. The first bit of the first input will be XORed with the corresponding bit of the second input as shown in Fig. 1.31. Similarly other bitwise operators operate on the operands at the bit level.

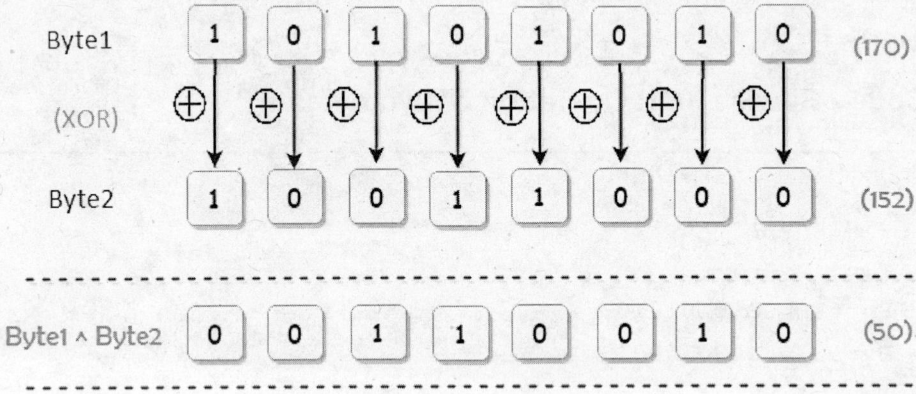

Fig. 1.31 Bitwise XOR operation

Output - Bitwise XOR Operation

```
First Byte: 170
Second Byte: 152
XOR operation of two bytes: 50
```

1.6.2.4 Compounded Operations

Compounded operations, combine arithmetic or a bitwise operation with assignment. They provide an easy way to modify a variable's value by performing an operation on it and storing the output back into the same variable.

Let us assume that a=20. The output of performing the different compounded operations on a is listed below:

Code: int a=20;

Code	Operation	Output
a+=4;	a=a+4	a = 24
a-=4;	a=a-4	a = 16
a*=4	a=a*4	a = 80
a/=4	a=a/4	a = 5

a%=4	a=a%4	a = 0
a++	a=a+1	a = 21
a--	a=a-1	a = 19
a&=5	a=a&5	a = 4
a|=5	a=a|5	a = 21

1.6.2.5 Pointer Access Operations

Pointers are a fundamental aspect of programming in Embedded C due to the need for direct memory manipulation, while dealing with hardware interfaces.

Pointer Initialization

Pointers allow direct access to the memory location where a variable is stored. The pointer initialization can be done with * operator and the declaration can be done using address-of operator (&). The value assigned to the variable can be changed in two ways, one using the pointer (dereference operator - *) and the other by using the variable itself. An example code of using pointers to a floating-point value is shown below:

Arduino Code - Pointer Initialisation and Dereferencing

```
void setup() {
  Serial.begin(9600); // Start serial communication at 9600 bits per
second
  // Define a variable
  int mysensorValue = 10.52;
  int *p_Sensor;              // Declare a pointer to an integer
  p_Sensor = &mysensorValue ;  // Assign the memory location of
mysensorValue to the pointer
  Serial.print("Sensor Value before modification: ");
  Serial.println(mysensorValue);
  *p_Sensor = 20.34;
```

```
  // Output the result to the Serial Monitor
  Serial.print("Sensor Value after modification: ");
  Serial.println(mysensorValue);
}
void loop() {
   // Nothing to do here, since we're demonstrating a one-time
operation in setup()
}
```

Output

```
sensorValue before modification: 10.52
sensorValue after modification: 20.34
```

Unit Recap

- The **Arduino Integrated Development Environment** (IDE) is a software tool that is used for writing, editing, compiling, and uploading code to Arduino boards.
- An **operator** in programming is a symbol that instructs the compiler to do a specific operation on one or more operands (values or variables). Operators are essential for performing calculations, making comparisons, and managing logical conditions.
- The different types of operators are

Arithmetic Operators
Boolean Operators
Bitwise Operators
Compounded Operators
Comparison Operators
Pointer access Operators

Mind map - Arduino IDE and operators

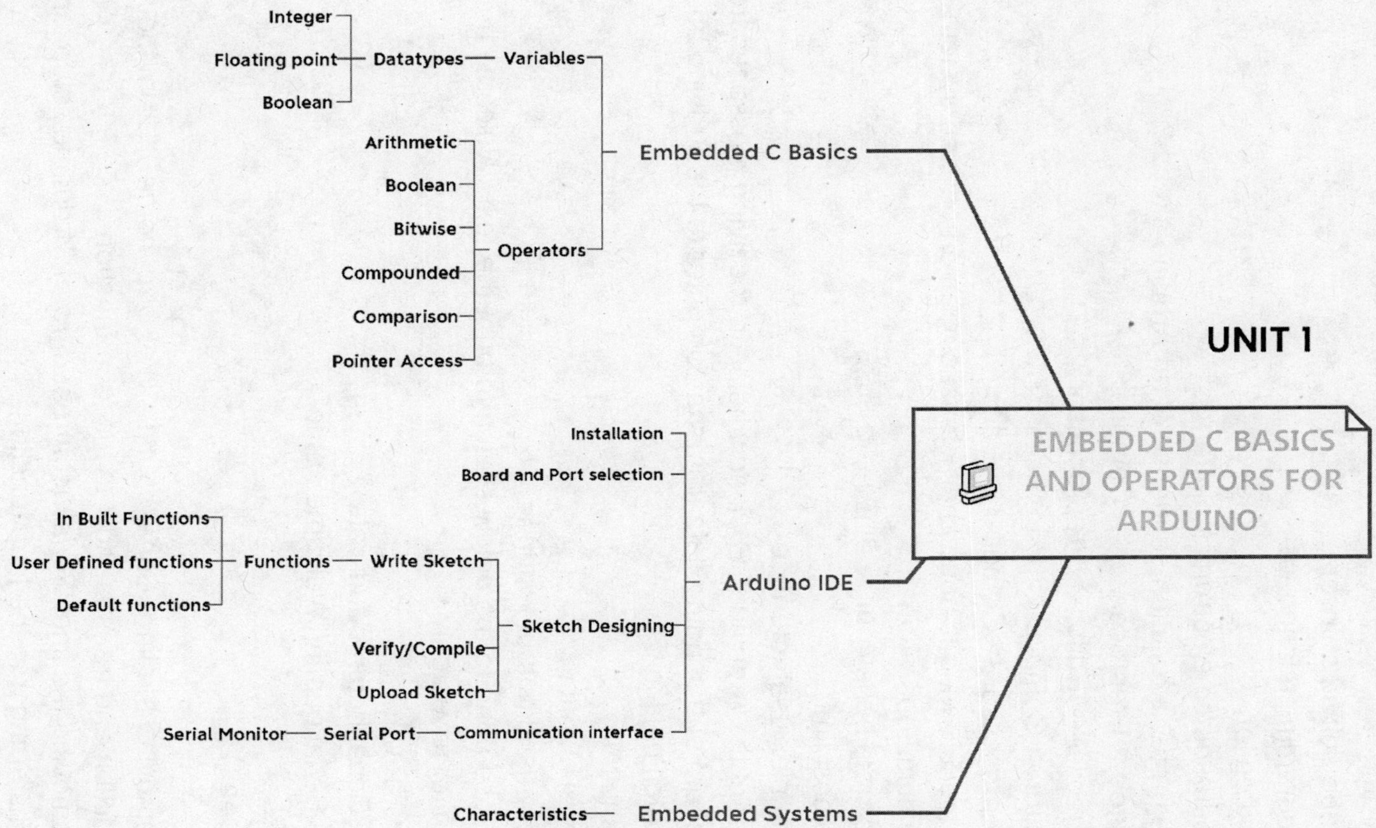

Multiple Choice Questions

1. What is Arduino?
    a. Image editing software
    b. Programming language
    c. Text editor
    d. Open-source electronics platform
2. Select the proper execution sequence of an Arduino sketch?
    a. Editor -> Preprocessor -> Compiler
    b. Compiler -> Editor -> Preprocessor
    c. Editor -> Compiler -> Preprocessor
    d. Preprocessor -> Compiler -> Editor
3. Which of the following is not a characteristic of an embedded system?
    a. Realtime operation
    b. Multirate behaviour
    c. No cost limit
    d. Complex user interface
4. Which part of the Arduino IDE window helps in receiving messages from the Arduino board and sending data from the computer to the Arduino board?
    a. Sketch editing
    b. Menu bar
    c. Serial monitor
    d. Command/output window
5. What must be done to the below sketch to print the text "Welcome home" on the serial monitor repeatedly.

```
void setup () {
        Serial.begin(baud_rate);”
        Serial println(“Welcome home”);
}
void loop () {
}
```

    a. Removing the line *“Serial.println ("Welcome home");”* from the setup function and transferring it to the loop function.
    b. Removing the line *“Serial.begin(baud_rate);”* from the setup function and transferring it to the loop function.

   c. Transferring both *Serial.begin(baud_rate); and Serial.println("Welcome home");* to the loop function.
   d. The code is correct, and no code edits are necessary.

6. Determine the output for the following program.

```
void setup() {
        Serial.begin(11200);
        Serial.print(sizeof(int));
}
```

   a. 11
   b. 6
   c. 4
   d. 2

7. The function that gets executed repeatedly inside the main code block?
   a. Setup
   b. Loop
   c. While
   d. None

8. A program written for Arduino using the IDE is called __________.
   a. Source code
   b. Cryptograph
   c. IDE source
   d. Sketch

9. Arduino does not require a separate ________ to dump the sketch on the board.
   a. Storage
   b. Programmer
   c. Initializer
   d. Oscillator

10. How does an embedded system interact with the external environment?
    a. Peripherals
    b. Output devices
    c. Memory
    d. Input devices

Programming Questions

1. Develop an embedded code using C language to set the 7th bit in a variable, A with the help of bitwise operators.
2. Create an Embedded C program using Boolean operators to check whether the given values lie in the range 0 to 10.
3. Develop an embedded code using C language to swap two numbers using pointers.

Know More

QR code for all the Arduino codes used in Unit 1

References

1. Banzi, M., & Shiloh, M. (2014). *Make: Getting Started with Arduino - The Open Source Electronics Prototyping Platform* (3rd ed.). Shroff/Maker Media. ISBN: 978-9351109075
2. Norris, T. (2018). *Beginning Arduino 4th Edition: A Complete Introduction to Arduino Programming*.
3. Pajankar, A. (2018). *Arduino made simple with interactive projects*. BPB Publications.
4. Schmidt, M. (2015). *Arduino: A quick-start guide* (2nd ed., illustrated). Pragmatic Bookshelf. ISBN: 1941222242, 9781941222249
5. Hughes, J. M. (2016). *Arduino: A technical reference*. O'Reilly Media, Inc. ISBN: 9781491934494
6. Wolf, W. (2008). *Computers as components: Principles of embedded computing system design*. Morgan Kaufmann Publishers.
7. Evans, B. (2011). *Beginning Arduino programming* [eBook]. Apress. https://doi.org/10.1007/978-1-4302-3778-5

2

Embedded C Control Structure Blocks

Unit Specifics

This Unit emphasizes the following aspects:

- Looping Mechanisms - For, Do and While loops
- Branching Operations based on Conditional Expressions - If, If-else Statements and Switch Case Statements
- Difference between the C language and Embedded C Language

IKS Insights

This section explores how concepts from Indian Knowledge Systems (IKS) align with and enrich contemporary practices and technologies.

Programming - Logic Redefined

Ancient Indian mathematicians developed algorithms and methods to solve complex problems, such as quadratic equations and trigonometric functions. Among these, Vedic mathematics, as proposed by Sri Bharati Krishna Tirthaji, introduced 16 sutras, including "Nikhilam Navatashcaramam Dashatah". It redefines the logic used in multiplication. By redefining logic, programming can be significantly simplified, making these ancient techniques a valuable reference for modern programming methods. Recent developments in electronics have applied these Vedic sutras to redesign logic and circuits, showcasing the timeless relevance of these ancient principles.

Power of Indian Mathematics - Precision and Accuracy

Aryabhatta's accurate calculations of planetary positions and eclipses exemplify the sophisticated techniques of measurement developed in ancient India. These traditional methods of precision and error minimization can inspire modern techniques for enhancing the accuracy of sensors and data acquisition systems. In programming, optimizing code not only reduces run-time errors but also improves system efficiency. Nature-inspired intelligent algorithms, such as Cuckoo Search, have significantly influenced the optimization of various parameters in complex system designs, further demonstrating the enduring impact of precise and accurate methodologies. Further, Traditional methods of measurement and analysis offer valuable insights and innovative approaches to sensor technology and data acquisition in embedded systems.

Rationale

This Unit introduces the fundamental control structures in Embedded C. Understanding loops and conditional branches enables students to write repetitive tasks and decision-making programs, which is critical for real-time embedded applications. This Unit will equip students with the skills to implement more dynamic and responsive processes within their code.

Prerequisites

Basic understanding of C programming concepts (variables, data types, and basic syntax and semantics, functions and arithmetic operations).

Unit Outcomes

At the end of this Unit, students will be able to

U2-O1: Describe and implement the different looping mechanisms in Embedded C.

U2-O2: Describe and implement branching operations using conditional expressions.

U2-O3: Identify scenarios where branching operations and looping mechanisms improve program functionality and efficiency.

UO - CO Mapping

Course Outcomes	Expected Mapping with Programme Outcomes (1- Weak Correlation; 2- Medium correlation; 3- Strong Correlation)				
	CO-1	CO-2	CO-3	CO-4	CO-5
U2-O1	2	1	3	1	2
U2-O2	2	1	3	1	2
U2-O3	2	1	3	1	3

2.1 Program Flow and Control Structures

In programming, managing the flow of execution is crucial in creating efficient and functional software. Control structures are the building blocks of a code that determine the sequence, decision-making, and repetition of instructions. They ensure that tasks are performed in correct sequence, conditions are evaluated, and actions are repeated as needed. Understanding these control structures is fundamental to mastering programming in embedded systems.

The control structures in Embedded C are divided into three different types as listed below:

1. Sequential Control Structure
2. Repetitive Control Structure
3. Selection Control Structure

2.1.1 Sequential Control Structure

Sequential control structures are of simplest form, where the statements are executed in the specified order, i.e., step by step or line by line flow of order.

Example - Sequential Control Structure

```
int SensorValue_1 = 10;
int SensorValue_2 = 20;
int combined = SensorValue_1 + SensorValue_2;
```

```
Serial.println("Combined Value = ");
Serial.println(combined);
```

In the above code, the statements are executed in sequential order: Sensor values (SensorValue_1, SensorValue_2) are declared, the combined value is calculated, and the result is displayed on the serial monitor.

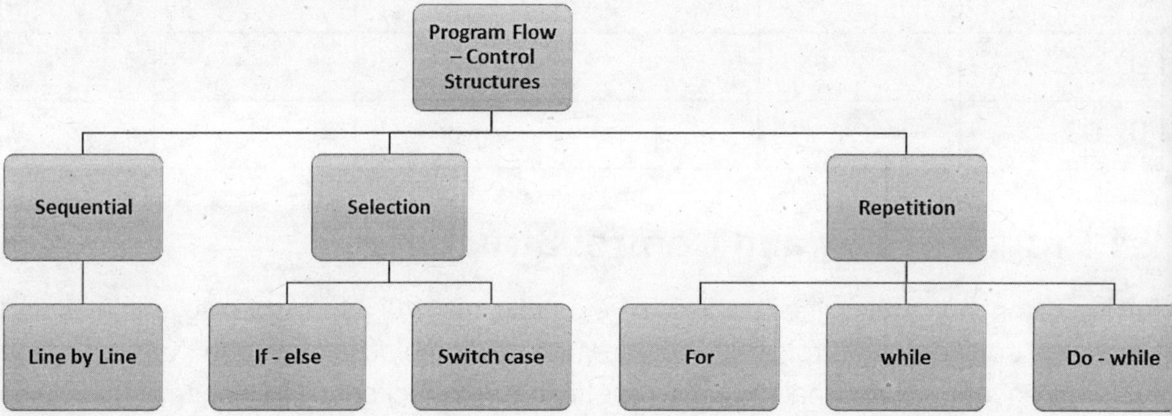

Fig. 2.1 Different Control structures

2.1.2 Repetitive Control Structure

Repetitive control structures allow a block of code to be repeated several number of times. The number of repetitions can be controlled with the help of conditional statements. These structures are also called looping mechanisms and the same will be further elaborated in Section 2.2.

2.1.3 Selection Control Structure

A selection control structure, also known as a conditional control structure, where different paths of execution are chosen depending on the conditional expressions. Branching refers to choosing between the several available paths of execution. This structure helps in decision making based on the specified conditions. These structures will be further elaborated with examples in Section 2.3.

2.2 Looping Mechanisms

Looping mechanisms allow repeated execution of a block of code, which is essential for tasks that involve continuous operations, such as monitoring sensor data, controlling actuators, and executing communication protocols. The different looping mechanisms that are available in Embedded C are **'for'** loop, **'do while'** loop and **'while'** loop. These loops allow the user to execute the same block of code multiple times without writing the code multiple times.

2.2.1 For Loop

A **for** loop in Embedded C is a control flow statement that allows a block of code to be executed repeatedly based on a given condition. 'For' loops are used in those cases where the block of code has to be repeated until a specific condition is met.

Know More

Conditions in the looping mechanisms evaluate to a Boolean output (1 for true and 0 for false respectively).

2.2.1.1 Syntax - For Loop

The syntax for 'For' loop is as given below. The syntax consists of a loop control variable that has three different phases, namely Initialisation, Condition Check and Increment/Decrement. When a block of code inside the loop gets executed once, it is called an iteration. The program flow of the For loop is depicted in Fig. 2.2.

```
for (initialization; condition; increment/decrement)
{
    // Code
}
```

- The **Initialisation** of the loop control variable happens only once at the beginning of the loop.
  eg: int i = 0;
  Here the variable i represents the loop control, which is initialized to 0.

- The **Condition Check** on the loop control variable happens every time before the loop gets executed.
  eg: i <=5;
  '<=' is a comparison operator which checks whether the current value of i is less than or equal to 5.
- The **Increment/Decrement** operation happens every time after the loop gets executed
  eg: i++;
  The value of loop control i is incremented by 1.
- The **Code** written inside the {} shall be executed for every iteration with the updated loop control variable.

The number of times the loop has to be executed/iterated depends on the initialisation value and the increment/decrement value.

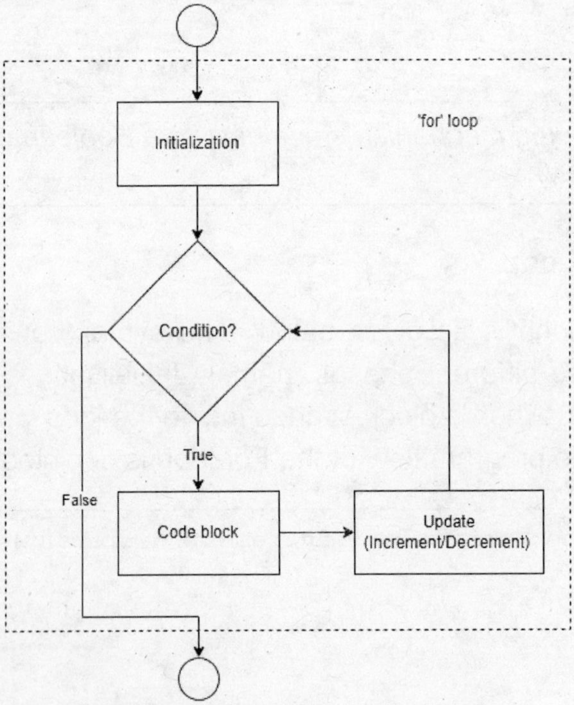

Fig.2.2 Flowchart - For loop

2.2.1.2 Example - For Loop

Let us consider an example to change the value of a Boolean variable continuously from 0 to 1 and from 1 to 0 for 10 times. It is equivalent to making an LED blink 10 times. Supplying a Boolean 1 to the LED makes it glow and supplying a Boolean 0 switches it OFF.

Arduino Code - Change the Boolean value 10 times

```
void setup() {
  Serial.begin(9600);
  bool myLED = 0;
  for (int i = 1; i < 11; i++) {
        // Toggle LED
        myLED = !myLED;
        // Delay for 500 milliseconds
        delay(500);
        Serial.print("**Iteration: ");
        Serial.println(i);
        Serial.print("LED Value: ");
        Serial.println(myLED);
    }
}
void loop() {
  // Nothing to do here, since we're demonstrating a one-time
operation in setup()
}
```

Output

**Iteration: 1 LED Value: 1 **Iteration: 2 LED Value: 0 **Iteration: 3 LED Value: 1 **Iteration: 4 LED Value: 0 **Iteration: 5 LED Value: 1	**Iteration: 6 LED Value: 0 **Iteration: 7 LED Value: 1 **Iteration: 8 LED Value: 0 **Iteration: 9 LED Value: 1 **Iteration: 10 LED Value: 0

2.2.2 Do While Loop

A Do-While loop is a control flow statement that executes a block of code at least once, and then it repeatedly executes as long as the given condition remains true. The program flow of the Do-While loop is depicted in Fig. 2.3.

2.2.2.1 Syntax - Do While Loop

The syntax for do-while loop is given below.

```
do {
    // Code to be executed
} while (condition);
```

- The **code** written inside the Do-While block {} is executed first before the condition is evaluated. The first-time execution of the Do Block happens even if the condition evaluates to false.

- The **condition** check happens at the end of block execution (before every new iteration). The do-while block gets executed continuously until the condition becomes false.

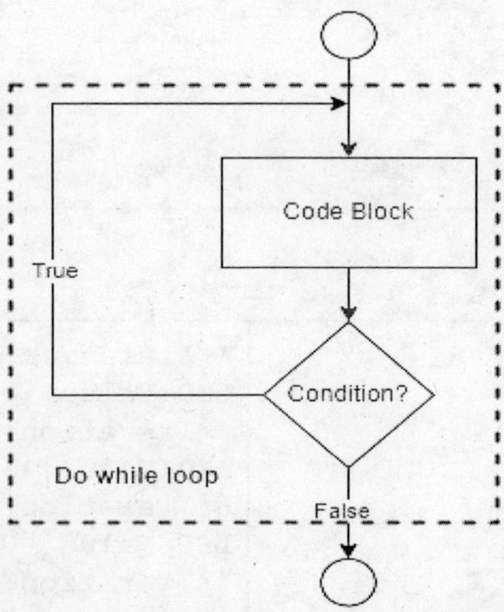

Fig. 2.3 Flowchart for Do-While loop

2.2.2.2 Example - Do-While Loop

Let us consider a scenario of a shopping cart, where the user tries to enter the quantity that he wants to purchase. Assuming that only 10 quantities are available, the following code shows how to validate whether the user input is within 1 to 10, using a do while loop. Here the user enters the input in the serial monitor and the output is printed back in the serial monitor. The loop repeats until the input lies between 1 and 10.

Arduino Code - User input validation

```
void setup() {
  Serial.begin(9600); // Start serial communication at 9600 bits per
second
  int quantity;
  do {
    char usr_Input[2]={'0','\0'}; // Define an array to store user
input (up to 2 characters)
    Serial.println("Enter quantity (1-10) for the item: ");

    // Read the user input from Serial Monitor
    while (!Serial.available()); // Wait until data is available
    Serial.readBytesUntil('\n', usr_Input, 10); // Read up to 10
characters or until newline

    // Print the entered quantity to Serial Monitor
    Serial.print("You entered: ");
    Serial.println(usr_Input);
    // Convert the input from string to an integer
    quantity = atoi(usr_Input);
       // Check if the quantity is within the valid range
    if (quantity < 1 || quantity > 10) {
      Serial.println("Invalid input! Please enter a quantity between
1 and 10.");
    }
```

```
  } while (quantity < 1 || quantity > 10);
  // Quantity is valid
  Serial.print("Quantity selected: ");
  Serial.println(quantity);
}
void loop() {
  // The loop function will not be executed
}
```

Know More

In order to perform the comparison operation without any errors, the two variables that are compared should be of the same datatype.

Output

```
Enter quantity (1-10) for the item:
You entered: 67
Invalid input! Please enter a quantity between 1 and 10.
Enter quantity (1-10) for the item:
You entered: 6
Quantity selected: 6
```

2.2.3 While Loop

A While loop is a conditional control flow statement that executes a block of code repeatedly as long as the given condition remains true. The difference between a For loop and a While loop is that, While loop does not know the exact number of times the code block will get executed. The program flow of the While loop is depicted in Fig. 2.4.

2.2.3.1 Syntax - While Loop

The syntax for the while loop is given below.

```
while (condition) {
    // Code to be executed as long as the condition is true  }
```

- The **Code** inside the while block {} is executed only if the condition check returns a true value
- The code might not get executed at all if the **condition** check fails for the first time itself.

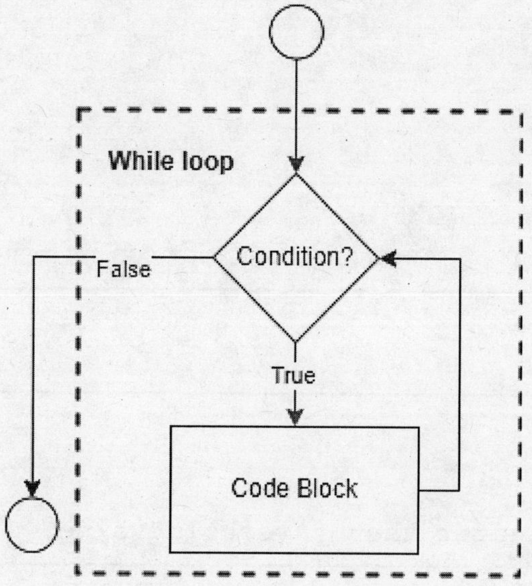

Fig. 2.4 Flowchart - While loop

2.2.3.2 Example - While loop

Let us consider that a variable mySensor gets updated inside the while loop. The while loop continues to execute until the condition evaluates to false.

Arduino Code - Check if sensorValue is less than threshold

```
void setup() {
  Serial.begin(9600);
  int threshold = 20;
  int mySensor = 5;
  while (mySensor < threshold) {
      mySensor += 5;          //Compounded operation
      delay(500);
```

```
      Serial.print("Sensor Value: ");
      Serial.println(mySensor);
    }
    Serial.print("Sensor value is greater than threshold value. The
while loop ends");
}
void loop() {
  // Nothing to do here, since we're demonstrating a one-time
operation in setup()
}
```

Output

```
Sensor Value: 10
Sensor Value: 15
Sensor Value: 20
Sensor value is greater than threshold value. The while loop ends
```

Know More

In a while loop, the condition is evaluated before the code inside the loop is executed. If the condition is false initially, the code inside the loop is never executed.

On the contrary, in a do-while loop, the code inside the loop is executed once before the condition is evaluated. If the condition is false after the first execution, the loop stops. Therefore, the do-while loop executes at least once regardless of the condition.

2.3 The Branching Operation based on Conditional Expressions

Branching operation uses conditional statements to change the flow of execution based on input conditions. Branching is used in decision making like responding to sensor inputs or selecting the different modes of operation or handling an error situation during the execution of the code. Conditional statements are used to manage constraints that may occur during the real-time execution of an embedded system.

For example, when we purchase something from a market and go for payment, there are different options available like cash, card or digital payments. Based on the user input selection, the corresponding code gets executed with the help of conditional branching.

The various constructs available in Embedded C for branching are **If-Else** statements and **Switch Case** statements.

2.3.1 If-Else Statement

The If-Else is a conditional branching statement where control can switch between two blocks of code depending on the given condition. The condition can either evaluate to true or false.

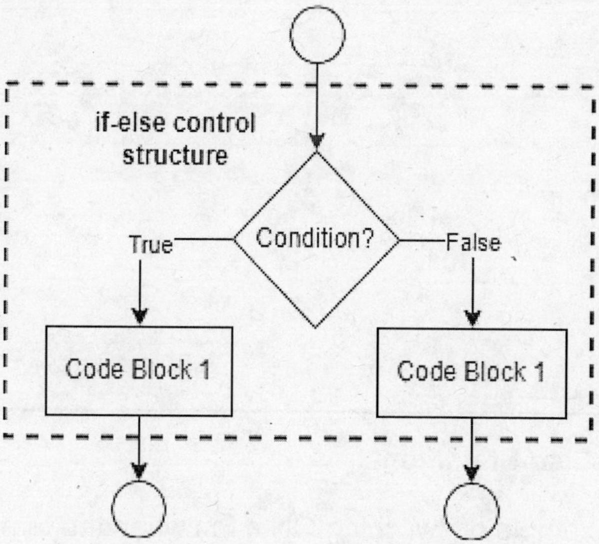

Fig. 2.5 Flowchart - if-else statement

2.3.1.1 Syntax - If-Else Statement

```
if (condition) {
// Code to execute if the condition is true
} else {
// Code to execute if the condition is false
}
```

- The **condition** in the If block can be as simple as a Boolean value or an expression which evaluates to a Boolean value.
- It consists of two blocks of code, one which gets executed when the condition is **true** and the other which gets executed when the condition is **false**.

Know More

If-Else can also be nested under other If-Else or Switch Case statements.

```
if (condition1) {
    if (condition2) {
    }
    else {
    }
}
else {
    if (condition3) {
    }
    else {
    }
}
```

2.3.1.2 Example - If-Else Statement

Let us consider the example of switching ON a fan when the temperature goes higher than a specified value. Let us use two variables temperature and fan to depict the real-world scenario. When the temperature variable is greater than 25, a high value '1' is assigned to the variable fan. Supplying a 1 to the fan switches ON the fan and supplying 0 switches OFF the fan.

Arduino Code - Switching on the fan when the temperature is high

```
void setup() {
  Serial.begin(9600);
  int temperature = 26;
  bool fan = 0;
```

```
  if (temperature > 25) {
    fan = 1;           //Switch on the fan
    delay(500);
    Serial.print("Temperature is : ");
    Serial.println(temperature);
    Serial.print("Fan is switched ON.");
  }
  else{
    fan = 0;
    delay(500);
    Serial.print("Temperature is : ");
    Serial.println(temperature);
    Serial.print("Fan is switched OFF.");
  }
}
void loop() {
  // Nothing to do here, since we're demonstrating a one-time
operation in setup()
}
```

Output

```
Temperature is: 26
Fan is switched ON.
```

2.3.2 Switch Case Statements

Switch Case statements are used to select between many of the different code blocks based on the value of a control variable. It helps in making complex decisions in embedded systems.

2.3.2.1 Syntax - Switch Case Statement

```
switch (control variable) {
case 1:
```

```
// Code for value1
break;
case 2:
// Code for value2
break;
default:
// Code for default case
break;
}
```

- The **control variable** selects between the different code blocks depending on its value.
- Each code block is written inside each **case**.
- **Break** statement is included inside each case in order to break the execution flow and go to the block after the switch statement.
- The **default** block is included as the last option within the Switch Case.

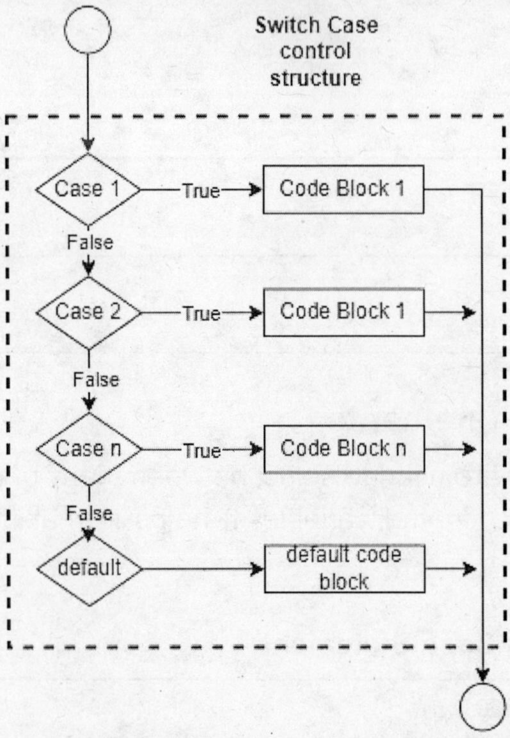

Fig. 2.6 Flowchart - switch case statement

2.3.2.2 Example - Switch Case

Let us consider the example of classifying the temperature from the sensor as Hot, Cold and Normal based on the specified temperature ranges. Let us describe the temperature as "Hot" when it exceeds 32 degrees Celsius, "Cold" when it is below 15 degrees Celsius, and "Normal" when it is between 15 and 32 degrees Celsius.

Arduino Code - Check temperature and classify

```
void setup() {
Serial.begin(9600); // Start serial communication at 9600 bits per
second
    int temperature = 25;
    Serial.print("Temperature = ");
    Serial.println(temperature);
        // Calculate the range for classification
    int range = 0;
    if (temperature <= 15) {
        range = 1; // Cold
    } else if (temperature > 15 && temperature <= 32) {
        range = 2; // Normal
    } else {
        range = 3; // Hot
    }
       // Determine the temperature category
    switch (range) {
        case 1:
            //Cold temperature
            Serial.println("The temperature is Cold.");
            break;
        case 2:
            //Normal temperature
            Serial.println("The temperature is Normal.");
            break;
        case 3:
```

```
            //Hot temperature
            Serial.println("The temperature is Hot.");
            break;
        default:
            printf("Invalid temperature range.\n");
            break;
    }
}
void loop() {
    // Nothing to do here, since we're demonstrating a one-time
operation in setup()
}
```

Output

```
Temperature = 25
The temperature is Normal.
```

2.4 Difference between the C Language and Embedded C Language

C language and Embedded C share the same core syntax, semantics and features. However, they differ in several ways, with distinct features and use cases as listed in Table 2.1.

Table 2.1: Difference between C and Embedded C language

C language	Embedded C
C is a general-purpose programming language developed by Dennis Ritchie in the early 1970s.	Embedded C constitutes a set of language extensions for the C programming language to support the features and capabilities of embedded systems.
It is used for system and application software development.	It is used with microcontrollers and microprocessors to control hardware.
A C program typically runs on General purpose processors with ample memory and processing power.	Embedded C programs run on resource-constrained devices with limited memory, Input/output ports/pins and processing capabilities.
C programs use general-purpose compilers and IDEs (e.g., GCC, Clang).	Embedded C programs use specialized compilers and toolchains/environments for specific microcontrollers (e.g., Energia, Keil, Arduino IDE, Code composer Studio).
Typical applications of C programs include developing operating systems, compilers, and applications for	Typical applications of Embedded C programs include enabling direct hardware control, efficient resource

implementing algorithms and data structures.	usage, development of firmware for embedded devices and real-time operation by programming microcontrollers for controlling sensors, actuators, and peripherals.
IO functions like printf(), scanf() are used to obtain user data or send data to the user.	Direct register manipulation and GPIO (General Purpose Input Output) can be accessed using the Pinmode function to set the pins.

Unit Recap

- Control statements like ***for, do-while*** and ***while*** loop control the flow of execution based on specified conditions.
- Iteration is the number of times a loop/code block gets executed.
- ***For*** loops are used in those cases where the number of times the code block has to be run is already known.
- ***Do-while*** loop will be executed at least once before checking the underlying condition.
- ***While*** loop is executed as long as the condition specified is true.
- ***C Language*** utilizes a rich standard library for a wide range of general-purpose programming tasks whereas ***Embedded C*** focuses on direct hardware manipulation with libraries and functions tailored for resource-constrained embedded systems.

Mind map - Control Structures

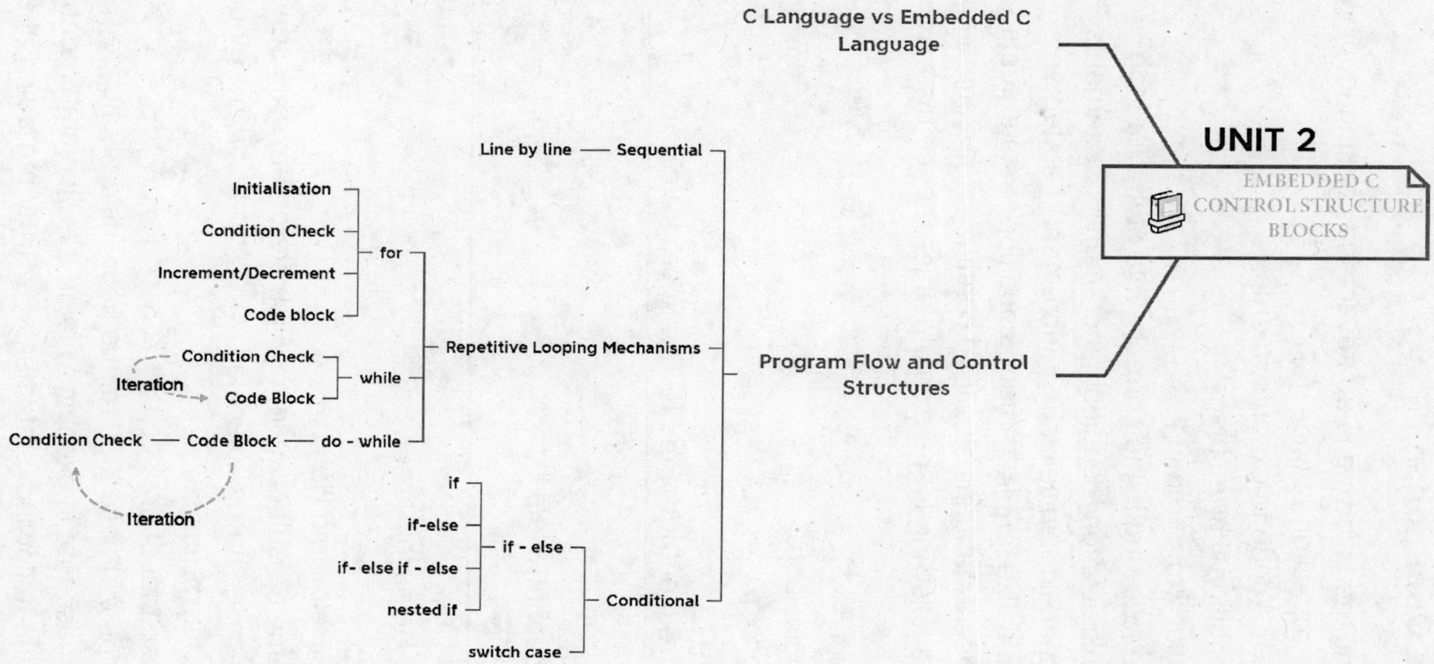

Multiple Choice Questions

1. Which among the following is an advantage of using looping mechanisms?
   a. Avoid repetition of code
   b. Allow the code to execute in order
   c. Unconditional branching
   d. Modular Programming
2. Which of the following is the correct syntax for a for loop?
   a. for (initialization; condition; increment) { statements }
   b. for (condition; initialization; increment) { statements }
   c. for (initialization; increment; condition) { statements }
   d. for (decrement; initialization; condition) { statements }
3. Which of the following loops execute at least once even if the condition is not satisfied?
   a. for loop
   b. do-while loop
   c. while loop
   d. if-else
4. Find the correct output of the following program?

```
int i = 0;
while (i < 3) {
        Serial.print("Help ");
        i++;    }
```

   a. Help Help
   b. Help Help Help
   c. Help
   d. Help Help Help Help
5. What does the default case in a switch statement represent?
   a. The case that is executed when none of the other cases match the switch expression.
   b. A case that cannot contain any code.
   c. An optional case that can be used instead of case 0.
   d. The case that is executed first in a switch statement.
6. Which of the following statements is true regarding if-else statements in Embedded C?

   a. The else block executes only if the condition in the if block is false.
   b. Nested if-else statements cannot be used in Embedded C.
   c. The if-else statement can only check for equality between two variables.
   d. The if-else statement is used only for arithmetic calculations.

7. What happens if the break statement is not included in each of the switch case statements?
   a. Only the particular case will get executed
   b. All the cases will get executed
   c. Only the default case will be executed
   d. All the cases below the selected case, including the default case will be executed

8. What does Serial.println("Data") do?
   a. Prints "Data" in the next line
   b. Prints "Data" and then goes to the next line
   c. Prints a new line before printing "Data"
   d. Does not print a newline

9. Find the output of the program

```
for (int k = 5; k > 0; k--) {
  Serial.print(k)          }
```

   a. 5 4 3 2 1 0
   b. 5 4 3 2
   c. 5 4 3
   d. 5 4 3 2 1

10. Find the output of the program below when the receivedChar is b.

```
switch (receivedChar) {
    case 'a':
        LED_ON();
        break;
    case 'b':
        LED_OFF();
        break;
    default:
        LED_BLINK();
        break;          }
```

   a. LED is switched ON

b. LED BLINKS
c. LED is switched OFF
d. LED switches ON for some time

Programming Questions

1. Develop an embedded code using C language to find the average of the 10 consecutive data from the sensor and print the same on the serial monitor. [Assume any 10 values for sensor data]
2. Develop an embedded program using C language to print all odd numbers between 1 and 25 using a for loop.
3. Develop an Embedded C Program for a countdown timer that counts until the timer hits 0. [Assume an initial value for the timer]
4. Develop an embedded program using C language to check whether the Sensor Value is positive or negative.
5. Develop an embedded code using C language to calculate and classify the individual based on their height (H in meter), weight (W in kg) and Body Mass Index (BMI). Use the formula: BMI = W/ (H * H)

BMI range	**Category**
BMI < 18.5	Underweight
18.5 <= BMI < 24.9	Normal weight
25 <= BMI < 29.9	Overweight
BMI >= 30	Obese

Know More

QR code for all the Arduino codes used in Unit 2.

3

Introduction to Arduino Mega

Unit Specifics

This Unit emphasizes the following aspects:

- Arduino Mega Specifications
- Arduino Mega Ports and Pins
- Digital and Analog Peripherals

IKS Insights

This section explores how concepts from Indian Knowledge Systems (IKS) align with and enrich contemporary practices and technologies.

Nature-Driven Nurture - Balance in Embedded Systems Design

Ancient Indian knowledge emphasizes the concept of "Nature-driven Nurture", where Prakriti (Nature) embodies patience, perseverance, and prosperity. This philosophy offers a robust model for integrating the best elements to create a balanced system within and around us. The “Pancha Mahabhuta” or the five elements of nature (Earth - Prithvi, Water - Jala, Fire - Agni, Air - Vayu, Space - Akash) and the seven chakras (Root - Muladhara, Sacral Chakra - Swadhisthana, Solar Plexus - Manipura, Heart - Anahata, Throat Chakra - Vishuddha, Third Eye - Ajna and Crown - Sahasrara), as described in Indian philosophy, bring balance to both body and mind, reflecting the interconnectedness of life. The Sankhya philosophy further explores this balance through the three gunas - Sattva, Rajas, and Tamas. It shows how their reciprocity in Prakriti leads to diversity and stability in creation.

This philosophy has clear parallels in the design of embedded systems, such as Arduino, where sensors, processors, and peripherals must work together to create a complete, balanced system with diverse applications. Just as the human body has the crown chakra and the root chakra, any active component requires a source and ground connection. Just as the balance of the three gunas in Prakriti leads to stability and order, balancing resources in embedded systems such as processing power, energy consumption, and memory utilization is crucial for achieving system stability and efficiency. This holistic approach can guide the development of more robust and effective embedded systems.

Rationale

This Unit provides a detailed understanding of the Arduino Mega microcontroller board, which is a robust and versatile platform with adequate input/output options and processing power. Being one of the ideal options for prototyping, understanding the aspects of the board is crucial for students to utilize in embedded systems projects. This Unit covers the essential specifications, power ratings, and detailed information about the ports and pins of Arduino Mega, as well as digital and analog peripheral interfacing with Arduino Mega.

Prerequisites

- Familiarity with fundamental concepts of Embedded C programming.
- Completion of introductory Units covering sketch design, serial communication, and basic coding techniques for Arduino.

Unit Outcomes

At the end of this Unit, students will be able to

U3-O1: Describe the technical specifications and power ratings of the Arduino Mega.
U3-O2: Identify the various ports and pins on the Arduino Mega board.
U3-O3: Interface and program the peripherals for simple applications.

UO - CO Mapping

Course Outcomes	Expected Mapping with Programme Outcomes (1- Weak Correlation; 2- Medium correlation; 3- Strong Correlation)				
	CO-1	CO-2	CO-3	CO-4	CO-5
U3-O1	1	1	1	3	2
U3-O2	1	1	-	3	2
U3-O3	1	1	2	3	3

3.1 Arduino Boards

Arduino is a sort after electronics prototyping platform due to a user-friendly coding environment, ease of use and the availability of powerful libraries that simplify interfacing with other external devices like cameras, scanners, displays, motors, printers, and remote controls. Like the Arduino software (IDE), Arduino platform's hardware design is also freely available open-source and hence it is useful for a broad spectrum of users, such as students, designers, hobbyists, and any embedded systems developer.

In real-time scenarios, tasks like turning ON a motor to fill a tank, waiting for a specified time, and then turning it OFF can be accomplished without requiring significant computing power. However, optimizing processes, such as minimizing wait times, relies on computational power. For instance, determining the time needed to fill a tank based on the water pressure from the tap requires computational calculations.

Starting from basic applications like an automatic water level indicator, progressing to automated plant watering system based on soil moisture levels, and addressing critical tasks like monitoring and communicating with caregivers of infants, all involve computational thinking and precise control. This kind of thinking is facilitated by microcontrollers in various applications.

Arduino UNO REV 3, Arduino Leonardo, Arduino Micro, Arduino Nano boards are some of the boards made for entry level users. Different Arduino boards may have different microcontrollers / processors. The Arduino Uno, shown in Fig. 3.1, is one of the boards in the series of Arduino boards connected using the USB and it is an ideal choice for beginners starting with the Arduino platform. This board employs the ATmega328P microcontroller, a popular and robust choice.

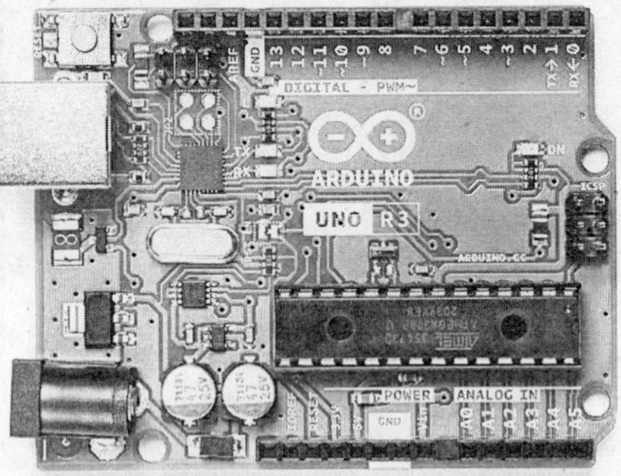

Fig. 3.1 Arduino Uno Rev3

The classic Arduino Nano, shown in Fig. 3.2 is the smallest board used to build projects based on ATmega328. Variants in the family include Arduino Nano, Arduino 33 IoT and Arduino Micro.

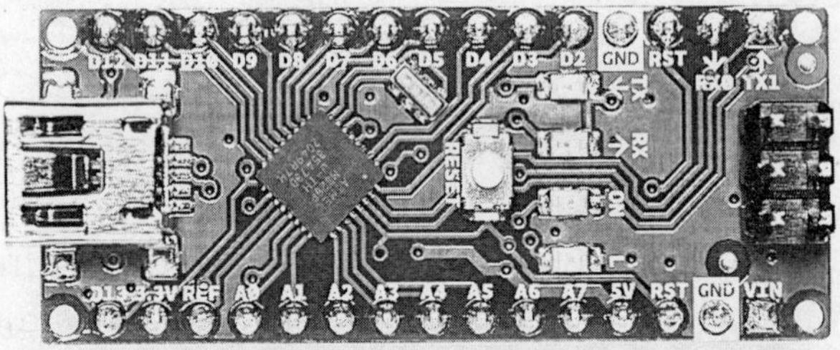

Fig. 3.2 Arduino Nano

The Arduino Zero, shown in Fig. 3.3 is a 32-bit extension of the Uno platform. The board features the Atmel's SAMD21 Microcontroller unit. The board runs at 3.3V.

Fig. 3.3 Arduino Zero

The Arduino Leonardo, shown in Fig. 3.4, features the ATmega32u4 which has a built-in USB communication, and does not require a secondary processor for USB communication. The Arduino Due, shown in Fig. 3.5, is based on a 32-bit ARM core microcontroller and it runs at 3.3 V.

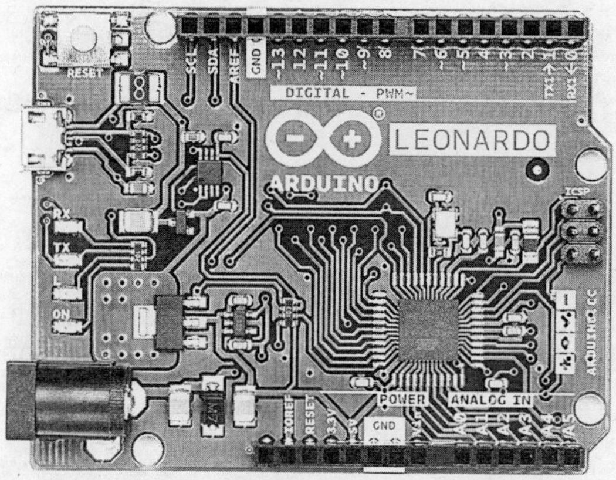

Fig. 3.4 Arduino Leonardo

Fig. 3.5 Arduino Due

3.1.1 Arduino Mega

The Arduino Mega is often preferred over the Uno. Its better capabilities make it more suitable, as shown in Table 3.1. For projects needing more I/O pins, memory, and speed, people choose the Arduino Mega. It supports multiple serial communications. For simple projects or educational purposes, the Arduino Uno is a popular, cheap choice.

Table 3.1: Comparison of performance parameters between Arduino Mega, Uno and Nano

Parameters	Arduino Mega	Arduino Uno	Arduino Nano
Number of Input/Output Pins	54 digital I/O pins (15 PWM), 16 analog inputs.	14 digital I/O pins (6 PWM), 6 analog inputs.	14 digital I/O pins PWM), 8 analc inputs.
Memory	256 KB Flash memory for the program, 8 KB SRAM, and 4 KB EEPROM	32 KB Flash memory, 2 KB SRAM, and 1 KB EEPROM	32 KB Flash memor 2 KB SRAM, and 1 K EEPROM
Processing Power	ATmega2560 is more capable in terms of memory and I/O	Uno uses ATmega328P	Nano us ATmega328

Serial Communication	4 hardware serial ports (UARTs)	1 hardware serial port	1 hardware serial port
Size	Larger physical footprint	Smaller and more compact.	Much smaller and more compact

3.2 Arduino Mega Specifications

The Arduino® Mega 2560 Rev3 development board is designed for building a variety of applications. It features the ATmega2560 microcontroller. The microcontroller operates at 16 MHz frequency. The board includes 54 digital input/output pins and 16 analog inputs. It also has 4 UART (Universal Asynchronous Receiver/Transmitter) hardware serial ports and a USB port for communication. The board features a power jack, an ICSP (In-Circuit Serial Programming) header and a reset button. Additionally, it has a USB serial processor called ATmega16U2, which serves as an interface between the USB port and the microcontroller. This enhances the board's flexibility in connecting with peripheral interfaces. The major features of the board are shown in Fig. 3.6.

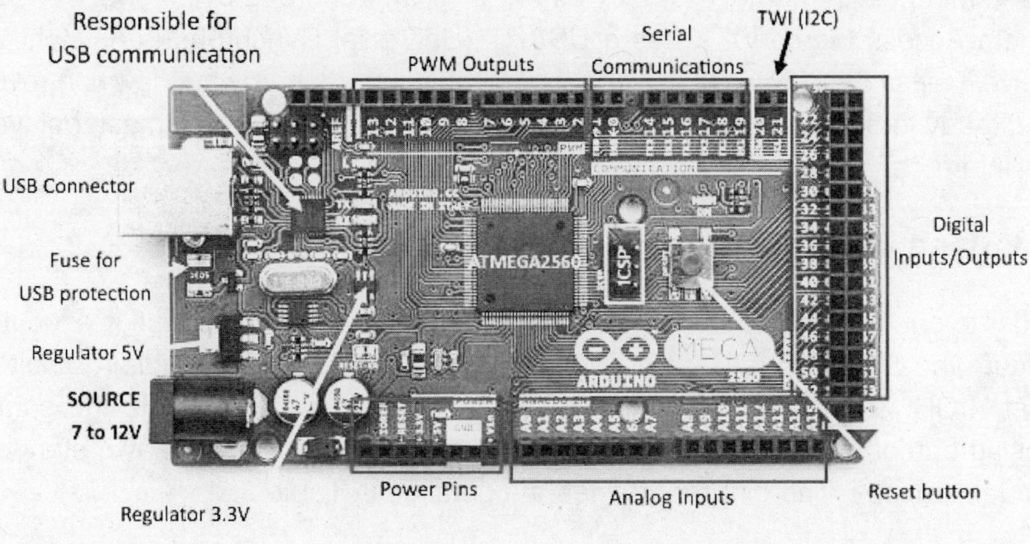

Fig. 3.6 Arduino® Mega 2560 Rev3 development board

The board includes

- Eight general-purpose working registers (32 bits each)
- A real-time counter with a separate oscillator
- Four 8-bit PWM channels
- Four programmable serial UART (Universal Synchronous Asynchronous Receiver/Transmitter) interfaces.
- An SPI (Serial Peripheral Interface).

3.2.1 ATmega2560 Processor

The ATmega2560 processor can execute up to 16 million instructions every second, and so its throughput is said to be 16MIPs (Million Instructions Per Second) when running at its maximum clock speed of 16 MHz. The processor has 256 kilobytes (kB) of memory (including 8 kB for the bootloader), 4 kB of EEPROM, and 8 kB of internal SRAM.

3.2.2 ATmega16U2 USB Serial Processor

ATmega16U2 runs at 16 MHz with 16 MIPS throughput. It has 16 kB of ISP (In-System Programming) flash memory, 512 bytes of EEPROM, and 512 bytes of SRAM (Static Random Access Memory). It has a USART (Universal Synchronous Asynchronous Receive/Transmit) with SPI master-only mode. It supports hardware flow control using RTS (Ready to Send) and CTS (Clear to Send) signals. It also has a master/slave SPI serial interface.

3.2.3 Sleep Modes

In order to put the Arduino board into sleep mode, a SLEEP instruction is executed to configure the Sleep Mode Control Register (SMCR). The Sleep Enable (SE) bit must be set HIGH. Sleep Mode Select bits (SM[2:0]) are used to activate the same by choosing one of the sleep modes among idle, power-down, power-save, standby, or extended standby. The different modes are detailed in Table 3.2.

Sleep Mode Control Register Format (SMCR format)

MSB (7)							LSB (0)
U	U	U	U	SM 2	SM 1	SM 0	SE

U - Unused

SM x - Sleep Mode Select Bits (x-> 0 to 2)

SE- Sleep Enable

Table 3.2 - Sleep Modes in Arduino Mega Board

S. No	Sleep Mode	Description
1.	Idle Mode	The CPU (Central Processing Unit) is halted while all other functions like peripherals and interrupts, remain active.
2.	ADC Noise Reduction	It turns OFF the CPU and all other clocks (clkCPU, clkI/O, clkFLASH) except for the ADC (Analog-to-Digital Converter). It is useful for precision ADC conversions without noise disturbances from other parts of the microcontroller.
3.	Power Save	Turns OFF the CPU clock but keeps the ADC, Timer/Counters, SPI, and USART running. It allows quick wake-up from external interrupts while saving more power than idle mode.
4.	Power Down	CPU and all peripherals are turned OFF except for the external interrupts. This mode minimizes power consumption allowing the CPU to wake up for an external event trigger.
5.	Standby	Provides a compromise between power consumption and wake-up time, keeping the external oscillator running while disabling the CPU and reducing other clock

		sources.

3.2.4 Power

- **USB Connection**

  The Arduino Mega board can be powered by connecting it to a computer or a USB power adapter using a USB Type-B cable. It supplies 5V power from the USB connection

- **External AC/DC Adapter**

  To power an Arduino Mega using an external AC/DC adapter, the DC barrel jack or the Vin pin on the board can be used. An appropriate AC/DC adapter can be chosen that provides a regulated DC voltage within the Arduino Mega's input voltage range (7 to 12 V DC). The Arduino can also be powered by applying a regulated 9-12 V DC power source to the Vin pin.

3.3 Arduino Mega Pins and Ports

3.3.1 Pins

This Section provides the pin details of the Arduino Mega board as labelled in Fig. 3.7

NC in Fig. 3.7 denotes no connection and serves as a placeholder. The IOREF pin is linked to the 5 V bus to provide the logical reference voltage (high). The RESET pin resets the microcontroller when set to low.

3.3.1.1 Power Pins

The 3.3 V pin delivers 3.3 V power at a maximum of 50 mA. The 5 V pin provides 5 V power. The GND pins are for ground connection. The Vin pin functions as an internal input for an externally regulated 7 - 12 V power supply for the board. If the board is powered via the power jack or USB, the Vin pin serves as a 5 V output.

3.3.1.2 Analog Input Pins

The sixteen analog input (ANALOG IN) pins on the Arduino Mega, as illustrated in Fig. 3.6, are labelled as A0 through A15. They are used to read signals from external analog sensors. Each pin has a 10-bit resolution, allowing it to work with 2^{10} different voltage levels, i.e., 1024 levels.

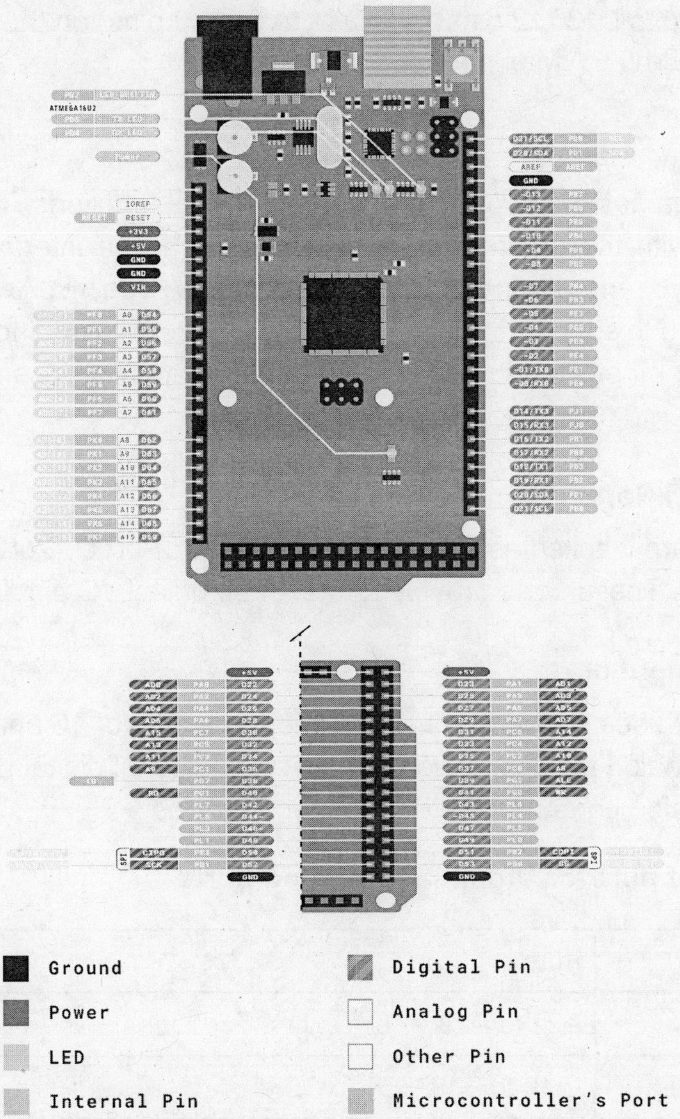

Fig. 3.7 Pin configuration grouping in the Arduino Mega board (Source: Pinout - Mega 2560 Rev 3 datasheet)

3.3.1.3 Digital I/O Pins

The Arduino Mega board has 54 digital I/O (DIGITAL) pins. They can be configurec for digital input or output. These pins operate at 5 V and can supply or receive up tc 20 mA of current. Current above 40 mA on any pin causes permanent board damage Additionally, fifteen of these pins support 8-bit PWM (Pulse Width Modulation) output Digital I/O pins D2 to D13 (12 pins) and D44 to D46 (3 pins) on the Arduino Mega are able to generate 8-bit PWM signals.

3.3.2 Ports

The Arduino Mega has many ports that serve different functions. These ports enable communication with the external world. Each port can be interfaced with sensors, actuators, displays, and other electronic components. Specific Arduino libraries anc functions are used to support the interface. This makes the Arduino Mega suitable fo complex projects that need many input/output capabilities and communicatior options.

3.3.2.1 Digital I/O Ports

Digital I/O ports are labelled as Port A, Port B, Port C, Port D, Port E, Port G, Port H, Port J and Port L. These ports provide a total of 54 digital I/O pins (D0 to D53).

3.3.2.2 Analog Input ports

Analog Input port uses Port F and Port K, offering a total of 16 analog input pins (AC to A15). These analog pins can also be used as additional digital pins. Table 3.3 lists all digital and analog ports and their corresponding pins.

Table 3.3: List of pins for Digital and Analog ports

Digital I/O Ports	Pins
Port A	D22 to D29
Port B	D 10 to D13, D50 to D53
Port C	D30 to D37
Port D	D18 to D21, D38

Port E	D0 to D3, D5
Port G	D4, D39, D40, D41
Port H	Digital I/O Pins: D6 to D9, D16 to D17
Port J	Digital I/O Pins: D14 to D15 (also used for serial RX/TX)
Port L	Digital I/O Pins: D42 to D49
Analog Input Ports	**Pins**
Port F	Analog input pins A0 to A7 (also used as D54 to D61 Digital pins)
Port K	Analog input pins A8 to A15 (also used as D62 to D69 Digital pins)

3.3.2.3 Serial Communication Ports

a) Serial (UART) Ports

Serial ports are used for serial communication, including programming the Arduino and communicating with external devices. The Mega board features a total of 4 UART ports, each port consisting of two pins (listed in Table 3.4), one for RX (Receive) which receives data and other for TX (Transmit) which transmits data. Each UART port on the Arduino Mega can be used independently for serial communication with external devices such as sensors, Bluetooth module, GPS module, and other microcontrollers.

Table 3.4: List of UART ports

Serial Port	Pin Numbers
Serial 0	Pins 0 (RX 0) and 1 (TX 0)
Serial 1	Pins 19 (RX 1) and 18 (TX 1)
Serial 2	Pins 17 (RX 2) and 16 (TX 2)
Serial 3	Pins 15 (RX 3) and 14 (TX 3)

b) SPI (Serial Peripheral Interface)

SPI enables fast communication between microcontrollers and peripherals like sensors, displays, and SD cards. It utilizes four signal lines: MOSI (Master Out Slave In), MISO (Master In Slave Out), SCK (Serial Clock), and SS (Slave Select). The clock frequency ranges from 125 kHz to 8 MHz. SPI supports full-duplex communication. It allows connection of multiple devices on the same bus. The Arduino Mega has one SPI port with signal lines as listed in Table 3.5.

Table 3.5: List of pins for SPI port

Signal line	Description	Pin Number
MISO	Master In Slave Out	Pin 50
MOSI	Master Out Slave In	Pin 51
SCK	Serial Clock	Pin 52
SS	Slave Select	Pin 53

c) I2C (Inter-Integrated Circuit)

I2C is a serial communication protocol. It supports multiple masters and slaves. It is commonly used to connect low-speed peripherals like sensors, EEPROMs, and microcontrollers. It uses two signal lines: SDA (Serial Data Line) and SCL (Serial Clock Line). Each I2C device has a unique address, allowing several devices to share the same bus.
The Arduino Mega has one I2C port and the pin numbers for the same are listed in Table 3.6.

Table 3.6: List of pins for I2C

Signal line	Pin Number
SDA	Pin 20
SCL	Pin 21

3.3.2.4 PWM (Pulse Width Modulation) Ports

PWM ports include digital I/O pins that can generate PWM output. These are pins D2 to D13 and D44 to D46. It allows analog-like control of devices such as motors and LEDs.

3.3.2.5 Special Purpose Ports

a. **ICSP (In-Circuit Serial Programming) header**: Used for programming the Arduino and for high-voltage programming.

b. **USB port**: Arduino boards feature a USB port primarily for uploading code and data exchange. It offers an easy way to upload sketches to the Arduino. It also allows serial data exchange between the Arduino and the computer.

3.4 Digital and Analog Peripherals

The Arduino Mega board designates 72 out of its 86 pins for input and output. It has 54 digital I/O pins (D0 to D53). They can be used with *pinMode(), digitalWrite(),* and *digitalRead().* There are 16 analog input pins (A0 to A15). Each has a 10-bit ADC (Analog to Digital Conversion). The *analogRead()* function is used to access the analog pins. All analog pins can also function as digital I/O pins. Also, digital I/O pins D2 to D13 (12 pins) and D44 to D46 (3 pins) can generate 8-bit PWM signals. These pins are controlled using the *analogWrite()* function.

3.4.1 Digital Peripherals

Digital peripherals typically refer to the external devices that interface with a microcontroller using digital signals (high or low voltage levels). The most common digital peripherals that will be used are LEDs (Light Emitting Diodes), Push Buttons and Switches.

3.4.1.1 Configuring the Digital Pins as Input/Output

Arduino Mega has digital pins numbered from 0 to 53. These digital pins can be initially configured as either input or output using the *pinMode()* function. The *setup()* function in Arduino sketches calls the inbuilt function pinMode().

3.4.1.1.1 Syntax - pinMode()

The syntax for the pinMode function is given below:

```
pinMode(pin_number, mode);
```

- **pin_number:** The Arduino Mega's pin number can be 0 to 53. It configures a pin as an input or an output.
- **mode**: The mode to set for the pin, specified by one of the following constants:
  - **INPUT**: Configures the pin as an input.
  - **OUTPUT**: Configures the pin as an output.
  - **INPUT_PULLUP**: Sets the pin as an input with a built-in pullup resistor.

3.4.1.1.2 Examples - pinMode()

Some examples depicting the usage of pinMode function is given below:

Code Snippets	Explanation
`pinMode(9, OUTPUT);`	Configure pin 9 as an output
`pinMode(11, INTPUT);`	Configure pin 11 as an input
`void setup() { pinMode(9, OUTPUT); pinMode(11, INPUT); }`	Providing configurations of multiple digital pins inside the setup function

3.4.1.2 Interfacing Output Devices to Arduino Board

Interfacing output devices such as LEDs, motors, and displays to an Arduino board is done through the digital pins. A sketch is then written to control them. This allows the Arduino to send signals to the devices. It enables functionalities like lighting/illumination, movement, and visual feedback.

3.4.1.2.1 Digital Write Function

The LEDs, relays, and other digital devices connected to Arduino pins can be controlled using the digitalWrite() function.

Syntax - digitalWrite()

The syntax for the digitalWrite() function is given below:

```
digitalWrite(pin_number, value);
```

- **pin_number**: The pin number which is configured as output. It can be a number from 0 to 53 on Arduino Mega.
- **value**: Specifies the state to be written to the pin, represented by constants:

1. HIGH (or 1): Sets the pin voltage to HIGH, typically 5 V.
2. LOW (or 0): Sets the pin voltage to LOW, 0 V or ground.

3.4.1.2.2 LED Interfacing

LEDs are commonly employed as visual indicators, or status displays in electronic projects. They are controlled using digital output pins. A built-in LED connected to the pin 13 on the Arduino Mega. This LED is often used for quick testing purposes as it can be controlled directly without external connections.

Example - Internal LED interfacing and blinking

Let us consider that the internal LED connected at pin 13 is to be turned ON and OFF using the Arduino board.

Arduino Code - Built-in LED Blinking

```
void setup() {
  pinMode(13, OUTPUT);  // Configure pin 13 as an output
}
void loop() {
  // Turn ON the LED using a HIGH signal
  digitalWrite(13, HIGH);
  delay(1000);                          // Wait for 1 second
```

```
  // Turn OFF the LED using a LOW signal
  digitalWrite(13, LOW);
  delay(1000);                          // Wait for 1 second
}
```

The pin 13, and in turn, the internally connected in-built LED is turned ON by supplying a HIGH value to the digitalWrite function. The LED is then turned OFF by a LOW value after a delay of 1 second. This ON and OFF operation is repeated inside the loop function block. This provides a blinking operation for the LED. Fig. 3.8 shows the internal LED glowing on the Arduino Mega board.

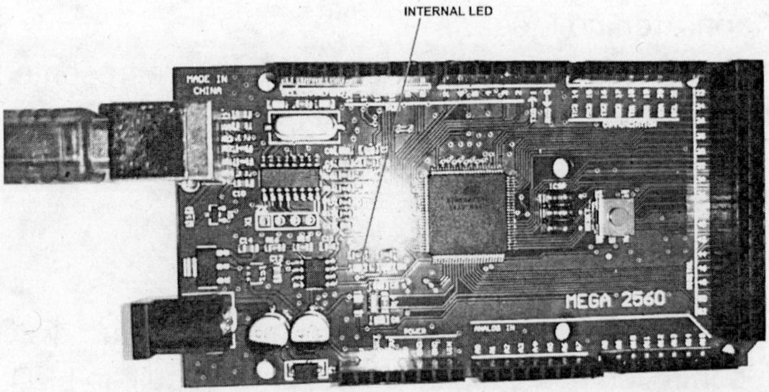

Fig. 3.8 Output showing the internal LED glowing

In a similar way, more LEDs can also be connected externally to the pins, and they can be controlled using the Arduino.

Example - External LED Interfacing and blinking

Let us consider an LED connected at pin 9 externally. The task is to turn it ON and OFF using the Arduino.

Arduino Code - External LED Blinking

```
int myled = 9;
void setup() {
  pinMode(myled, OUTPUT);       // Configure pin 10 as an output
}
```

```
void loop() {
  digitalWrite(myled, HIGH);    // Turn the LED ON
  delay(1000);                  // Wait for 1 second
  digitalWrite(myled, LOW);     // Turn the LED OFF
  delay(1000);                  // Wait for 1 second
}
```

One end of the LED is connected to digital pin 9 on the Arduino Mega as shown in Fig. 3.9. The other end is connected to one end of a 220 Ω resistor. The other end of the resistor is connected to the digital GND on the Arduino Mega. The resistor acts as a current limiter, limiting the current flow to the LED. If the LED is connected directly without any resistor, the LED will initially shine brightly. The component overheats and fails or burns out from too much current.

Alternating HIGH and LOW voltages are supplied to the LED (connected at pin 10) using the Arduino board to create a blinking effect as shown in Fig. 3.10.

Fig. 3.9 Schematic for Interfacing - External LED connected to Mega board

Fig. 3.10 Output of an external LED connected to Arduino board

Know More

A ***breadboard*** *is a versatile platform enabling easy component placement and adjustments. It is used to prototype electronic circuits without the need for soldering, it includes a rectangular grid of interconnected holes where discrete components and jumper wires can be inserted to assemble circuits.*

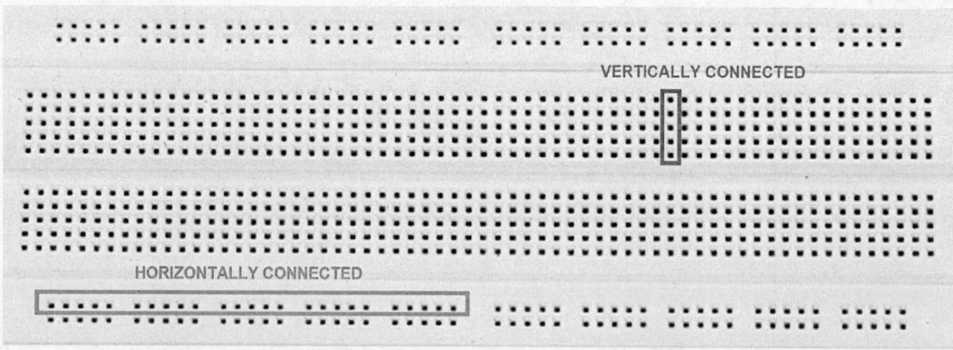

Front side of a breadboard

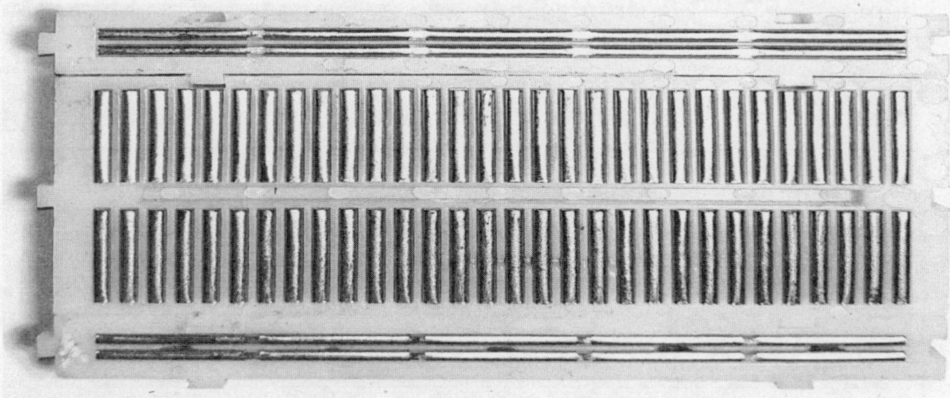

Back side of a breadboard

3.4.1.2.3 Seven - Segment LED Interfacing

A seven segment LED display comprises 7 individual LEDs configured in a rectangular layout as shown in Fig. 3.11 to form numbers and some letters. Each segment can be lit independently, allowing for the display of digits 0-9 and some alphabetic characters. The 7-segment LED which is used in our experiment is SUN056CA (Common Anode configuration).

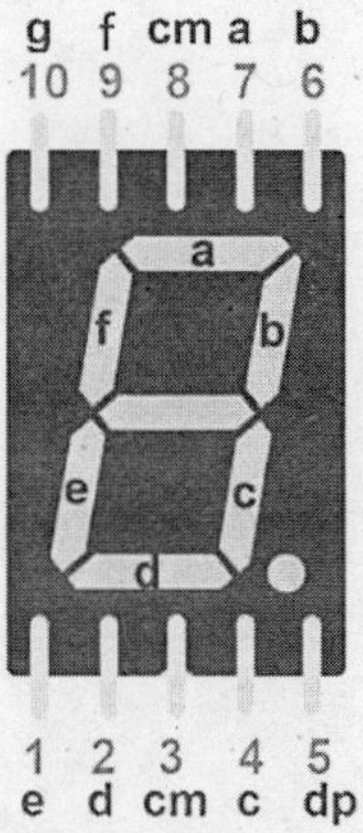

Pin 1- e-segment
Pin 2- d-segment
Pin 3- common
Pin 4- c-segment
Pin 5- Dot
Pin 6- b-segment
Pin 7- a-segment
Pin 8- common
Pin 9- f-segment
Pin 10- g-segment

Fig. 3.11 Pin Configuration and different segments of 7-segment LED

To interface a 7-segment LED display to an Arduino Mega board the display's segments are connected to the digital pins of the Arduino board as in Table 3.7. Then, it is programmed to display numbers. The setup shown in Fig. 3.12 shows the pin configuration diagram. It connects the Arduino Mega's digital pins to specific segments of the 7-segment LED. This creates numeric or alphanumeric characters on the display.

Table 3.7 Hardware connection between 7-segment display and Arduino Mega

7-segment display pin	Segment representation	Arduino Mega pin
1	e	4
2	d	5
3&8	common	Vdd (5 V/3.3 V)
4	c	6
5	dp	-
6	b	7
7	a	8
9	f	3
10	g	2

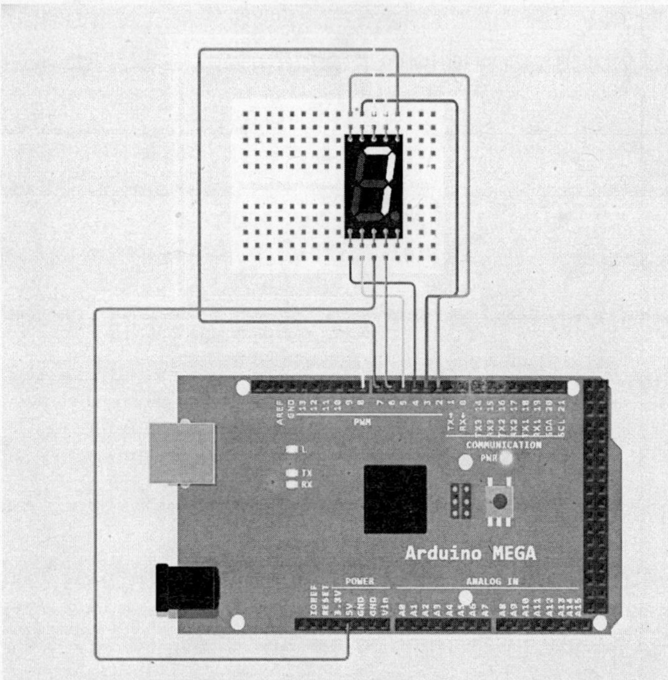

Fig. 3.12 Schematic diagram for connecting 7-segment display to Arduino Mega

Know More

Configurations of 7 segment display

A 7-segment display has two configurations: a common anode and a common cathode. In a common anode setup, all the anodes of the LEDs connect to a common positive voltage (anodes are positive terminals). To turn ON a specific segment, the corresponding cathode (negative terminal) is connected to the ground. In a common cathode configuration, cathodes unite at a single ground in a common cathode setup. To light the segments, a positive voltage is applied to their anodes.

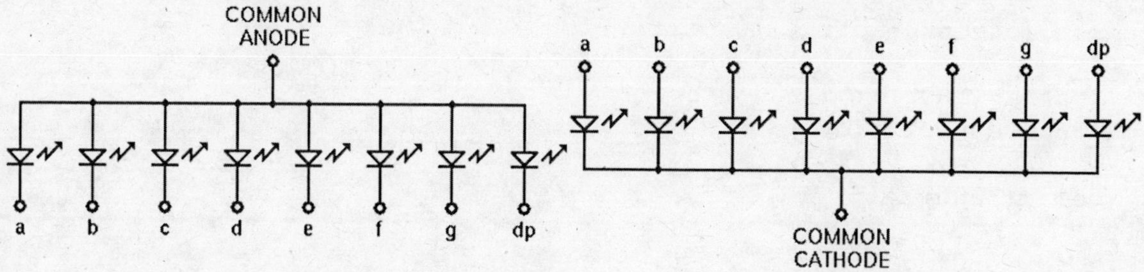

Arduino Code - Interfacing 7-segment LED

The Arduino code for connecting 7-segment LEDs in Common Anode configuration is given below. The common terminal of the 7-segment LED is connected to 5 V. It is illuminated by providing a LOW signal to the segment.

```
// Segment representations for numbers
//                          { a,b,c,d,e,f,g }
int array_num[10][7] = {    { 0,0,0,0,0,0,1 },  // segment values - 0
                            { 1,0,0,1,1,1,1 },  // segment values - 1
                            { 0,0,1,0,0,1,0 },  // segment values - 2
                            { 0,0,0,0,1,1,0 },  // segment values - 3
                            { 1,0,0,1,1,0,0 },  // segment values - 4
                            { 0,1,0,0,1,0,0 },  // segment values - 5
                            { 0,1,0,0,0,0,0 },  // segment values - 6
                            { 0,0,0,1,1,1,1 },  // segment values - 7
                            { 0,0,0,0,0,0,0 },  // segment values - 8
                            { 0,0,0,1,1,0,0 }}; // segment values - 9
void number_write(int);        //User defined function declaration
int ctr,j;
void setup()
```

```
{ //Setting pinmodes for 7 digital pins
  //Segments a to g configured as output
  pinMode(8, OUTPUT);
  pinMode(7, OUTPUT);
  pinMode(6, OUTPUT);
  pinMode(5, OUTPUT);
  pinMode(4, OUTPUT);
  pinMode(3, OUTPUT);
  pinMode(2, OUTPUT);
}
void loop()
{ //Counter loop - displaying numbers from 0 to 9
  for (ctr = 0; ctr < 10; ctr++)
  {
    delay(1000);
    number_write(ctr);      //Calling the user defined function
  }
  delay(3000);
}
// User Defined function to write a value to the 7 segments
void number_write(int num)
{
  int pin_no = 8;
  for (j=0; j< 7; j++) {
    digitalWrite(pin_no, array_num[num][j]);
    Pin_no--;  }
}
```

The 7 digital pins (Digital Pins 2 to 8) connected to each segment (a to g) as shown in Table 3.7 are configured as OUTPUT. The variable num_array is an array of values to be supplied to each segment for creating different numbers on the display segment as per the common anode configuration. User defined function "Num_Write" controls the segments to be lit up to display numbers from 9 to 0. The output of the 7-segment display along with the Arduino board connectivity is shown in Fig. 3.13. The segments a, b and c are lit up to show the number 7 on the display, by supplying a LOW value to the digital pins 7, 6 and 4 respectively as per the values supplied by the num_array.

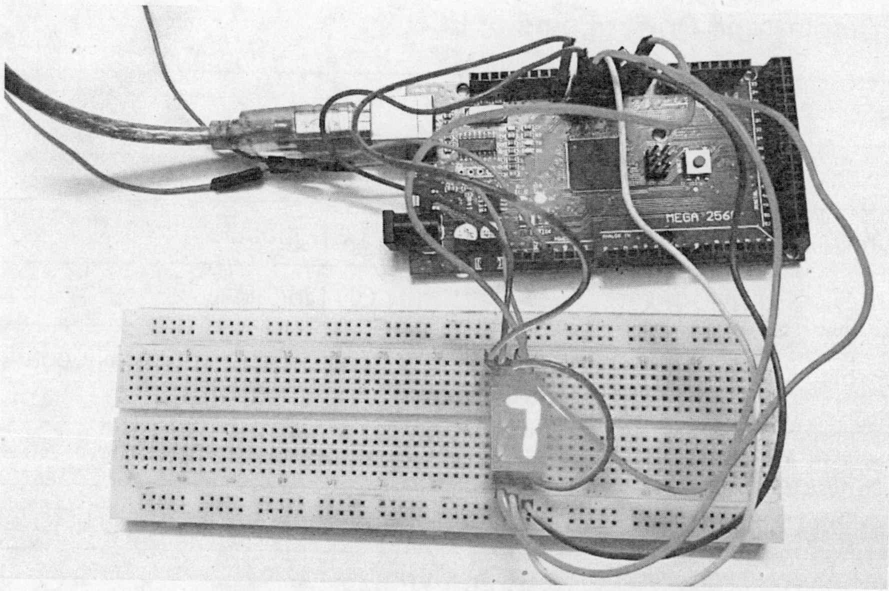

Fig. 3.13 Output of a 7 segment LED connected to an Arduino board

3.4.1.2.4 LCD Interfacing

An LCD (Liquid Crystal Display) is a technology with a flat panel commonly used to show alphanumeric characters and simple graphics. It uses electric signals to control liquid crystals. They can block or allow light, creating visible images. The pin configuration of a typical LCD is shown in Fig. 3.14. LCD pins are usually divided into display and control pins, as in Table 3.8.

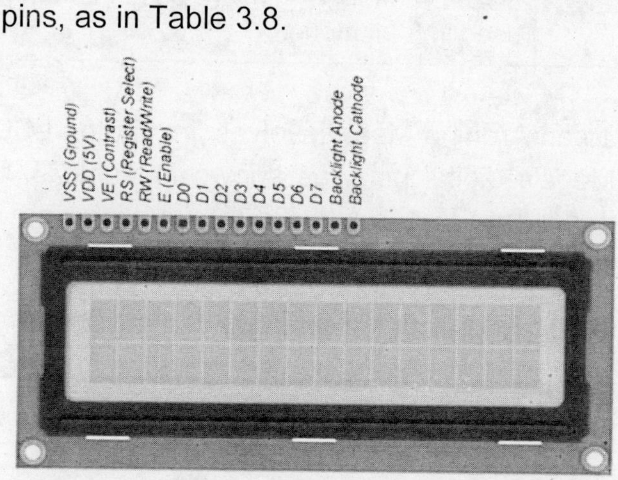

Fig. 3.14 Pin Configuration of a typical LCD

Table 3.8: Display and Control pins of LCD

LCD Pins	Description
	Display Pins
VSS (Ground)	Ground connection for LCD module
VDD (+5 V)	Power Supply to the LCD Module
VE (Contrast)	Controls the display contrast and is typically connected to a potentiometer for adjustment.
BLA+ (Backlight Anode)	Positive terminal for backlight
BLA- (Backlight Cathode)	Negative terminal for backlight
	Control Pins
RS (Register Select)	If RS = 1, it selects the data register and if RS = 0, it selects the command register
RW (Read/Write)	Controls the direction of data flow (RW=1 for read and RW=0 for write)
E (Enable)	Enables the display module to accept commands or data.
D0-D7 (Data Pins)	Data lines for transferring data between the Arduino and the LCD. Data bits D4-D7 are used in 4-bit mode; and D0-D7 are used in 8-bit mode.

Connecting an LCD to an Arduino Mega involves linking the LCD display's data and control pins to the Mega's digital pins, as shown in Table 3.9. This process also requires configuring the library for the specific display type and writing code to send text or data to be displayed.

Table 3.9: Hardware Interfacing - LCD Display

Pins in the LCD	Digital pin in Arduino board
VDD	5 V/3.3 V

Vss	GND
RS	9
E	8
RW	Vcc (To read register), Gnd (To write register)
D4 - D7 (4 bit mode)	2 - 5
Backlight Anode	Through 1 kΩ resistor to 5 V
Backlight Cathode	GND

Linking library files to Arduino IDE

In order to connect an Arduino Mega with an LCD, appropriate library files are to be downloaded and installed. The most commonly used library for LCDs is the LiquidCrystal library and the latest version can be downloaded from https://www.arduino.cc/reference/en/libraries/liquidcrystal/ as shown in Fig. 3.15. The downloaded file will be available in zip file format.

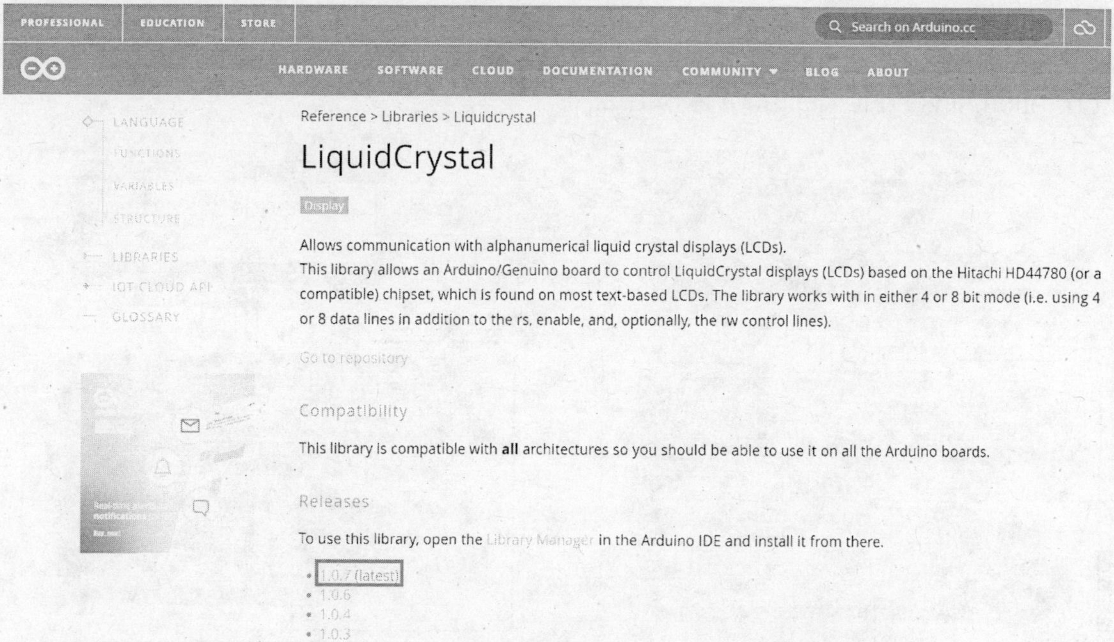

Fig. 3.15 Liquid Crystal library from arduino.cc

The .zip file can be added to the sketch by clicking the "Add .ZIP library…" under the Sketch menu as shown in Fig. 3.16. Select the .zip file from the recently downloaded location and click on the Open button.

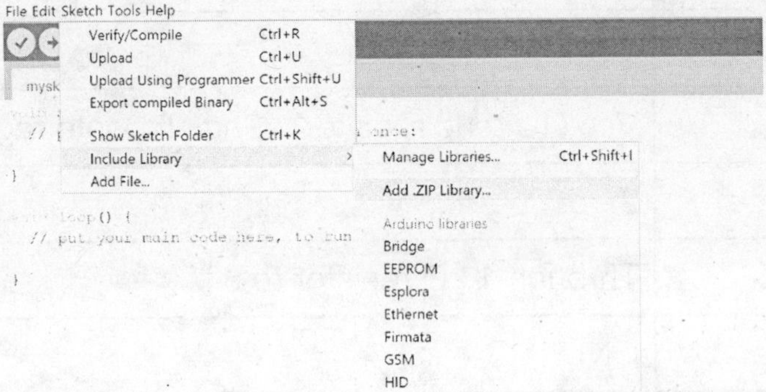

Fig. 3.16 Including libraries from the Sketch menu

Once the downloaded library is added, it can be included in the Arduino sketch by including the following line at the top of the Arduino sketch.

```
#include <LiquidCrystal.h>
```

The connections are made between the LCD and the Mega board as per Table 3.9 and the schematic diagram is shown in Fig. 3.17. Data pins d4 to d7 handle 4-bit information, linking to digital pins 5 to 2.

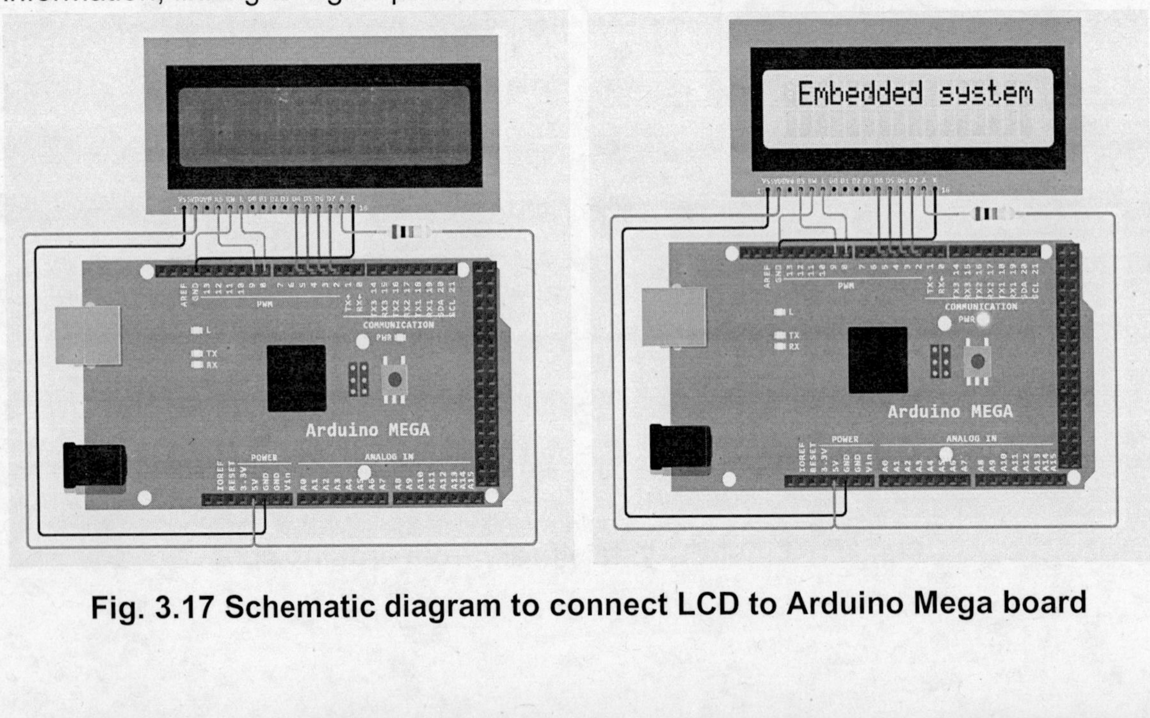

Fig. 3.17 Schematic diagram to connect LCD to Arduino Mega board

Arduino Code - LCD Display

```
#include <LiquidCrystal.h>            //including header files
const int rs = 9, en = 8, d4 = 5, d5 = 4, d6 = 3, d7 = 2;
LiquidCrystal lcd(rs, en, d4, d5, d6, d7);
void setup()
{
lcd.begin(16, 2);      // Initialize LCD with 16 columns and 2 rows
delay(500);
}
void loop() {
lcd.setCursor(0, 0);  // Positions the cursor to first row, first
column
lcd.print("Embedded systems!");  //Print the message
for (int j = 0; j < 29; i++)
{
lcd.scrollDisplayLeft();  // Scroll display towards left
delay(250);
}
}
```

This code initializes the LCD library, sets up the LCD dimensions and pins, and prints "Welcome to the Embedded systems!" on the display. The function lcd.scrollDisplayLeft() will continuously scroll the message "Welcome to the Embedded systems!" across the screen from right to left. The output of the LCD interfaced with Mega board is shown in Fig. 3.18.

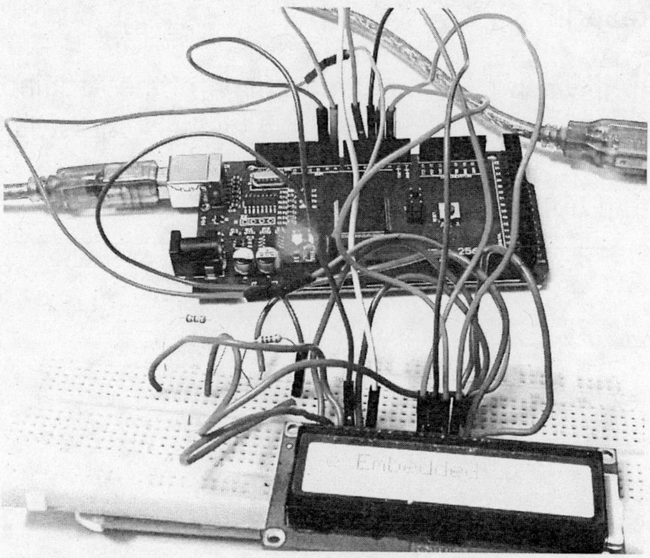

Fig. 3.18 Interfacing LCD with the Mega board

3.4.1.3 Interfacing Input Devices to Arduino Board

Input devices like buttons, switches, and sensors like temperature sensor, light sensor, sound sensor etc., can be interfaced to an Arduino board by connecting via the digital input pins. In embedded C code, a *digitalRead()* function is used to read the values of input devices from the pin states or values.

3.4.1.3.1 Digital Read Function

The *digitalRead()* function gets the current state of a pin. This allows the Arduino to respond in real-time to changes in connected devices, like buttons and sensors.

Syntax - digitalRead()

The syntax for the *digitalRead()* function is given below:

```
return_value =digitalRead(pin_number);
```

- **return_value:** The input pin reads HIGH when the switch is not pressed and LOW when it is pressed.
- **pin_number**: The pin number configured as input. It can be a number from 0 to 53 on Arduino Mega.

Example - digitalRead()

Let us consider that a switch is connected to pin 4 of the Arduino Mega. Pin 4 is an input. The *digitalRead()* function reads its value to check the switch's status.

Arduino Code - Read button state

```
void setup() {
  // Set pin 4 as input with internal pull-up resistor
  pinMode(4, INPUT_PULLUP);      // Button is connected to Pin 4
  Serial.begin(9600);
}
void loop() {
  // Read button's state or the value at pin 4
  int button_state = digitalRead(4);
```

```
  if (button_state == LOW) {
    Serial.println("Switch pressed!");
    // Your code here
  } else {
    // Switch is not pressed
    // Your code here
  }
  delay(100);                // Delay to avoid reading input too quickly
}
```

3.4.1.3.2 Push Button Interfacing

Push Buttons and switches are used for user input or as digital triggers. They can be connected to digital input pins to detect state changes (pressed or released). The pin configuration for connecting the push button with the Mega board is shown in Fig. 3.19.

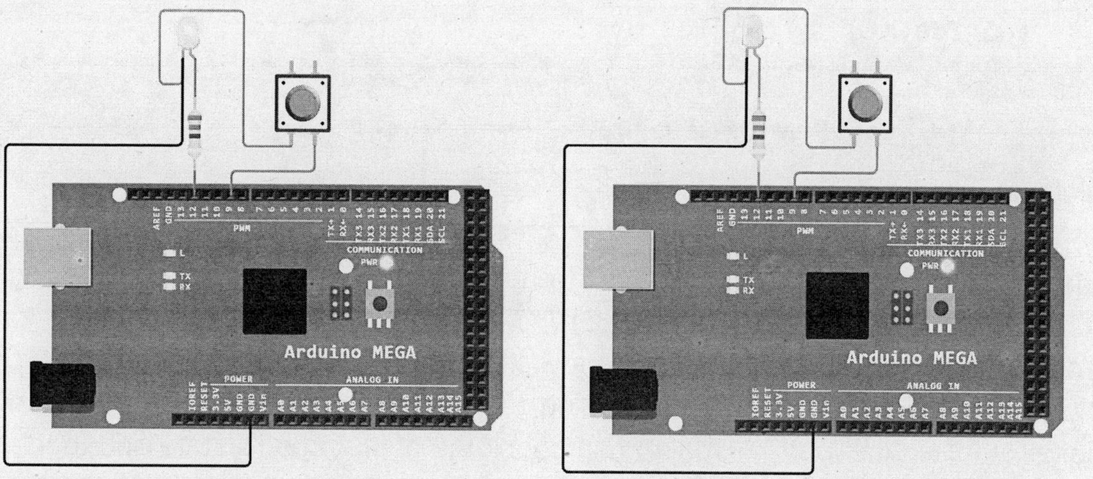

a) Push button pressed state **b) Push button released state**

Fig. 3.19 Configuration diagram for connecting a push button with Arduino

Arduino Code - Push button Interfacing

The Arduino code for interfacing push button and LED is given below. The LED attached to digital pin 12 operates as an output device. The push button connected to digital pin 9 functions as an input device.

```
int myledPin = 12;         // LED to PIN 12
int mybuttonPin = 9;       // Button on PIN 9
int toggleState = false; // Button toggle is OFF
void setup()
{
  // mybuttonPin configured as input
  pinMode(mybuttonPin, INPUT_PULLUP);
  // myledPin configured as output device
  pinMode(myledPin, OUTPUT);
}
void loop()
{
  //check for button press
  if (digitalRead(mybuttonPin) == false)
  {
    toggleState = !toggleState; // Reverse current state of variable
    digitalWrite(myledPin, toggleState); // LED to toggleState
  }
  while (digitalRead(mybuttonPin) == false);
  delay(50);                     // Add a delay of 50ms
}
```

The loop() function uses digitalRead() to read the push button's state. Pressing the button makes digitalRead() return LOW. This means the pin is connected to the ground through the button. When the switch is not pressed, digitalRead() will return HIGH. This is due to the internal pull-up resistor pulling the pin to 5 V. By calling digitalRead() in the loop(), Arduino can check the push button's state and toggle the LED connected to it. Fig. 3.20 shows the output of a push button, and an LED connected to the Mega board.

Fig. 3.20 Output of a Push button and LED interfaced with Arduino board

3.4.2 Analog Peripherals

Analog peripherals, such as temperature sensors, light sensors, and potentiometers, provide continuously varying signals that represent physical quantities like temperature, light etc.,

3.4.2.1 Analog Read Function

The analog input pins are used to connect the analog peripherals to the Arduino Mega board. The voltage on a specified analog input pin is read using the *analogRead()* function which converts the varying voltage levels to a digital value between 0 and 1023. It corresponds to a 0 to 5 V range. It allows for precise measurement of analog signals.

3.4.2.1.1 Syntax - analogRead()

The syntax for the analogRead() function is given below:

```
int sensorValue = analogRead(pin_number);
```

- **pin_number**: The analog input pin to be read (A0 to A15).

- **sensorValue** : The read value converted to a digital between (0 to 1023) will be stored

3.4.2.1.2 Interfacing Potentiometer

Let us consider that a potentiometer is connected to analog input A1 as shown in Fig. 3.21. The hardware pin mappings are done as per Table 3.10.

Table 3.10 - Hardware Interfacing - Potentiometer

Potentiometer Pin	Arduino Mega Pin
Pin 1	5 V
Pin 2	A1
Pin 3	GND

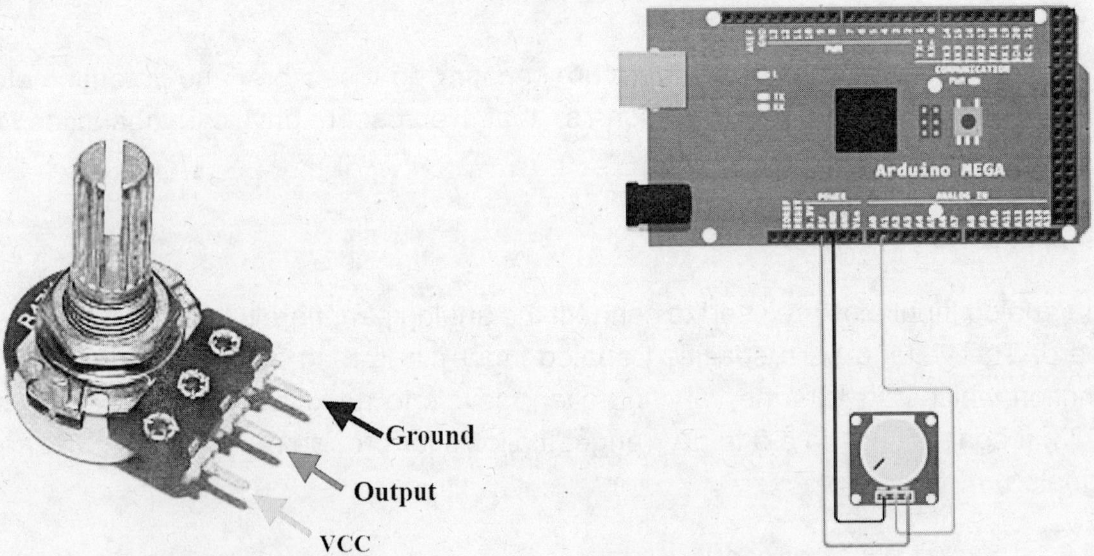

a) Potentiometer pinouts b) Interfacing with Mega board

Fig. 3.21 Interfacing potentiometer with Arduino Mega board

Arduino Code - Interfacing Potentiometer

```
void setup() {
  // Start serial communication to print the sensorValue in the
Serial Monitor
  Serial.begin(9600);
}
void loop() {
  int mysensorValue = analogRead(A1);   // read the analog input from
A0
  // Convert analog reading(0 - 1023) to a voltage range(0 - 5V)
  float myvoltage = mysensorValue * (5.0 / 1023.0);
  Serial.print("Voltage read from the sensor:");
  Serial.println(myvoltage);     // Display voltage on the Serial
Monitor
}
```

This code continuously reads the value from analog input pin A1, converts it to a voltage and displays in the Serial Monitor. The read analog value (0-1023) is scaled to a voltage range of 0-5V using a conversion factor. The potentiometer connected to the Mega board is shown in Fig. 3.22. The output on the Serial Monitor while varying the potentiometer is shown in Fig. 3.23.

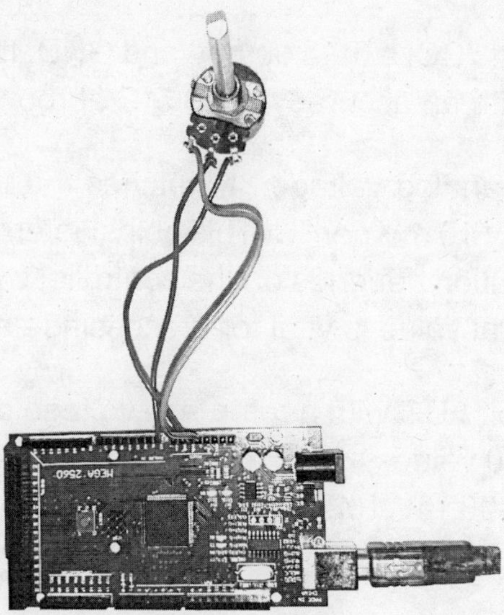

Fig. 3.22 Potentiometer connected to Analog pin A1 of the Mega board

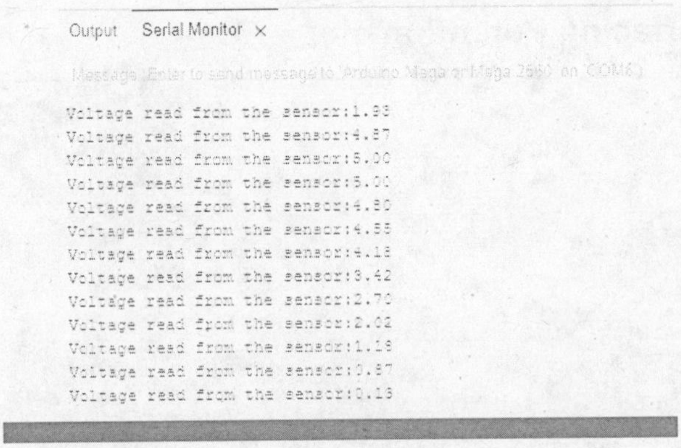

Fig. 3.23 Output of the varying potentiometer captured on the Serial Monitor

3.4.2.1.3 Interfacing Temperature Sensor

Popular temperature sensors on the market may be analog or digital. LM35 and TMP36 are analog sensors, while DS18B20 and DHT11 are digital sensors. They also vary in their specifications, such as range and accuracy. The example below shows the use of the analogRead function for the LM35 temperature sensor. It is an analog sensor. An instance of DHT11 is demonstrated in the forthcoming Unit 4, Section 4.2.6.

LM35 features three pins: VCC, a data output, and GND. It can measure temperatures from -55°C to +150°C, with an accuracy of ±0.5°C at room temperature.

The sensor output is an analog voltage. It matches the temperature in Celsius. The output voltage changes by 10 mV per °C. This helps determine the sensor's resolution. The LM35 sensor's resolution depends on the controller's ADC, i.e., the Arduino Mega in this example. The digital value is vital for processing and controlling applications.

Arduino Mega has a 10-bit ADC with a reference voltage of 5V. Hence, the values can be mapped from 0 to 2^10 values, i.e., 0 to 1023 steps or 1024 values or the step size. This is approximately 5000 mV/1024 steps = 4.88 mV per step. The output voltage changes by 10 mV per °C. So, the temperature measured = 4.88 mV/10 mV per °C. This is 0.488 °C per step.

The schematic for interfacing the temperature sensor with the Arduino Mega is shown in Fig. 3.24. The hardware connections between the temperature sensor and the

Arduino Mega are done as shown in Table 3.11. The interfacing of LM35 with Arduino Mega is shown in Fig. 3.25.

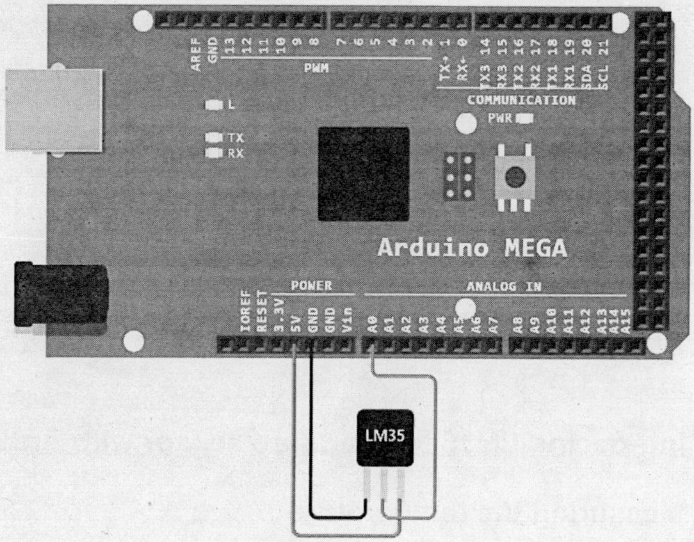

Fig. 3.24 Schematic for interfacing LM35 with Arduino Mega

Table 3.11 - Hardware Interfacing - Temperature Sensor

LM35 Pin	Arduino Mega Pin
Pin 1	5 V
Pin 2	A0
Pin 3	GND

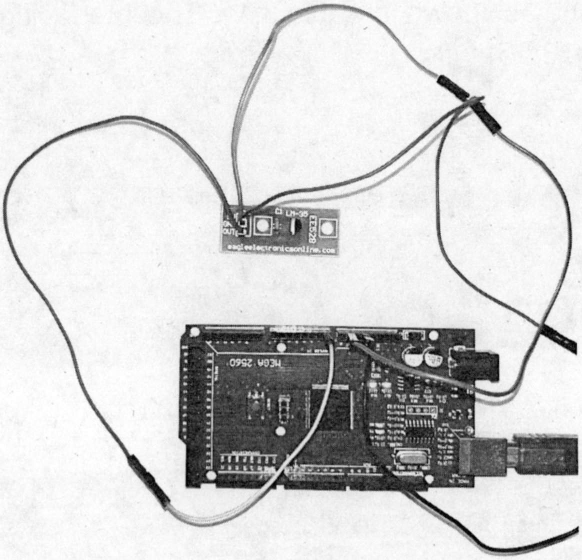

Fig. 3.25 Interfacing LM35 temperature sensor with Arduino Mega

Arduino Code - Measuring the temperature

The code reads the analog temperature from an LM35 sensor. It converts it to a digital value in degrees Celsius. The Serial monitor displays the temperature every second, as shown in Fig 3.26. The conversion uses the formula based on the LM35 sensor's output of 10 mV per degree Celsius.

```
const int ouputpin = A0;  // LM35 analog dataout pin
void setup() {
  Serial.begin(9600);}
void loop() {
  int tempsensor;
  float tempsensornew;
  tempsensor = analogRead(ouputpin); //read live Temperature value
  tempsensornew = (tempsensor * 4.88); //Convert analog value
                                       //equivalent digital value
  tempsensornew = (tempsensornew/10); //LM35 outputs 10mv/°C
  Serial.print("Temperature = ");
```

```
Serial.print(tempsensornew);
Serial.print("deg celsius\n");
delay(1000); }
```

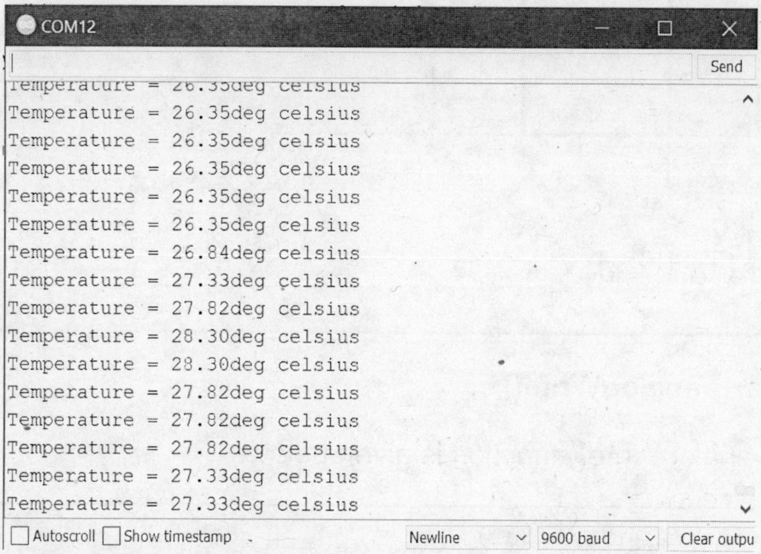

Fig. 3.26 LM35 module connected to the Arduino Mega for temperature sensing

3.4.2.2 Analog Write Function

The analogWrite() function is used to generate a PWM (Pulse Width Modulation) signal on certain specified digital pins. The duty cycle of the generated PWM signal can be varied by providing a value between 0 and 255. 0 indicates 0% duty cycle (completely OFF) and 255 indicates 100% duty cycle (fully ON). This varying duty cycle can be used to control the speed of motors, brightness of LEDs, and other analog-like outputs. It is important to note that analogWrite() does not produce a true analog signal, but a PWM signal that can simulate 256 varying levels of power.

Know More

Duty cycle
The duty cycle is the percentage of time a signal is in its ON state compared to the entire period of the signal.

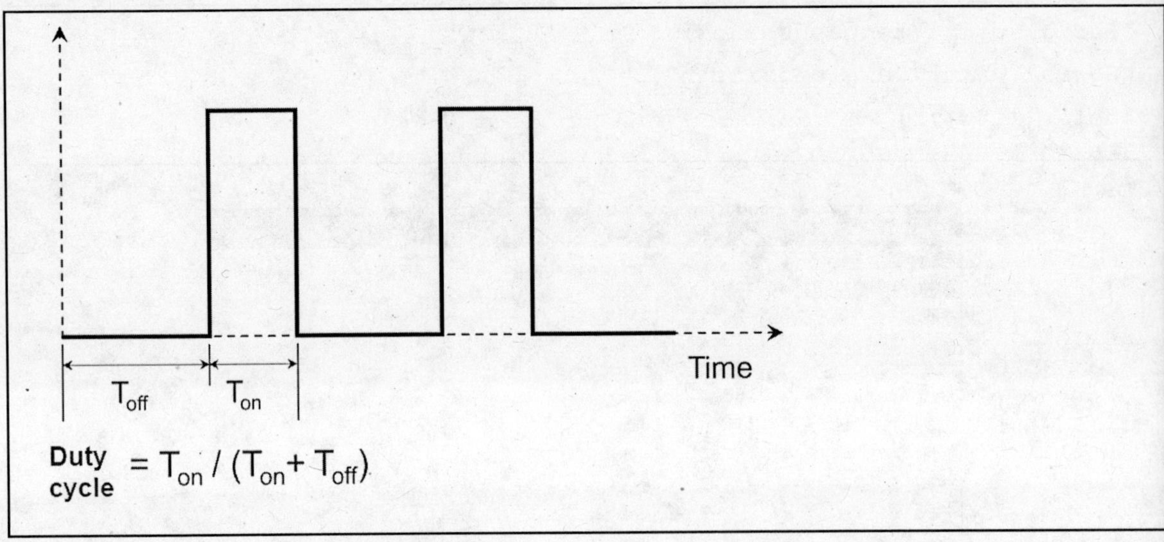

3.4.2.2.1 Syntax - analogWrite()

The syntax for analogWrite() function is given below:

```
analogWrite(pin_number,value);
```

- **pin_number**: The digital pin number where PWM output will be generated (D2 to D13 and D44 to D46)
- **value:** Value of the duty cycle ranging from 0 (always OFF) to 255 (always ON).

3.4.2.2.2 Varying the Brightness of LED using PWM Signal

To vary an LED's brightness with a PWM signal on an Arduino Mega, the LED is connected to a PWM pin on the board. This pin, set as an output, uses the Arduino's PWM. It sends a signal that changes the LED's brightness.

Arduino Code - LED Brightness variation using PWM signal

```
const int myLED = 9;          // Arduino pin connected to LED
int i = 0;
void setup()
{
```

```
  pinMode(myLED, OUTPUT);          //set myLED as an output
}
void loop()
{
  for (i = 0; i < 255; i++)
  {
    analogWrite(myLED, i);         //Increase the brightness of the LED
    delay(10);
  }
}
```

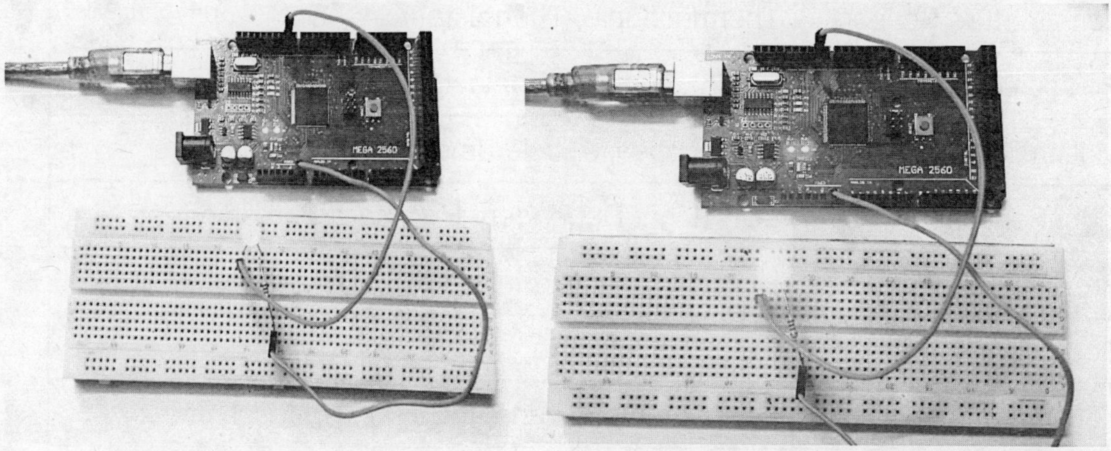

Fig. 3.27 Output of PWM signal varying the brightness of LED

In the above code, Pin 9 is set as an output to control the LED. In the loop(), the LED's brightness is gradually increased from OFF (0) to fully ON (255) over 255 steps. Each step increases the brightness by 1 and pauses for 10 milliseconds using the delay(10) creating a smooth effect. Here, analogWrite(myLED, i) sets the brightness of the LED to level 'i' at each iteration. Thus, the LED is continuously made to gradually brighten from OFF to fully ON in a loop. Fig. 3.27 shows the output of the LED showing varying brightness levels controlled by a PWM signal.

3.5 Applications - Sensor Interfacing

A sensor detects and responds to physical inputs from the environment, like light, heat, motion, moisture, and pressure. It converts these inputs into readable signals. These signals are often used in electronic systems to monitor and respond to changes in conditions. Sensors have many uses. These include industrial automation, medical devices, environmental monitoring, and consumer electronics.

Different types of sensors exist. Each measures a specific physical quantity. Table 3.12 provides the different types of sensors and their measuring physical quantities.

Table 3.12 Different types of sensors with examples

Type of Sensor	Typical Examples
Temperature Sensor	Thermocouple, Thermistor
Pressure Sensor	Strain gauge, Piezoelectric sensor
Motion Sensor	Gyroscopes, Accelerometers
Light Sensor	LDR (Light Dependent Resistor), Photodiodes
Proximity Sensor	Ultrasonic sensor, Infrared Sensor
Sound Sensor	Microphone
Touch Sensor	Resistive touch sensor, Capacitive touch sensor
Chemical Sensor	Liquid chemical sensor, Gaseous chemical sensor

In this Unit, interfacing of sensors with some typical proximity sensors like Ultrasonic sensor and Infrared sensor is discussed.

3.5.1 IR Sensor Interfacing

The Infrared (IR) obstacle avoidance sensor module has an IR transmitter and an IR receiver. The sensors are available in the market in different models like FC-51, HW-201 and MH-B. The transmitter part uses an IR LED to send out infrared light that propagates through the air, hits an object and gets reflected. The receiver part uses a photodiode to detect the infrared light reflected back by the object. The detected light signal is converted to electrical signal and then processed (amplified, filtered and compared to a threshold) and converted into digital signal. The module has two onboard built-in LEDs, one to indicate power availability and the other one turns on when the sensor detects an object. If the object is close, a strong light is reflected and detected at the photodiode sensor, and the module output is LOW. If the object is far away, a weak light is detected, and the normal sensor module output is HIGH. The distance for proximity sensing using an IR sensor can be adjusted with a trimpot. The components of the IR sensor module are shown in Fig. 3.28.

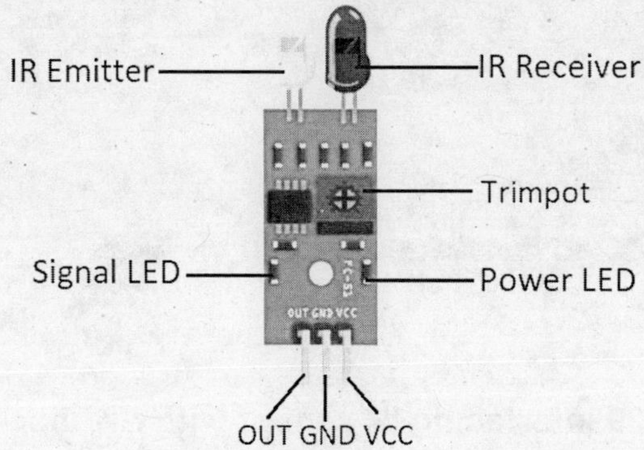

Fig. 3.28 IR Sensor Module

There are three terminals to interface the IR sensor with the Mega board as shown in Table 3.13. The schematic diagram for interfacing the IR sensor module with the Arduino board is shown in Fig. 3.29.

Table 3.13 Interfacing IR Sensor with Arduino Mega board

Pin Description (IR Sensor)	Connection to Arduino
Vcc	5 V
OUT (5V TTL logic output)	Pin 49
GND	GND

Fig. 3.29 Interfacing IR sensor with Arduino Mega

Arduino Code - Interfacing IR sensor

The Arduino code for interfacing IR sensor module with Arduino Mega for obstacle detection is given below:

```
int ledPin = 13;
int sensorPin = 49;  //IR sensor Output connected to pin 49 in Arduino
int obstacleDetected= LOW; // LOW refers to no obstacle
void setup() {
  pinMode(ledPin, OUTPUT);
  pinMode(sensorPin, INPUT); //pin 49 receives IR sensor output
  Serial.begin(9600);
}
void loop()
{
  obstacleDetected= digitalRead(sensorPin);
  if (obstacleDetected == LOW) {
    Serial.println("Stop! obstacle detected");
    digitalWrite(ledPin, HIGH);
  }
  else {
    Serial.println("No Obstacle, Go ahead!");
    digitalWrite(ledPin, LOW);
  }
  delay(200); }
```

Firstly, the sensor OUT pin, here named as variable 'sensorPin' is read using *digitalRead()* function. The value (HIGH/LOW) is stored in a status variable 'obstacleDetected'.

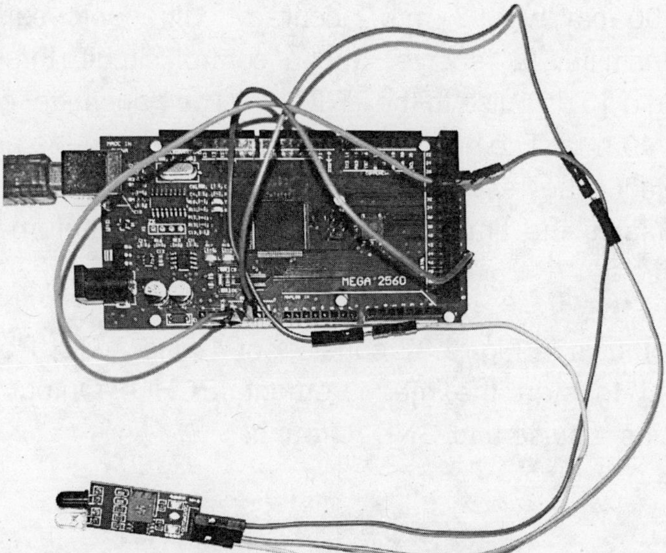

Fig. 3.30 Output observed of interfacing IR Sensor with Arduino Mega board

A HIGH sensor output denotes that no object is detected and a message to go ahead, is displayed in the serial monitor window. A LOW output from the module at pin 49, indicates the object is detected, and a warning message to stop is displayed. Fig. 3.30 shows the real time interfacing of the IR sensor with the Arduino Mega board and Fig. 3.31 shows the Serial Monitor output window when the object is placed in the path of the IR Sensor.

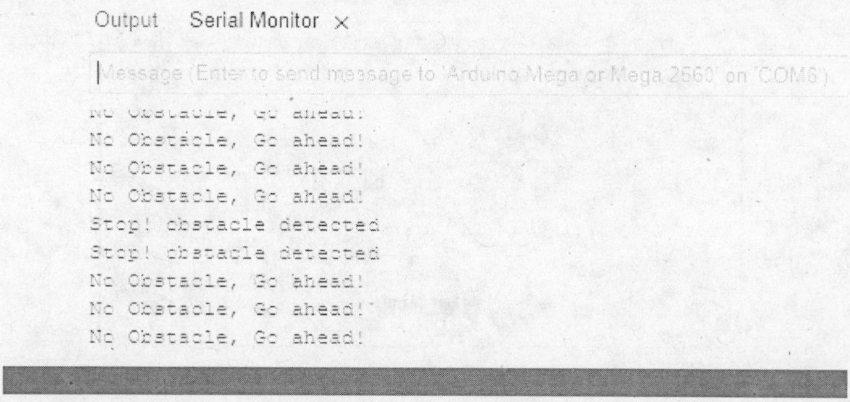

Fig. 3.31 Serial Monitor Output when IR Sensor detects an object ahead

3.5.2 Ultrasonic Sensor

The HC-SR04 is an ultrasonic sensor used to measure distances accurately in the range 2 cm to 400 cm with 3 mm accuracy. Ultrasonic sensors have three components: a transmitter, a receiver and a control circuit. Firstly, the sensor is triggered by sending a 10 µs pulse to the TRIG pin. The transmitter emits an ultrasonic burst of 8 cycles at 40 kHz. The emitted waves travel through the air and reflect back upon hitting an object. The receiver detects the reflected waves or the echo. The control circuit calculates the time taken for the waves to return and uses this to compute the distance.

HC-SR04 module, shown in Fig. 3.32 consists of 4 pins. VCC: Power supply (5 V), TRIG: Trigger input to start the measurement, ECHO: Output pin to send the measured distance as a pulse and GND: Ground.

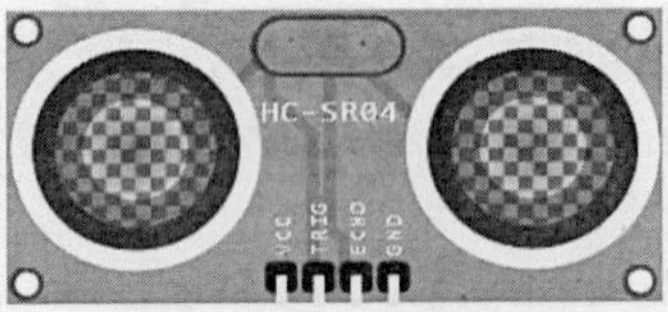

Fig. 3.32 HC-SR04 Ultrasonic Sensor Module

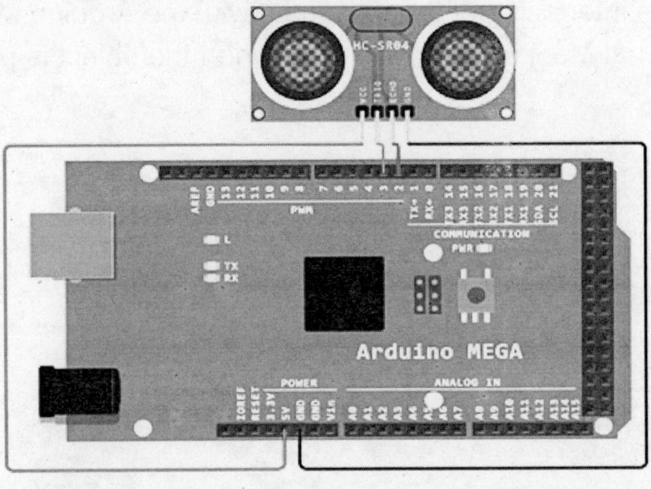

Fig. 3.33 Schematic for Interfacing ultrasonic sensor with Arduino mega

Pins 3 and 2 on the Arduino are connected to the TRIG and ECHO pins, respectively, in the sensor module. See the schematic in Fig. 3.33. They are named trig (output from Arduino) and echo (input to the Arduino from the sensor). To make sure that the trig is clear, it is set to LOW state for 2 μs initially. To generate the ultrasound wave, trig is set to HIGH state for 10 μs and then lowered.

Using the pulseIn() function, the travel time of the ultrasonic signal is recorded by reading the ECHO pin. The sensor sets the ECHO pin to HIGH after sending an 8-cycle ultrasonic burst. It waits for the wave. Then, it goes LOW once it receives the reflected wave from the object. This duration for which the ECHO pin remained HIGH, is returned by the pulseIn() function in microseconds. It is stored in a long variable named, 'roundtriptime'.

Speed of sound value is 340m/s, i.e., 0.0343 centimetres per microsecond (cm/μs)

Distance = Speed x (roundtrip time taken / 2)

Distance (cm) =0.034 cm/μs x (roundtrip time (μs) /2)

For getting the distance, the round-trip time is divided by 2 and then multiplied by speed (0.034).

Arduino Code - Interfacing Ultrasonic sensor

The Arduino code for Interfacing the Ultrasonic sensor to detect the distance of the obstacle from the sensor is given below:

```
// define pins numbers
const int trig = 3;
const int echo = 2;
// define variables
long roundtriptime;
int dist;
void setup() {
  pinMode(trig, OUTPUT); // Set the pin 3 as an Output from Mega to TRIG
in HC-SR04
  pinMode(echo, INPUT); // Set the pin 2 as an Input to Mega from the
ECHO in HC-SR04
  Serial.begin(9600); // Start serial communication
}
```

```
void loop() {
  // Clear the TRIG for 2 microseconds
  digitalWrite(trig, LOW);
  delayMicroseconds(2);
  // Set the TRIG on HIGH state for 10 microseconds
  digitalWrite(trig, HIGH);
  delayMicroseconds(10);
  digitalWrite(trig, LOW);
  // Read the ECHO and return the sound wave travel time in microseconds
  roundtriptime= pulseIn(echo, HIGH); //unit: microseconds
  // Calculate the distance
  dist = (roundtriptime/2)* 0.034);
  // Display distance
  Serial.print("Distance: "); // unit - cm
  Serial.println(dist);
}
```

This Arduino code uses an HC-SR04 ultrasonic sensor to measure distance. It sends a pulse from the “trig” pin and measures the time it takes for the echo to return on the “echo” pin. The distance is then calculated and printed to the Serial Monitor. Fig. 3.34 illustrates the ultrasonic sensor interfacing with the Arduino Mega. The distance sensed by the sensor is displayed on the serial monitor as shown in Fig. 3.35.

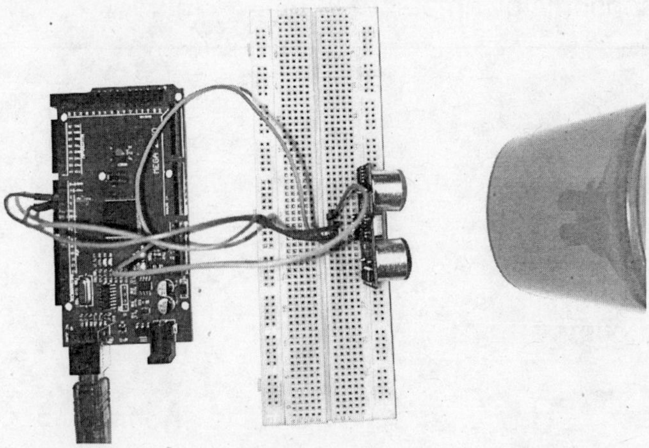

Fig. 3.34 Interfacing ultrasonic sensor with Arduino Mega

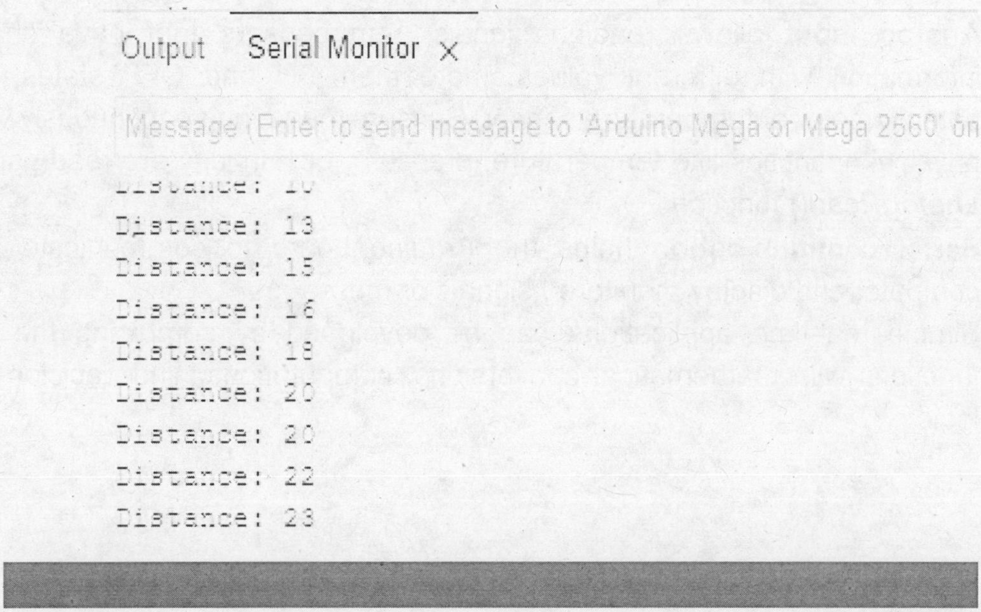

Fig. 3.35 Output Interfacing ultrasonic sensor with Arduino Mega

Unit Recap

- The Arduino Mega board features the ATmega2560 microcontroller operating at 16 MHz with a 5V operating voltage. It has 54 digital I/O pins (including 15 PWM output pins) and 16 analog input pins.
- The Arduino Mega includes 4 UARTs, an SPI, and an I2C port.
- Pin 13 has an inbuilt LED.
- The ***pinMode*** keyword is used in the program to configure a pin as either input or output.
- **Digital output** is used for controlling peripherals like LEDs, buzzer, motor and seven-segment displays. It uses the ***digitalWrite*()** function to turn the devices ON or OFF.
- **Analog output** is used to control the brightness of the LED, speed of a motor etc., Control is done by sending signals through the ***analogWrite*()** function.
- **Digital input** allows reading the state of sensors that indicate either ON or OFF, such as push buttons or switches. The status of these switches and buttons is read using the **digitalRead()** function.

- **Analog input** allows reading signals from sensors that have changing information with different values, more than ON and OFF states, like a potentiometer or temperature sensor. Sensors measuring continuously varying physical quantities like temperature, pressure, or humidity are read using the ***analogRead*()** function.
- **Serial communication** helps the Arduino board to communicate with a computer and display monitored signals or messages.
- Simple real-time applications can be developed by combining the above functions with mathematical conversions, computations, and decision-based logic.

Mind map - Arduino Mega and its peripherals

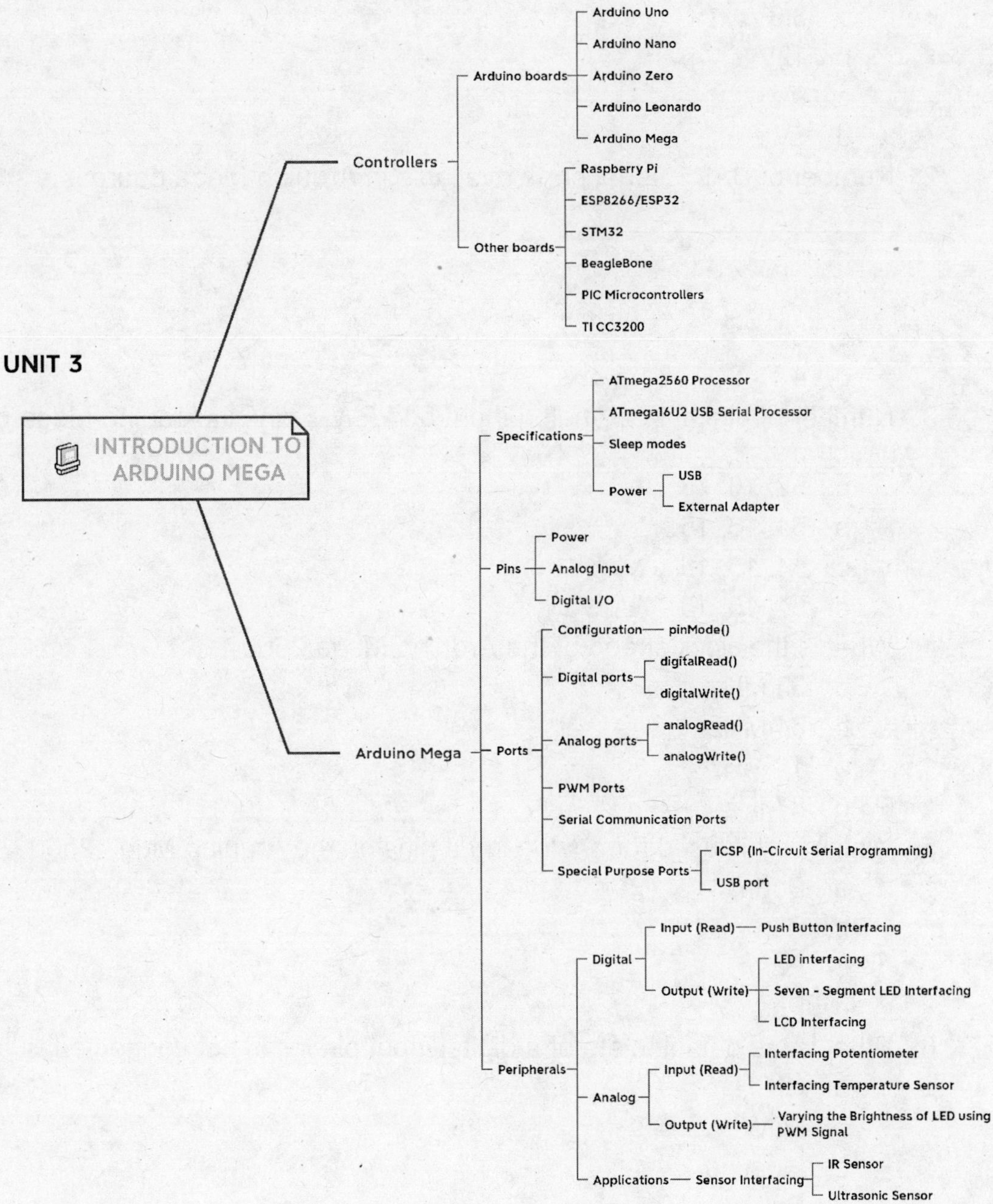

Multiple Choice Questions

1. The operating voltage of the Arduino Mega board is ____________.
    a. 3.3V
    b. 12V
    c. 9V
    d. 5V
2. Number of UART serial ports available in Arduino Mega board is ________________
    a. 1
    b. 2
    c. 3
    d. 4
3. Number of digital I/O, Analog input and PWM pins in Arduino Mega board are ______________
    a. 52, 16, 15
    b. 54, 16, 15
    c. 54, 15, 16
    d. 54, 15, 15
4. What is the clock speed of the Arduino Mega 2560?
    a. 32 MHz
    b. 64 MHz
    c. 16 MHz
    d. 8 MHz
5. Which port is used for analog input pins on the Arduino Mega 2560?
    a. Port B
    b. Port F
    c. Port D
    d. Port C
6. What is the default state of a digital input pin if it is not connected to anything?
    a. HIGH
    b. LOW
    c. Floating
    d. Pull-up
7. What is the range of values returned by the analogRead() function?
    a. 0 to 1023

   b. 0 to 255
   c. 0 to 4095
   d. 0 to 65535
8. Which among the following is not a serial port?
   a. UART
   b. I2C
   c. ICSP
   d. SPI
9. PWM is generated by
   a. analogRead
   b. analogWrite
   c. digitalRead
   d. digitalWrite
10. Iteration count "n" in a for loop and delay(100) in body of the loop
    a. (n/2) s
    b. (2n)s
    c. (0.1n)s
    d. (1/n)s
11. The travel duration taken by pulseIn() function to return the echo (sound) signal is 2ms, then distance of the object is ________
    a. 34m
    b. 0.34cm
    c. 3.4cm
    d. 34cm
12. Find the most suitable output of the following code:

```
int y = 4;
void setup()
{  Serial.begin(9600); }
void loop()
{ Serial.print("The value of y is:");
  Serial.println(y);
  Serial.print("cm.");
  delay(500); }
```

    a. cm.The value of y is:4
    b. The value of y is:4cm.
    c. The value of y is 4cm.

   d. The value of y is:4.

13. The distance of the proximity sensing using IR sensor is adjusted by
   a. Vcc
   b. program
   c. Trimpot
   d. PWM pin
14. Match the following

A. Analog input	E. Servomotor
B. Digital input	F. Switch
C. Digital output	G. LED
D. Analog output	H. Temperature sensor

   a. A-G, B-F, C-E, D-H
   b. A-H, B-F, C-G, D-E
   c. A-E, B-H, C-G, D-F
   d. A-F, B-G, C-H, D-E

Programming Questions

1. Write a program to read the state of a button connected to pin 2 and turn on an LED connected to pin 13 when the button is pressed.
2. Write a program to read the value from a potentiometer connected to analog pin A1, and switch on a LED if the value from the potentiometer is more than 2.5V.
3. Write a program to control the brightness of an LED connected to pin 9 using an Ultrasonic sensor distance, let the LED glow bright when an object is closer and fade away as the object moves away.
4. Write a program to generate a PWM signal on pin 9 with a duty cycle that varies from 0% to 100% in steps of 10%.
5. Write a program to read the value of the light sensor connected to analog pin A1 and turn on an LED connected to pin 13 if the light level is below a certain threshold.

6. Write a program to read the value from a light sensor connected to analog pin A1 and turn on an LED connected to pin 13 if the light level falls below a specified threshold.

Know More

QR code for all the Arduino codes used in Unit 3.

References

1. George, K., Davis, B., & Prasanna, S. R. M. (2013). *Arduino Projects For Dummies* (For Dummies Series). Wiley. ISBN: 978-1118551479
2. Banzi, M., & Shiloh, M. (2014). *Make: Getting Started with Arduino - The Open Source Electronics Prototyping Platform* (3rd ed.). Shroff/Maker Media. ISBN: 978-9351109075
3. Pajankar, A. (2018). *Arduino made simple with interactive projects*. BPB Publications.
4. Wolf, W. (2008). *Computers as components: Principles of embedded computing system design*. Morgan Kaufmann Publishers.
5. Arduino. (n.d.). *Arduino Mega 2560 Rev3.*, from https://docs.arduino.cc/hardware/mega-2560/
6. Adafruit. (n.d.). *Learn Arduino*. Adafruit. https://learn.adafruit.com/category/learn-arduino
7. Spoken Tutorial: https://spoken-tutorial.org/tutorial-search/?search_foss=Arduino&search_language=English

4 Communication with Arduino

Unit Specifics

This Unit emphasizes the following aspects:

- Different communication modules available with their real-life application
- Communication interface

IKS Insights

This section explores how concepts from Indian Knowledge Systems (IKS) align with and enrich contemporary practices and technologies.

Unity in Diversity: Interfacing and System Optimization

India's rich tapestry of languages, cultures, and lifestyles exemplifies the concept of 'Unity in Diversity'. This idea finds a parallel in the Arduino interfacing modules, where diverse units effectively communicate and interlace to deliver a significant output for an application. Just as different Indian cultures and traditions contribute to a cohesive society, diverse components in an embedded system work together to optimize performance.

Ancient Indian architectural principles, such as Vastu Shastra, emphasize the optimization of space and resource usage, a form of system optimization that can be applied to embedded systems. Adopting these principles in the design and integration of interfacing modules in embedded systems can enhance efficiency and support the development of robust subsystems.

Holistic Approach of Indian Origin: Subsystems and Holistic Data Analysis

Traditional Indian practices like Ayurveda, Yoga, and Meditation emphasize a holistic approach. They consider multiple factors and their interrelationships to gain a comprehensive understanding. This philosophy can be applied to embedded systems by integrating multiple sensor inputs to achieve a complete understanding of the environment. A holistic approach also aids in mitigating co-design issues that arise during the integration of subsystems. It ensures smoother and more effective system development.

Indian Culture as the Epitome of Sustainability: Sustainable Practices

Indian culture deeply values sustainability and harmony with nature, influencing traditional methods of measurement, construction, and living. This emphasis on sustainability can inspire the design of energy-efficient sensors and data acquisition systems using sustainable materials. By adopting these best design practices, engineers can create systems that are efficient, precise and sustainable with minimised environmental impact. This approach aligns with the broader Indian tradition of creating solutions that live in harmony with the environment, balancing precision with sustainability.

Rationale

In embedded systems, communication interfaces are essential for enabling devices to exchange data and work cohesively. These interfaces facilitate the interconnection of sensors, actuators, and other peripherals to the microcontroller for creating efficient and functional systems. By learning about communication modules such as UART, SPI, I2C, Wi-Fi and their integration and utility with Arduino Mega, students will be equipped with a practical foundation to design and implement functional embedded system projects for solving problems.

Prerequisites

Before starting this Unit, students should have:

- A basic understanding of digital electronics and familiarity with microcontrollers
- Experience with the Arduino platform and basic coding in Embedded C
- Understanding of basic electronics, including reading circuit diagrams and using common electronic components

Unit Outcomes

At the end of this Unit, students will be able to

U4-O1: Understand and describe the different communication such as UART, SPI, I2C, and Wi-Fi modules used in embedded systems.

U4-O2: Implement Arduino Mega based real-life applications by interfacing UART, SPI, I2C, and Wi-Fi modules.

UO - CO Mapping

Course Outcomes	Expected Mapping with Programme Outcomes (1- Weak Correlation; 2- Medium correlation; 3- Strong Correlation)				
	CO-1	CO-2	CO-3	CO-4	CO-5
U4-O1	-	2	-	2	3
U4-O2	-	2	2	3	3

4.1 Communication Modules

Communication modules in embedded systems are essential for data exchange between devices, enabling remote monitoring and control. They ensure integration and interoperability among various components using standard protocols. Additionally, they also support real-time communication, which is essential for timely responses in critical applications. Data exchange between devices (between microcontroller and peripheral devices or between two microcontrollers) can be done in a parallel manner or in a serial manner. Data to be sent or received is represented in binary format consisting of 0s and 1s, where the Most Significant Bit (MSB) is the bit with the highest value position in the binary number, and the Least Significant Bit

(LSB) is the bit with the lowest value position. In a serial data transmission, the MSB is often transmitted first, followed by the LSB.

Parallel Data Transfer

In parallel arrangement, there is a dedicated bus line for each bit. In Fig. 4.1, there are 8 bus lines dedicated for 8-bit simultaneous transfer. These bus lines may be unidirectional (bus that can carry data in only one direction) or bidirectional (bus that can carry data in both directions). But parallel transfer requires more space than the serial transfer.

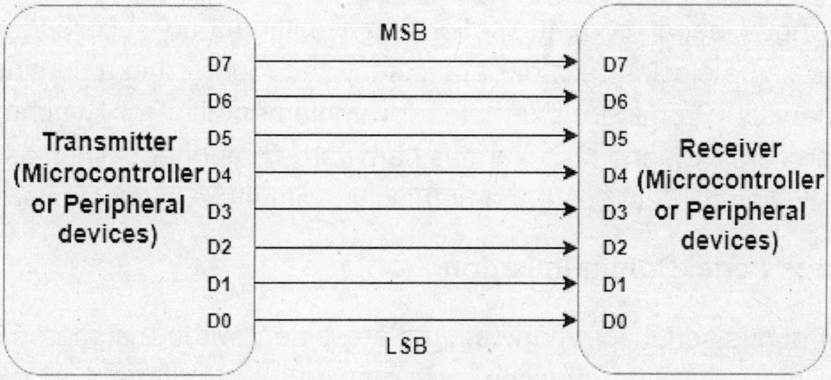

Fig. 4.1 Parallel Interface

Serial Data Transfer

Serial communication involves the bit-by-bit transfer of data through a single bus line, also known as a serial bus, is shown in Fig. 4.2. The sending device is the transmitter (Tx). and the receiving device is the receiver (Rx). To enable bidirectional communication, the Tx terminal of one device is connected to the Rx terminal of the other device and vice versa. Serial communication takes place in either synchronous or asynchronous mode.

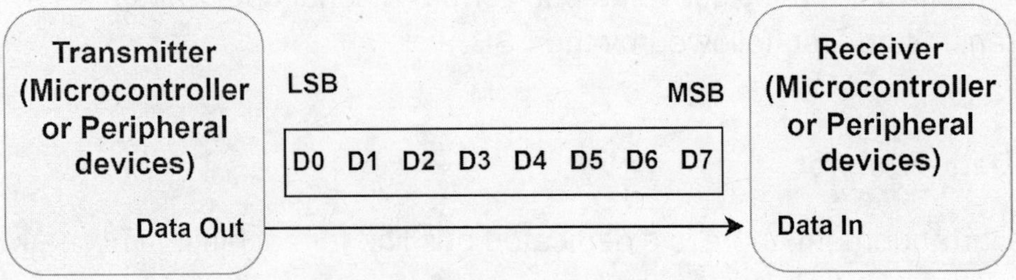

Fig. 4.2 Serial Interface

Synchronous Serial Communication

In a synchronous serial communication, transmitting and receiving devices are running at the same clock rate. So, data is sent and received in a continuous stream at regular intervals. Prominent examples for implementation of Synchronous Serial Communication are SPI, and I2C. Various hardware components such as LCD, OLED make use of I2C and SPI buses to communicate with the Arduino's microcontroller.

Asynchronous Serial Communication

In an asynchronous serial communication, data is sent without a shared clock signal. Transmitting and receiving devices are running at a different clock rate. This communication relies on start and stop bits attached to each byte of data. Example for implementation of Asynchronous Serial Communication is serial communication to serial monitor. UART is an example for Synchronous and Asynchronous communication. Asynchronous Serial requires only two lines. The transmitter and receiver agree on a common data rate, also called the baud rate for the data exchange. Baud rate is defined as the number of bits transmitted per second and the typical Baud rates used in communication are 9600, 115200, etc.

4.1.1 UART (Universal Asynchronous Receiver/Transmitter) Communication

There are four hardware UART (Universal Asynchronous serial Receiver and Transmitter) ports namely UART 0, UART 1, UART 2 and UART 3 in the Arduino Mega 2560, allowing serial communication with multiple devices like computers, other Arduino boards, or peripheral devices, by sending and receiving data in a sequential manner. This is done through a serial interface, typically using the TX (transmit) and

RX (receive) pins. The data is transferred bit-by-bit over a single line or wire, where both the communicating devices agree upon the same communication speed or the Baud rate. The data transmission can be of two types:

- **Half duplex communication:** The data transmission can happen between two devices (a transmitter and a receiver) in both directions but cannot transfer at the same time. When one device only transmits, the other will only receive.
- **Full duplex communication:** Two communicating devices can send and receive data simultaneously.

4.1.1.1 UART Ports on Arduino Mega

The Arduino Mega's UART ports are used for serial communication, supporting both synchronous and asynchronous modes. The primary Serial0 interface is connected to the USB, facilitating communication with a computer. Serial1, Serial2, and Serial3 can be used to interface with several serial devices, like GPS modules, Bluetooth modules, and other microcontrollers.

Table 4.1 Pin Configuration of UART Ports in Arduino Mega

Serial Port in Arduino Mega	Digital Pins and Type	
	TX (Transmit)	RX (Receive)
Serial	0	1
Serial1	18	19
Serial2	16	17
Serial3	14	15

Each UART port can be independently configured for different baud rates and communication parameters. Table 4.1 lists the Digital pins associated with the serial ports. Fig. 4.3 highlights the different communication modules available in Arduino Mega.

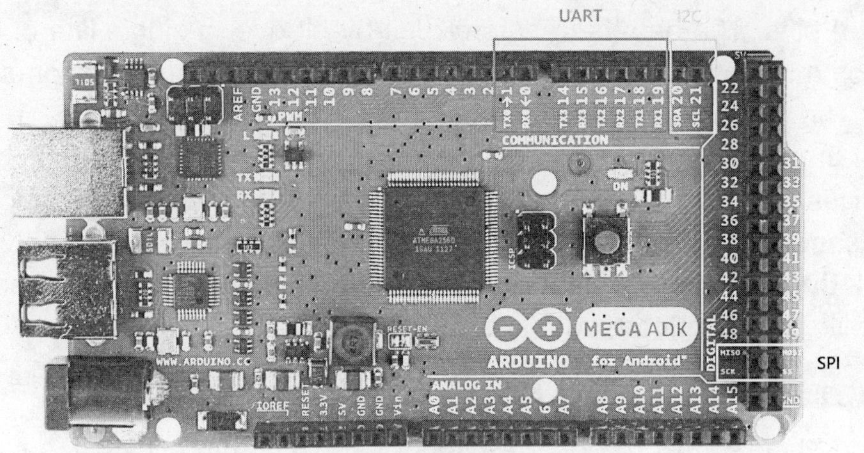

Fig. 4.3 Pins used for communication modules in Arduino Mega

4.1.1.2 Half Duplex Communication - Arduino Uno and Arduino Mega

Half duplex communication is established between an Arduino Uno and Arduino Mega board where the data transmission can happen in both directions, but only one acts as a sender device at a time. For example, the Mega sends a message while the Uno listens. In this scenario, Mega serves as a Master device and Uno serves as a Slave device.

For example, let us assume that Arduino Mega communicates to Arduino Uno through UART communication and controls the LED connected to the Arduino Uno. As the control happens from the Mega, the Mega is said to be the Master, and Uno acts as a slave. An LED is connected to both the boards as shown in Fig. 4.4. Both the LEDs are controlled by the Arduino Mega board by sending numbers as signals ('1' to switch ON the LED and '0' to switch OFF the LED). Table 4.2 provides the hardware pin configurations of the Arduino Mega and Arduino Uno. The ground (GND) and power supply connections are respectively connected together in both the boards.

Mega board sends the command ('1' or '0') to the Uno board, which is interpreted, and the LEDs are switched ON or OFF respectively. Mega acts as a Transmitter (TX) of data and Uno acts as a Receiver (RX). So, the transmit pin of the UART (Serial 1 - Mega board) is connected to the Receiver port of Arduino Uno. The pin 18 (TX 1) on Arduino Mega is connected to pin 10 on Arduino Uno, which acts as a Virtual Receiver pin. The data is transmitted via pin 18 (Arduino Mega) to pin 10 (Arduino Uno) in a serial manner.

Table 4.2 Hardware Configuration for Half Duplex Communication between Arduino Mega and Arduino Uno

Board	Pin Number	Connection
Arduino Mega	18 (TX 1)	Connected to pin 10 on Arduino Uno
	10	Connected to Red LED (Fig. 4.3)
Arduino Uno	12	Connected to Green LED (Fig. 4.3)
	10	Configured as Virtual Receiver pin

The Arduino code for Arduino Mega and Arduino Uno are given below.

Arduino Code - UART Master (Arduino Mega)

This Arduino Mega code establishes half-duplex communication with an Arduino Uno using Serial port. Serial is used to configure the Serial Monitor for sending data to Uno. Serial1 refers to the Serial port 1 on Mega board, which is physically connected to the Uno board. Whenever the data is available on Serial, it reads and sends it via Serial1 to the Uno. It also toggles the LED ON or OFF based on the characters received '0' or '1'.

```
//Interfacing Arduino Mega with Arduino Uno - Half Duplex Communication
int myLED = 10;                                    // Connect an LED to pin 10
void setup() {
    pinMode(myLED, OUTPUT);
    Serial.begin(9600);          // Start Serial Monitor communication
    Serial1.begin(9600);        // Start serial communication on Serial 1
USART port (18 pin - TX)
}
void loop() {
    if (Serial.available() > 0) {
```

```
        char received = Serial.read();          //Read the character
entered in the Serial Monitor
        delay(200);
        Serial1.write(received);                    //Write the
character to Serial 1 connected to Uno
        if (received == '0') {
            digitalWrite(myLED, LOW);     //Switch OFF the LED
connected to the Mega board
            delay(500);
        } else if (received == '1') {
            digitalWrite(myLED, HIGH);    //Switch ON the LED connected
to the Mega board
            delay(500);
        }
    }
}
```

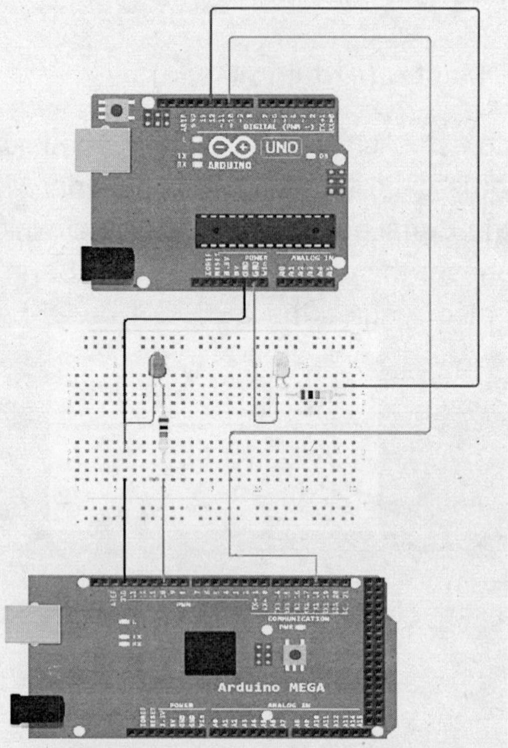

Fig. 4.4 Interfacing Arduino Mega with Arduino Uno using UART

Arduino Code - UART Slave (Arduino Uno)

This Arduino Uno code establishes half-duplex communication with an Arduino Mega using Serial port. To configure the virtual serial port on Arduino Uno board, the inbuilt library “SoftwareSerial.h” is included. Virtual serial ports are declared on pins 10 and 9, which are configured as Receiver (RX) and Transmitter (TX) respectively using the Serial1. The Receiver of Serial1 (pin 10) is physically connected to the Transmitter of the Mega Serial1 (pin 18). Whenever the data is available on the Serial1 (RX), it is used to switch ON or OFF the LED connected at pin 12, based on the received character.

```
#include <SoftwareSerial.h>
SoftwareSerial Serial1(10, 9);      // RX, TX
int myled=12;
void setup() {
    pinMode(myled, OUTPUT);          // LED configured as output
    Serial.begin(9600);        // Start Serial Monitor communication
    //Start serial communication with Arduino Mega
    Serial1.begin(9600);
}
void loop() {
    if (Serial1.available() > 0) {
        //Read the character entered from Mega
        char received = Serial1.read();
        Serial.println(received);
        if (received == '0') {
            // Switch OFF the LED connected to Uno
            digitalWrite(myled, LOW);
            delay(500);
        } else if (received == '1') {
            // Switch ON the LED connected to Uno
            digitalWrite(myled, HIGH);
            delay(500);
        }
    }
}
```

4.1.1.3 Full Duplex Communication between Arduino Mega and Arduino Uno

Full duplex communication is also called two-way data transmission. Two devices can send and receive data at the same time simultaneously, through separate channels for sending and receiving data.

Example: Live chat between Arduino Uno and Arduino Mega

Let us make a live chat between Arduino Mega and Arduino Uno using USART communication. The RX pin on Arduino Mega is connected to TX pin on Arduino Uno and TX pin on Arduino Mega is connected to RX pin on Arduino Uno creating two separate channels for sending and receiving. The hardware connection is as shown in Fig. 4.5.

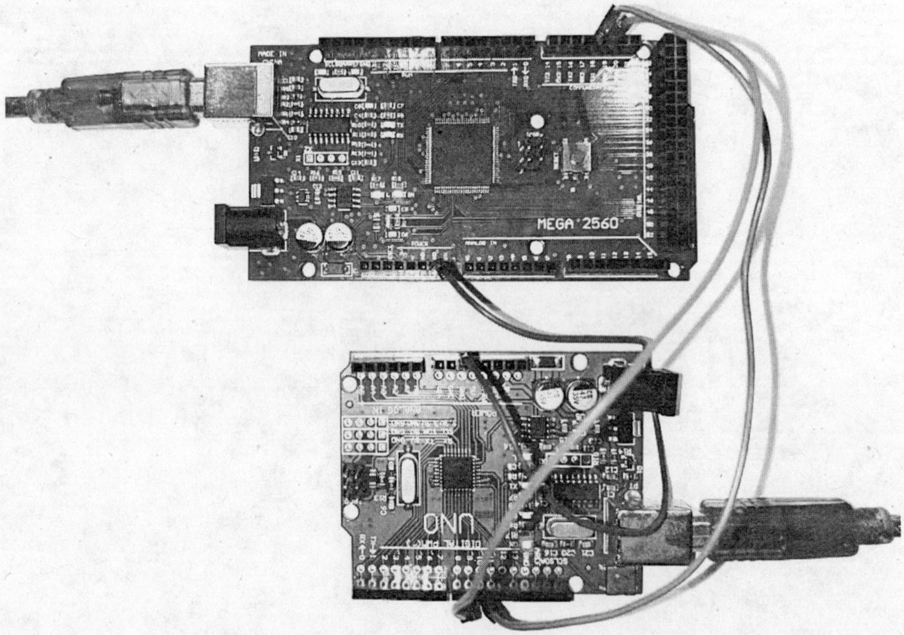

Fig. 4.5 Full duplex communication between Arduino Mega and Arduino Uno

Arduino Code - Uno (Full duplex communication)

A virtual serial port is created in Arduino Uno for communicating with Arduino Mega boards using the pins 10 and 9 as RX and TX respectively. The inbuilt serial port 'Serial', available in Arduino Uno is configured for serial monitor. 'Serial1', configured as a virtual serial port, is used for physical connection to the Mega board as per Table 4.3. The grounds of both the boards are connected together and the boards are powered separately. Fig. 4.6 shows the schematic for interfacing Arduino Mega and Uno for establishing full duplex communication.

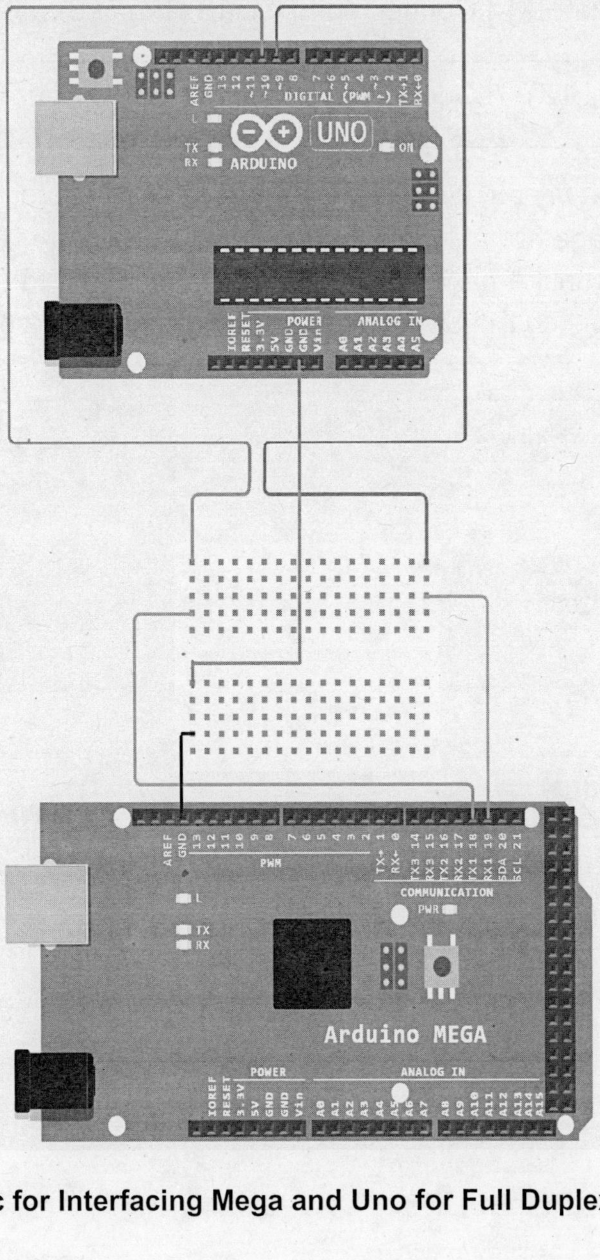

Fig. 4.6 Schematic for Interfacing Mega and Uno for Full Duplex Communication

Table 4.3 Hardware Configuration for Full Duplex Communication with Arduino Mega

Board	Pin	Connection
Arduino Uno	10 (Virtual RX)	Connected to pin 18 (TX) of Serial 1 in Arduino Mega
	9 (Virtual TX)	Connected to pin 19 (RX) of Serial 1 in Arduino Mega

If data is available on Serial1, it reads the message, then prints it to the Serial Monitor prefixed with "Message from Mega:". If data is entered on the Uno's Serial Monitor, it reads the message until a newline character, and sends it to the Mega via Serial1, and displays the same on the Serial Monitor with the prefix "Message sent from Uno:"

```
#include <SoftwareSerial.h>
SoftwareSerial Serial1(10, 9); // RX pin and TX Pin
void setup()
{
  Serial.begin(9600); // Start Serial Monitor
  Serial1.begin(9600);// Start Serial communication with Mega
}
void loop()
{
  if (Serial1.available()) {
    String msgFromMega = Serial1.readStringUntil('\n');
    Serial.print("Message from Mega:");
    Serial.println(msgFromMega); // Print message from Mega to Serial
Monitor
    delay(100);
  }
  if (Serial.available()) {
    String msgFromPC = Serial.readStringUntil('\n');
    Serial.print("Message sent from Uno:");
    Serial.println(msgFromPC); // Display message on Serial Monitor
    Serial1.println(msgFromPC); // Send message from PC to Mega
```

```
    delay(100);
  }
}
```

Arduino Code - Mega (Full duplex communication)

If data is entered into Mega's Serial Monitor, it reads the message, sends it to the Uno via Serial1, and displays it on the Serial Monitor with prefix **"Message sent from Mega:"**. If data is available from the Uno via Serial1, it reads the message and prints it to the Serial Monitor with the prefix **"Message from Uno"**.

```
void setup() {
  Serial.begin(9600);   // Start Serial Monitor
  Serial1.begin(9600);  // Start Serial1 for communication with Uno
}
void loop() {
  if (Serial.available()) {
    delay(100);
    String msgFromPC = Serial.readStringUntil('\n');
    Serial1.println(msgFromPC);       //Send message from Serial
Monitor to Uno
    Serial.print("Message sent from Mega:");
    Serial.println(msgFromPC);        //Display the message from Mega
on Serial Monitor
  }
  if (Serial1.available()) {
    delay(100);
    String msgFromUno = Serial1.readStringUntil('\n');
    Serial.print("Message from Uno:");
    Serial.println(msgFromUno);       // Print message from Uno to
Serial Monitor
  }
}
```

The output screen on the Serial Monitor (Arduino Uno) is shown in Fig. 4.7.

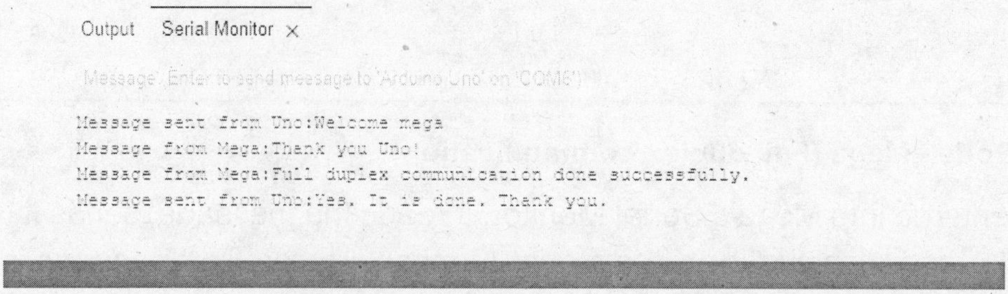

Fig. 4.7 Serial Monitor output (Uno) screen for live chat between Uno and Mega boards

4.1.2 SPI (Serial Peripheral Interface) Communication

SPI (Serial Peripheral Interface) is a synchronous serial communication protocol developed by Motorola in the 1980s. It is used for short-distance communication in embedded systems. SPI consists of four main signals: MISO (Master In Slave Out), MOSI (Master Out Slave In), SCK (Serial Clock), and SS (Slave Select). It allows high-speed, full-duplex data transfer between one master device and one or more slave devices, making it ideal for interfacing sensors, memory cards, and other peripherals. A major drawback is that SPI can only have a single master device, limiting its flexibility in complex networks. Fig. 4.8 provides the block diagram of a single master slave configuration for SPI communication.

Table 4.4 lists the pins associated with SPI communication in Arduino Mega.

Table 4.4 SPI Pin configuration for Arduino Mega

Pin Number	SPI Configuration
Pin 50	MISO (Master In Slave Out)
Pin 51	MOSI (Master Out Slave In)
Pin 52	SCK (Serial Clock)
Pin 53	SS (Slave Select)

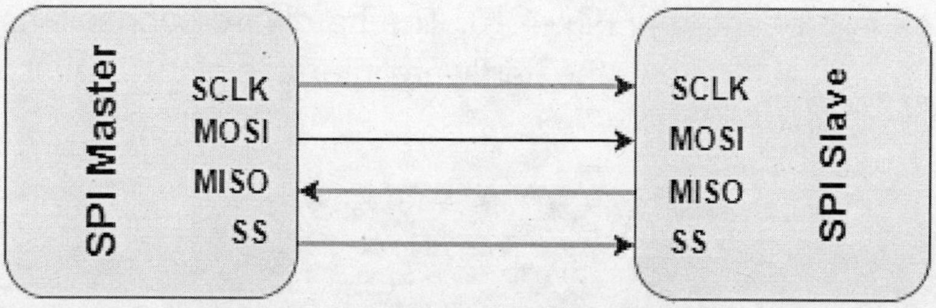

Fig. 4.8 Master Slave Configuration for SPI Communication

4.1.2.1 Digital Potentiometer using Arduino Mega

A digital potentiometer is an electronic component that adjusts resistance electronically rather than manually. It uses digital signals from a microcontroller to change the resistance value in a circuit. This adjustment is often controlled using communication protocols like SPI or I2C. Digital potentiometers are commonly used for volume control, calibration, and other applications requiring precise resistance adjustments.

The pin configuration of a digital potentiometer (MCP 4131) is shown in Fig. 4.9. The potentiometer is connected between the two terminals A (P0 A) and B (P0 B). They can be connected to 5V and Gnd or vice versa. The Wiper terminal (P0 W) can be digitally controlled to change the resistance in the circuit.

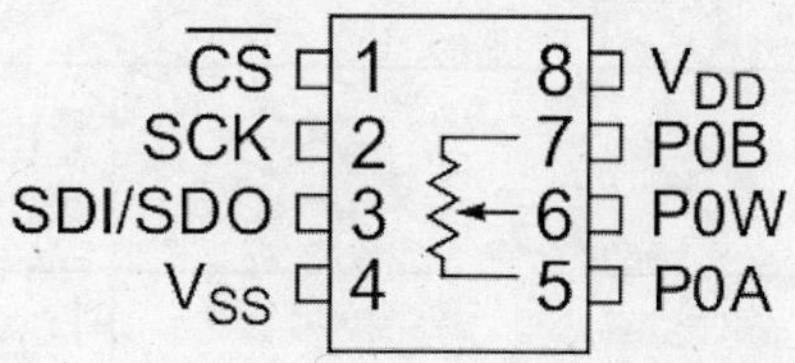

Fig. 4.9 Pin Configuration of a Digital Potentiometer (MCP 4131)

Let us consider an application to connect a digital potentiometer to an Arduino Mega and communicate using SPI protocol. Apart from the power and ground connections provided to the potentiometer, communication pins (SCK, SDI/SDO) in the potentiometer are connected to the corresponding pins on the Arduino. The brightness of the LED connected to Arduino Mega is varied by the variation in resistance provided by the digital potentiometer. The schematic for interfacing a Digital Potentiometer with an Arduino Mega is presented in Fig. 4.10. The hardware connections are given as listed in Table 4.5. Fig. 4.11 shows the hardware interface of the Digital potentiometer.

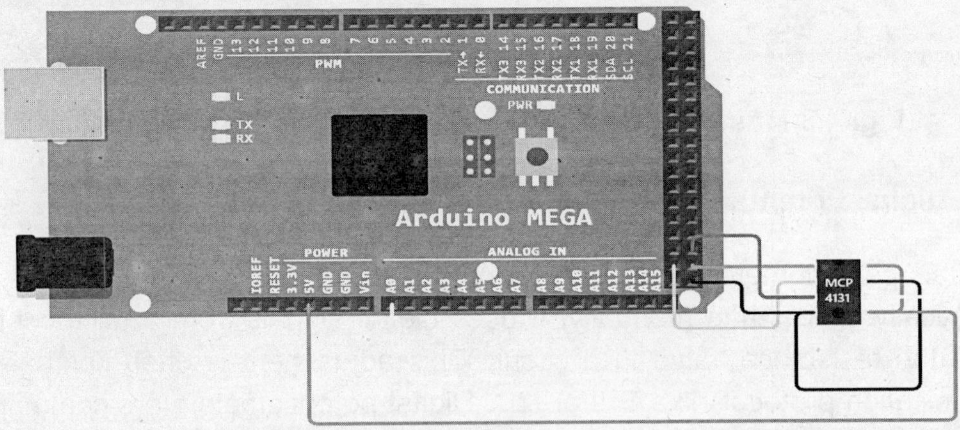

Fig. 4.10 Schematic for interfacing Digital Potentiometer with Arduino Mega

Table 4.5 Hardware connections between Digital Potentiometer and Arduino Mega

Digital Potentiometer (MCP 4131)		**Arduino Mega Pins**
Pin Description	**Pin Number**	
CS (Chip Select)	Pin 1	Pin 53
SCK (Serial Clock)	Pin 2	Pin 52
SDI/SDO (Serial Data Input/Serial Data Output)	Pin 3	Pin 51
VSS and P0B (Terminal B of the potentiometer)	Pin 4 and 7	GND
VDD and P0A (Terminal A of the potentiometer)	Pin 8 and 5	5V
P0W (Wiper terminal of the potentiometer)	Pin 6	A0

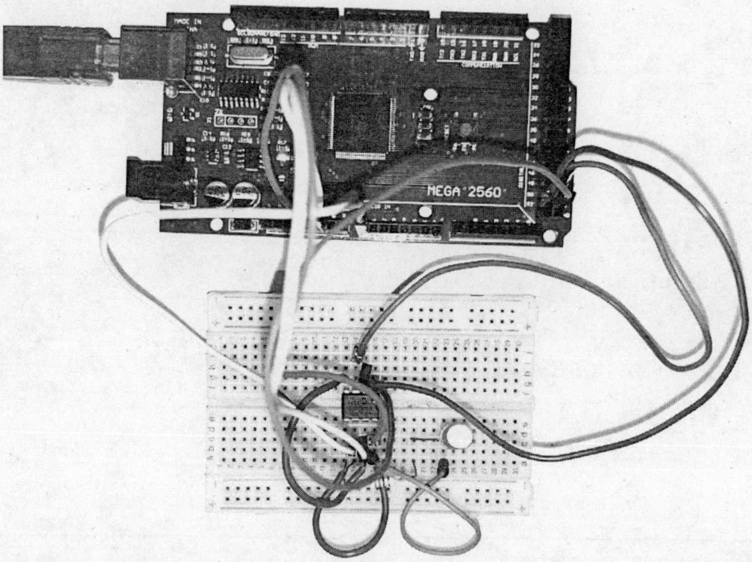

Fig. 4.11 Hardware Interfacing of Digital Potentiometer to Arduino Mega

Arduino Code - Interfacing Digital Potentiometer to Arduino Mega using SPI protocol

The Arduino code for controlling the value of the wiper on MCP4131 digital potentiometer using SPI is given below. The Chip Select (CS) is connected to pin 53 on Arduino Mega. The CS pin is set to LOW to enable communication to digital potentiometer, and a for loop iterates through wiper values from 0 to 128, sending each value to the MCP4131 through SPI protocol. The analog value from pin A0 is read and printed to the serial monitor. After the loop, the CS pin is set to HIGH in order to disable communication:

```
#include <SPI.h>
int cspin = 53;
void setup() {
  pinMode(cspin, OUTPUT); // set CS pin 53 as output
  SPI.begin();          // Start the SPI library
  Serial.begin(9600);
}
```

```
void loop() {
  digitalWrite(cspin, LOW);              // set the CS pin to LOW
  for(int wiper_val = 0; wiper_val <=128; wiper_val ++) {
    SPI.transfer(0x00);              // send a write command to the
MCP4131 to write at registry address 0x00
    SPI.transfer(wiper_val);        // send a new wiper value
    Serial.println(analogRead(A0)); // read the value from analog pin
A0 and send it to serial
    delay(500);
  }
  digitalWrite(cspin, HIGH);             // set the CS pin HIGH
}
```

4.1.3 I2C (Inter-Integrated Circuit) Communication

Inter Integrated Circuit (I2C) was invented by Philips semiconductor. I2C is a type of Synchronous Serial Synchronous bus used to connect low-speed peripherals to microcontrollers. Arduino mega has built-in I2C support.

I2C eliminates the drawbacks of Asynchronous serial and SPI communication and combines their positive aspects. Like asynchronous serial communication, I2C also requires only two lines, SDA (data line) - Pin 20 and SCL (clock line) - Pin 21. Unlike SPI it can have multiple master nodes and multiple slaves. Multiple devices (slaves) can be connected to the same bus and controlled by the master (Arduino Mega). Each device on the I2C bus is denoted by a unique address. Arduino provides a built-in Wire library to facilitate I2C communication. I2C Supports various speed modes, including standard mode (100 kHz), fast mode (400 kHz), and high-speed mode (up to 3.4 MHz). By default, the Arduino Wire library sets the I2C speed to 100 kHz.

Know more

I2C supports 7-bit addressing, allowing for 128 unique addresses (0x00 to 0x7F). However, addresses from 0x00 to 0x07 and 0x78 to 0x7F are reserved for special purposes. Theoretically one can connect up to 112 devices. Due to practical considerations and constraints like the electrical load, wire length, bus speed and power requirements for all devices, realistically, only 10 to 20 devices are manageable without significant issues.

4.1.3.1 Interfacing OLED using I2C

The OLED (Organic Light Emitting Diode) allows controlling individual pixels of the display. Both text and graphics can be displayed. Unlike LCDs, OLED does not require backlighting and hence it consumes lesser energy and has better contrast. It can be interfaced with any Arduino board through I2C or SPI. Popular libraries like Adafruit_SSD1306, Adafruit_SH1106, Adafruit_GFX, or U8g2 are used in the programming part to support the display. OLED is available in varying screen size and resolution in the market.

The OLED display used in the demonstration that follows is a SH1106 1.3 Inch OLED Display Module with a resolution of 128*64 pixels. It can be interfaced using the I2C communication interface. It has an on-board voltage regulator and can work with 3.3V or 5V systems without requiring any converters.

Table 4.6 and Fig. 4.12 shows the connections between the OLED and Arduino Mega board.

Table 4.6: Hardware connections between the OLED and Arduino board

OLED (SH1106) Pin	Arduino Mega Pin
GND (0V)	GND
VDC (3.3V - 5V DC)	5V
SCL (Serial I2C Clock)	SCL (Pin 21)
SDA (Serial I2C Data)	SDL (Pin 20)

In the setup function, an OLED object is initialized using the begin() function, with parameter, SH1106_SWITCHCAPVCC that turns on the internal charge pump circuitry, and another parameter to set the OLED display's I2C address. The address of the I2C object may be 0x3C or 0x3D based on the model used. The address of the I2C object for SH1106 is 0x3C (Hexadecimal 3C).

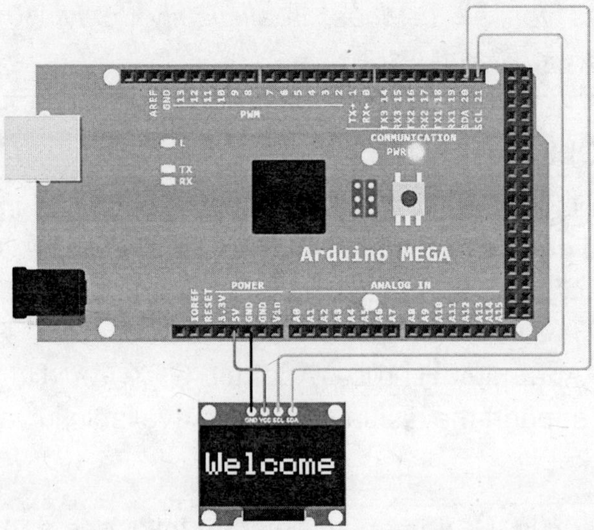

Fig. 4.12 Schematic for Interfacing OLED with Arduino mega

Arduino Code - Interfacing OLED through I2C with Arduino Mega

```
#include <Wire.h>
#include <Adafruit_SH1106.h>
#include <Adafruit_GFX.h>
#define OLED_rst -1
Adafruit_SH1106 display(OLED_rst); //Object of class Adafruit_SH1106
void setup() {
  display.begin(SH1106_SWITCHCAPVCC, 0x3C);//Initialize display with
I2C address 0x3C
  display.clearDisplay(); //Clear display
  display.setTextColor(WHITE);
  display.setTextSize(2);    //set font size of text
  display.setCursor(0,0);    //top left corner
  display.println("Embedded Systems");
  display.display();
  delay(500);
}
void loop() {  //do nothing   }
```

The Arduino code initializes an Adafruit SH1106 OLED display. The display is initialized with an I2C address of 0x3C, cleared, and configured with white text of font size 2. The text "Embedded Systems" is set to appear at the top-left corner of the display, which is then updated to show the text. Fig. 4.13 shows the output “Embedded system” displayed on the OLED display panel.

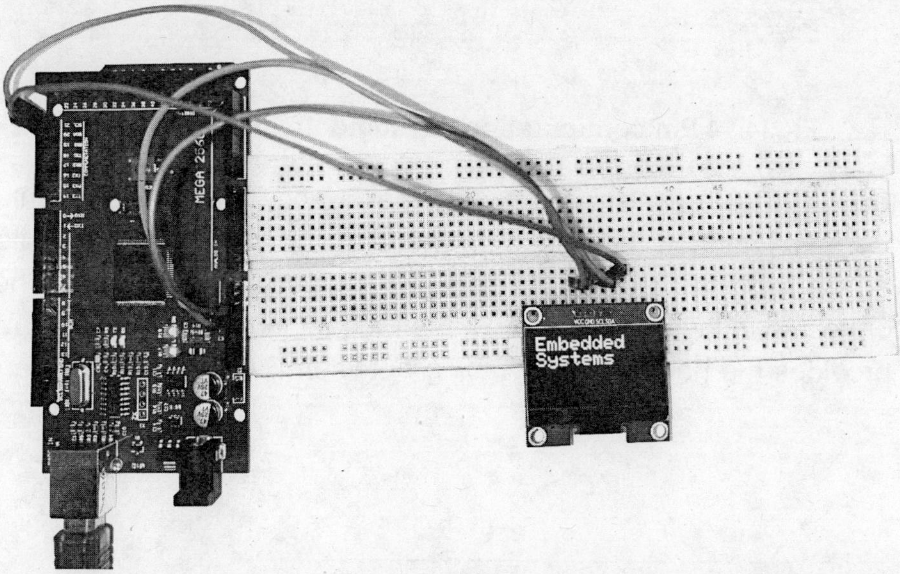

Fig. 4.13 Arduino Mega communicating with the OLED module via I2C interface for displaying a message

4.1.4 Interfacing Bluetooth Module with Arduino

Bluetooth is a wireless technology. It lets devices connect and exchange data over short distances. It runs at 2.4 GHz and supports applications like audio streaming and file transfer. Bluetooth provides a low-power, secure connection for short-range data exchange, up to 100 meters. Devices such as smartphones, headphones, and computers typically use this technology.

Similar to UART interfacing, Bluetooth is interfaced to the Arduino Mega using RX and TX pins and the *SoftwareSerial* library is used to establish communication and access the Bluetooth module. Fig. 4.14 shows the Bluetooth module to be interfaced with the Arduino Mega.

Fig. 4.14 Pin configuration of Bluetooth module (HC 05)

The Bluetooth module consists of two pins RXD and TXD for communicating with other devices. To interface the Bluetooth module with Arduino, connect its TXD and RXD pins to the Arduino Mega's RX1 and TX1, respectively. The VCC and the GND pins are connected to the 5V and GND of the Mega board respectively. Table 4.7 and Fig. 4.15 provides the hardware interfacing between Bluetooth module and Arduino Mega.

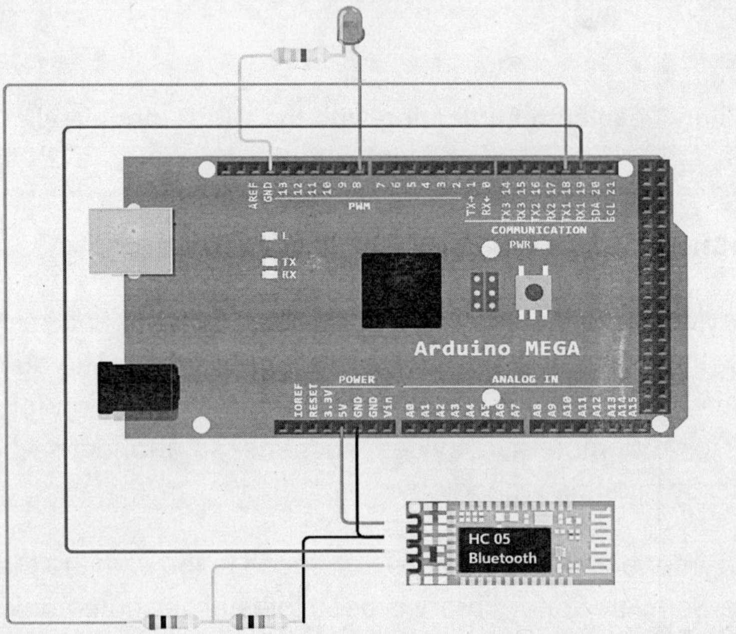

Fig. 4.15 Schematic for interfacing Bluetooth module with Arduino Mega

Table 4.7: Hardware Interfacing between Bluetooth module and Arduino Mega

Bluetooth Module (HC 05)	Arduino Mega
VCC	5V
GND	GND
TXD	RX 1 (Pin 19)
RXD	TX 1 (Pin 18)

The data is communicated to the Bluetooth module using an application (Mobile app) on the mobile phone.

4.1.4.1 Bluetooth Connectivity using Mobile Phone

The Bluetooth connectivity is established using the mobile phone as outlined in the steps below:

Step 1: The Bluetooth connection is switched on and connected to the Bluetooth network "HC-05" as shown in Fig. 4.16.

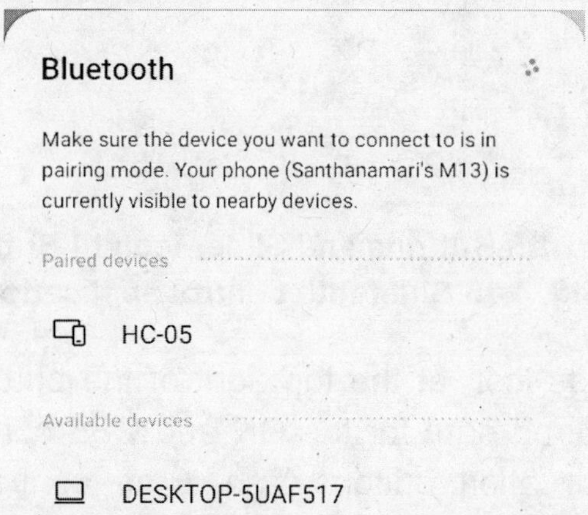

Fig. 4.16 Establishing connection with the Bluetooth module HC 05

Step 2: Any Bluetooth application can be downloaded from the Play Store (for eg: Arduino BlueControl). Fig. 4.17 shows the application installed in the mobile phone for controlling Bluetooth enabled devices.

Fig. 4.17 Bluetooth Control application installed in the mobile phone

Step 3: Open the Bluetooth control application and the window opens as shown in Fig. 4.18 (a). Click on buttons and slider icons in the home screen and the buttons control page opens as shown in Fig. 4.18 (b).

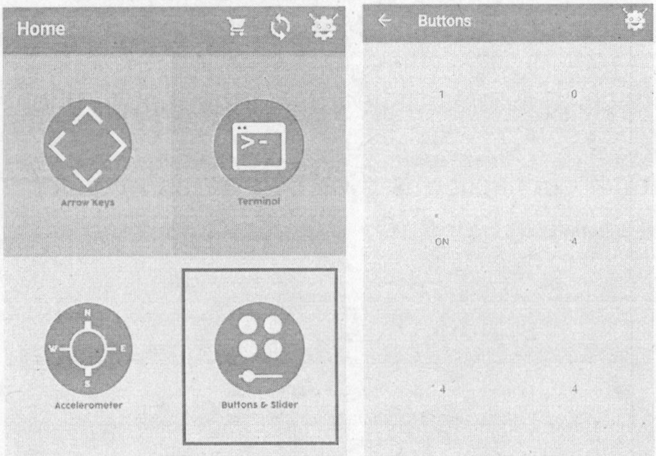

a)Launch window with Buttons and Slider icon b) Buttons Control page

Fig. 4.18 Bluetooth control application

Step 4: Click the Settings icon at the top right of the buttons page. Configure the buttons to send the required data for the ON and OFF conditions as shown in Fig. 4.19. For the current application, buttons A and B are configured to send data 1 and 0 respectively. The button A switches on the LED by sending a 1 to Arduino and the Button B switches OFF the LED by sending a 0 to Arduino through the Bluetooth module.

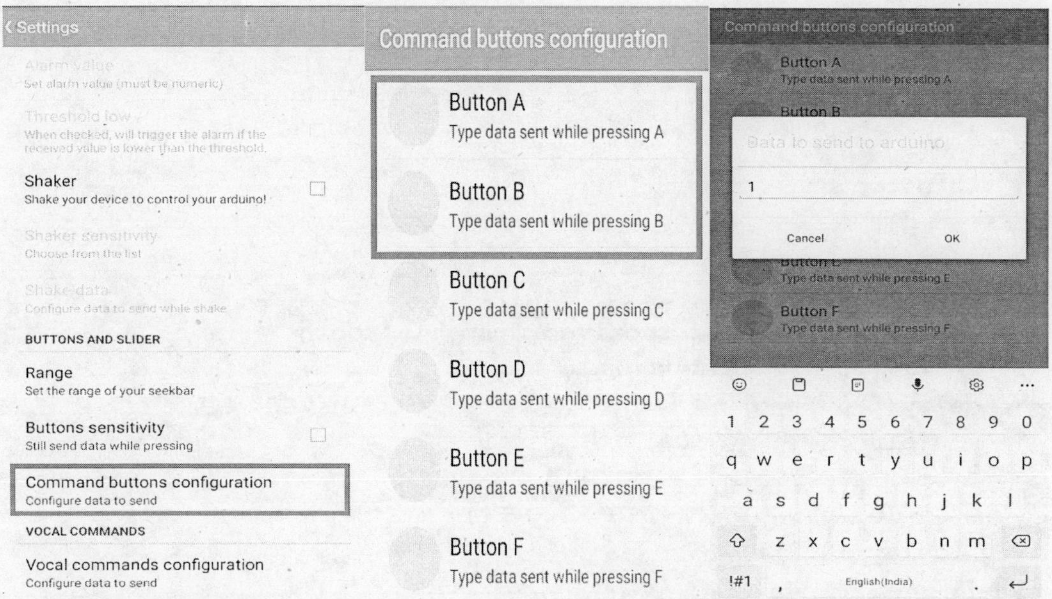

Fig. 4.19 Data to be sent to Arduino on clicking the respective buttons

Step 5: On pressing Button A, the data “1” is sent to the Arduino board through the Bluetooth module; Button B sends data “0” to the Bluetooth module. The received data turns ON or OFF the LED.

Arduino Code - Bluetooth Control

The Arduino code sets up Bluetooth communication to control an LED connected at pin 8 on Arduino Mega. Serial communication is initialized for both Serial Monitor (Serial0) and Bluetooth (Serial1). If the data is available from the Bluetooth module (Serial1), Arduino reads it and displays the received data on the Serial Monitor. If the received data is '0', it turns OFF the LED; if the data is '1', it turns ON the LED. Fig. 4.20 shows the hardware interfacing done between the Bluetooth module - HC 05 and Arduino Mega. The Bluetooth module connects to the mobile phone in a wireless fashion. The Serial Monitor shows the data from the mobile phone via the Bluetooth module, as in Fig. 4.21.

```
//Bluetooth Control
#define myled 8
void setup() {
  pinMode(myled, OUTPUT); // LED configured as output
```

```
  Serial.begin(9600);  //Start Serial Monitor
  Serial1.begin(9600); //Initialise serial port for Bluetooth
connection
}
char bluetooth;
void loop() {
  if (Serial1.available()) {
    char bluetooth= Serial1.read();   // Listen/receive from bluetooth
    Serial.print("data received from bluetooth:");
    Serial.println(bluetooth);
    delay(1000);
    if (bluetooth == '0') {
      digitalWrite(myled, LOW);
      Serial.println("myLED is OFF");
      delay(1000);
    }
    else if (bluetooth == '1') {
      // Switch ON the LED connected to Arduino
      digitalWrite(myled, HIGH);
      Serial.println("myLED is ON");
      delay(1000);
   }
  }
}
```

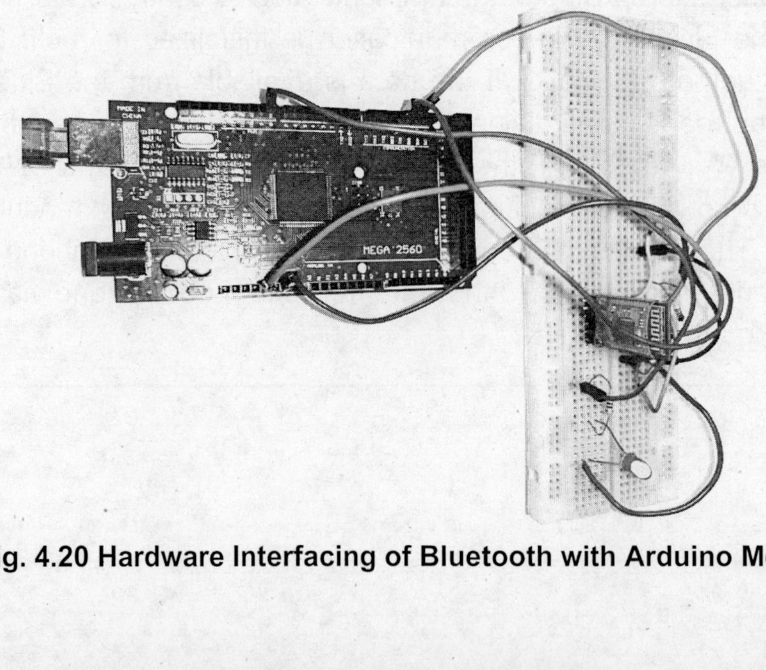

Fig. 4.20 Hardware Interfacing of Bluetooth with Arduino Mega

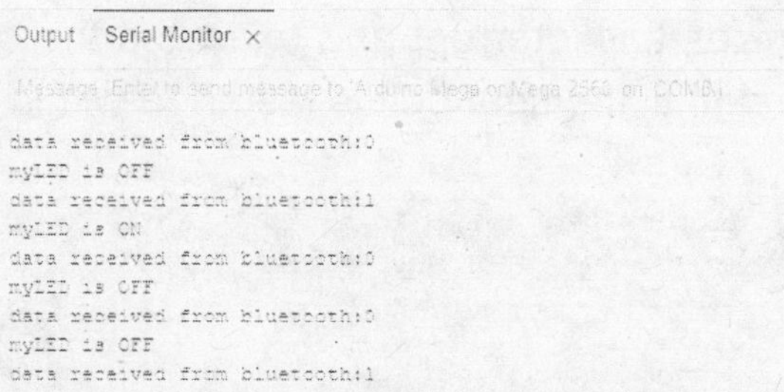

Fig. 4.21 Serial Monitor showing the control from a mobile device

4.2 Demonstration of Real-life Applications

Ports, timers and interrupts are the essential built-in peripherals for any real time embedded systems application development. This Section throws light on these peripheral interfacing with examples demonstrating the potentiality of Arduino Mega in real time applications and prototyping.

4.2.1 Interrupts

An interrupt is a signal which temporarily stops the regular flow of a program to address a high-priority task. Imagine a fast-moving car that is suddenly struck by another car coming from the opposite direction. The car's accelerometer detects a sudden deceleration and triggers an interrupt to the car's microcontroller. This interrupt prompts the microcontroller to send an electric signal to deploy the airbags. The microcontroller continuously senses various parameters. It checks the car's speed via the speedometer, the air conditioning temperature, and the seat belt status. When a car is hit by another vehicle, the vibration sensor senses the sudden vibration changes and interrupts the normal operation. The microcontroller recognizes this interrupt and promptly initiates the deployment of the airbags.

Technically, an interrupt is a process by which I/O devices (hardware interrupt), or instructions (software interrupt) can pause the normal execution flow of a microcontroller. After pausing the normal flow, the interrupt gets serviced by executing a subprogram called Interrupt Service Routine (ISR). For example, when a person sits in the driver's seat, a load sensor detects it and generates an interrupt. The car's microcontroller recognizes this interrupt and executes the corresponding ISR, which initiates a buzzer sound until the seat belt is fastened within a predefined interval.

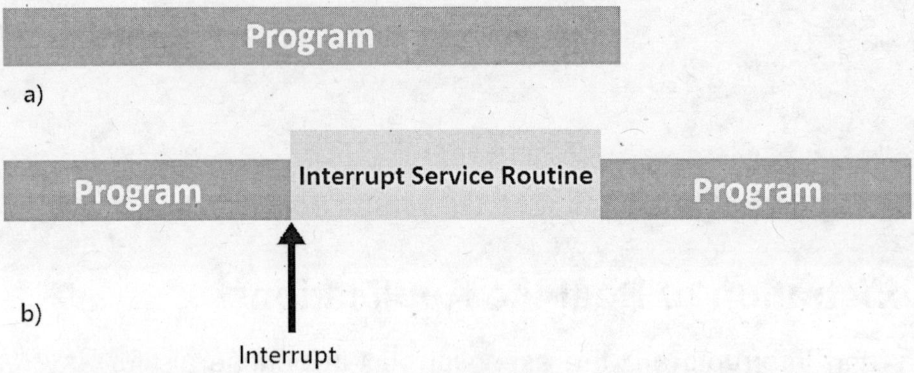

Fig. 4.22 Program Execution a) Without interrupt b) With interrupt

Interrupts can be triggered by different sources. In this case of a car accident, a hardware interrupt is generated when the state of the digital pin changes. Most of the Arduino boards have two hardware interrupts (namely "interrupt0" and "interrupt1") hard-wired to digital I/O pins 2 and 3, respectively. The routine to be executed when an interrupt is sensed is written using a special function or a subprogram called an "Interrupt Service Routine" (ISR) as shown in Fig. 4.22. This routine/ function can be specified to execute at the rising edge, falling edge, or both, automatically each time an event occurs on the input pin. More details about the level at which interrupt is recognised is discussed in 4.2.1.2.

4.2.1.1 Types of Interrupts

Interrupts are generally of two types: hardware and software interrupts.

Hardware Interrupt: An external event causing a state change on a microcontroller's digital pin, such as from low to high or high to low, triggers a hardware interrupt. For example, pressing a switch connected to a digital pin (causing a low to high transition) can be recognized as a hardware interrupt.

Software Interrupt: When an instruction in the main program causes the execution flow to jump to the corresponding ISR, it is called a software interrupt. For instance, when the delay() function is called, timer0 (discussed in the section 4.2.2) operates to generate a time delay by executing a separate routine.

The Arduino Mega features six hardware interrupts represented by pin numbers, as shown in Table 4.8.

Table 4.8 Different interrupts in Arduino Mega board

Interrupt number	Arduino pin
INT 0	2
INT 1	3
INT 2	21
INT 3	20
INT 4	19blu
INT 5	18

Since pins 20 and 21 are used for I2C communication (SDA and SCL), they are not available for interrupts while engaged in I2C communication.

4.2.1.2 Application Development using Interrupts

To develop an application using interrupts, the hardware interrupt pin and the condition to be evaluated is set up using *attachInterrupt()*. The Interrupt Service Routine (ISR) is defined to take the appropriate action when the interrupt occurs. The ISR manages the interrupt events efficiently, while the main program loop can handle other tasks.

Syntax - attachInterrupt()

```
attachInterrupt(digitalPinToInterrupt(pin_number), service_routine,
mode);
```

- **pin_number**: The number of the digital pin to which the interrupt is attached.
- **service_routine**: The name of the interrupt service routine (ISR) that will be executed when the interrupt occurs.

- **mode**: The condition that triggers the interrupt, it can be LOW, CHANGE, RISING, or FALLING.

It is generally recommended to use *digitalPinToInterrupt(pin_number)* instead of specifying the interrupt number directly in the sketch. *digitalPinToInterrupt(pin_number)* converts the digital pin to the corresponding interrupt number, ensuring compatibility and clarity in the code.

Arduino Code - Interrupt Handling

This Arduino code blinks an LED connected to pin 12 in the normal program execution function. This normal execution will be interrupted by any change in the push button. It uses an interrupt to monitor the push button connected to pin 2; when the button state changes, an ISR updates the state of a blue LED connected to pin 11. Fig. 4.23 shows the schematic for connecting the Arduino board for interrupt handling.

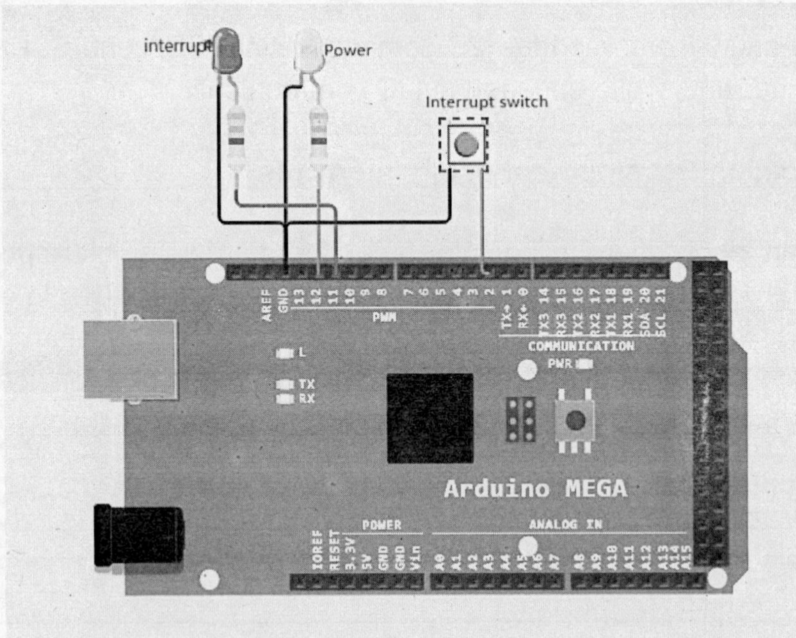

Fig. 4.23 Schematic for providing an interrupt through a push button

The ISR turns the blue LED on if the button is pressed (LOW) and OFF if the button is released (HIGH). The *attachInterrupt()* function is used to trigger the ISR on changes to the state of the button pin.

```
int normal_LED = 12;
int intrpt_LED = 11;
int button_pin = 2;
int button_State;
void button_interrupt_ISR(){     //interrupt service routine
  button_State=digitalRead(button_pin);
  if (button_State == LOW) {
    digitalWrite(intrpt_LED, HIGH);
  }
  if (buttonState == HIGH) {
    digitalWrite(intrpt_LED, LOW);
  }
}
void setup() {
  pinMode(normal_LED, OUTPUT);
  pinMode(intrpt_LED, OUTPUT);
  pinMode(button_pin, INPUT_PULLUP);
  //define the interrupt pin and attach it to the ISR
  int interruptPin = digitalPinToInterrupt(button_pin);
  attachInterrupt(interruptPin,button_interrupt_ISR, CHANGE);
}
void loop() {     //Normal program execution
  digitalWrite(normal_LED, HIGH);
  delay(150);
  digitalWrite(normal_LED, LOW);
  delay(150);
}
```

4.2.2 Timers

A timer, also known as a counter in Arduino, is a hardware component built into the microcontroller that counts clock pulses. It can be used to measure time events or generate time delays by counting the pulses. There are two types of timers: internal (counting the system clock pulses) and external (counting external clock pulses).

Timers are essential for various tasks such as generating precise time delays, creating PWM signals, and handling time-based interrupts. Arduino boards typically come with multiple timers of different bit resolutions (e.g., 8-bit, 16-bit), each capable of different functions which can be programmed by the registers given in Table 4.9.

Table 4.9: Registers used in Timer or Counter operations

Registers	Explanation
TCNTx	Timer/Counter Register (Actual timer value)
TCCRx	Timer/Counter Control Register (Pre-scaler)
ICRx	Input Capture Register (only for 16-bit timer)
OCRx	Output Compare Register
TIMSKx	Timer/Counter Interrupt Mask Register (Enable/disable timer interrupts)
TIFRx	Timer/Counter Interrupt Flag Register (Indicates a pending timer interrupt)

The Arduino Mega board features multiple timers: Timer0 and Timer2 are 8-bit timers, while Timer1 is a 16-bit timer. These timers are used for various functions such as *delay()*, *millis()*, *micros()*, PWM generation, and the *tone()* function. The Arduino Mega series includes additional 16-bit timers (Timer3, Timer4, and Timer5) for more advanced timing applications.

Timer behavior can be modified through timer registers. Important aspects include clock frequency and timer frequency.

Let us calculate the delay for Timer1 on an Arduino Mega to generate a 4Hz signal (0.25 second delay).

1. **CPU frequency** - 16MHz
2. **Maximum value of the timer/counter** - Maximum count of 65,536 for a 16-bit timer and a maximum count of 256 for an 8-bit timer. Timer 1 is a 16-bit timer.

3. **Timer Frequency** = CPU frequency/chosen pre-scaler (16,000,000 / 256 = 62,500).
4. **Timer Count = Timer Frequency/Desired Frequency** (62500/4 = 15625)
5. **The result against the maximum timer/counter value**: (15625 < 65,536). Choose a different prescaler if the result does not fall within the maximum value.

4.2.3 Interfacing Motors with Arduino Mega

Actuators are devices that convert electrical signals into physical movement or action. A motor is a typical actuator that can be used for controlling robotics, such as driving wheels and manipulating robotic arms, and for home automating like opening curtains or controlling fans.

Let us control the speed and direction of the motor using Arduino mega. A potentiometer is used to control the speed of the motor. The motor driver (L293D) is used as an interface between the microcontroller and the motor. The driver can be connected to two motors simultaneously. Its function is to amplify the low current control signals from the microcontroller to a higher current that can drive the motors. Fig. 4.24 shows the pin configuration of the motor driver. A motor driver is required to connect a DC motor with Arduino Mega because it handles higher current demands, provides directional control, and regulates motor speed using PWM signals. Two push buttons are used for controlling the direction of the motor, one for forward movement and the other for backward movement.

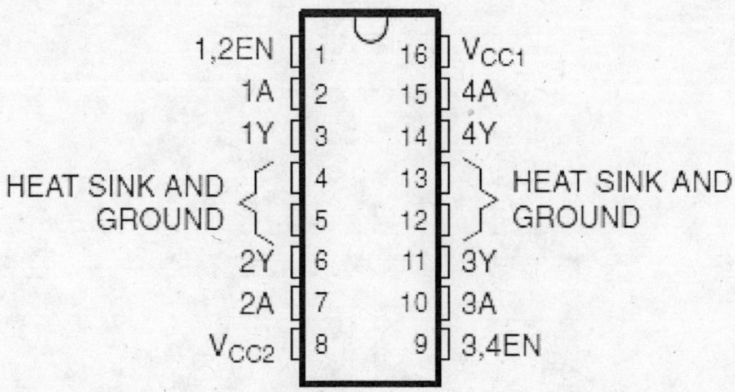

Fig. 4.24 Pin Configuration of a typical Motor Driver

Table 4.10 and Fig. 4.25 provides the hardware connections for controlling the DC motor, motor driver (L293D) and push buttons.

Table 4.10: Hardware Connection for Interfacing a motor with Arduino Mega

Component	Pin Number	Arduino Pin/Component
Motor Driver IC (L293D)	1 & 8	Vcc
	2	10
	7	11
	5	GND
	3 & 6	DC Motor
Potentiometer	2	A0
Push Button (Red)		13
Push Button (Green)		12
DC Motor		Motor Driver IC

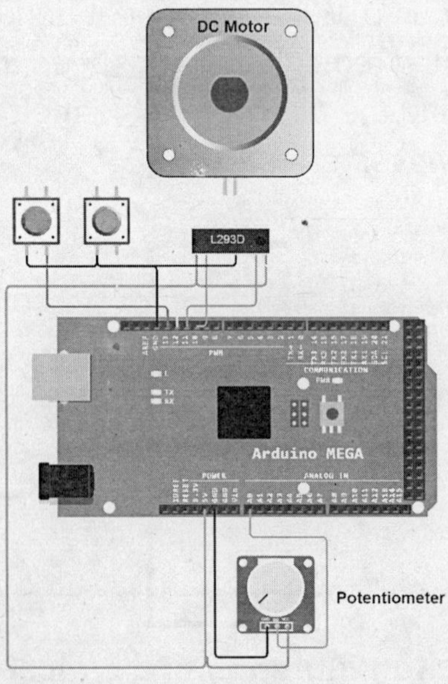

Fig. 4.25 Schematic of interfacing motor with Arduino Mega

Fig. 4.26 gives the connectivity established for controlling the motor speed and direction using a potentiometer and push buttons.

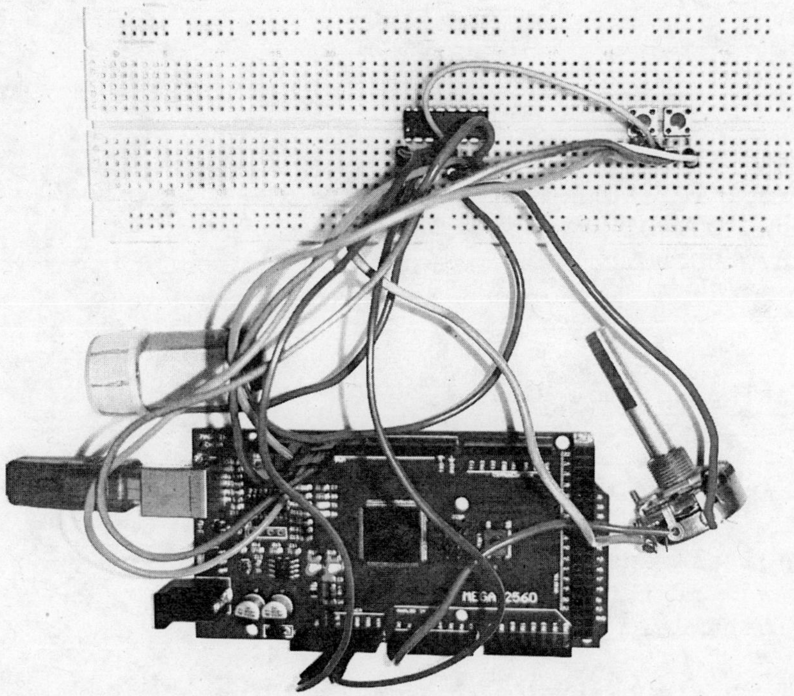

Fig. 4.26 Interfacing push buttons and motor with Arduino Mega

Arduino Code - Interfacing DC Motor with Arduino Mega

When the RED push button is pressed, the motor drives in the forward direction with the speed determined by the potentiometer value. When the GREEN push button is pressed, the motor drives in the backward direction with the speed read from the potentiometer. analogRead function reads the value from the potentiometer. The potentiometer values are scaled from 0-1023 to 0-255 for PWM control using the map function. If a button is pressed, analogWrite sets the PWM value to the corresponding motor control pin, controlling motor speed along with the direction of control.

```
const int pot_Pin = A0;
const int fwdPin = 13;    //Red push button
```

```
const int bckPin = 12;    //Green push button
const int ICpin2 = 11;  //driver IC pin 2 connected to 11 in Mega
const int ICpin7 = 10; //driver IC pin 7 connected to 10 in Mega
int potValue = 0;
int motorValue = 0;
int fwdState = 0;
int bckState = 0;
void setup()
{
pinMode(fwdPin, INPUT_PULLUP);
pinMode(bckPin,INPUT_PULLUP);
pinMode(ICpin2, OUTPUT);
pinMode(ICpin7, OUTPUT);
}
void loop()
{
potValue = analogRead(pot_Pin);
//Map the potentiometer value (0 to 1023) to a range of 0-255 for
PWM
motorValue = map(potValue, 0, 1023, 0, 255);
//Note the state of the forward button
fwdState = digitalRead(fwdPin);
//Note the state of the backward button
bckState = digitalRead(bckPin);
delay (500);
// Check whether either button is pressed
if(fwdState == LOW || bckState == LOW)
{
// Write the PWM value to the appropriate pin for motor speed
analogWrite(fwdbuttonState == LOW ? ICpin2 : ICpin7, motorValue);
// Ensure the opposite direction pin is LOW
digitalWrite(fwdbuttonState == LOW ? ICpin7 : ICpin2, LOW);
}
else
{
digitalWrite(ICpin2, LOW); // If no button is pressed, stop the
motor
digitalWrite(ICpin7, LOW); // Set both motor control pins to LOW
}
}
```

4.2.4 Interfacing Keypad with Arduino Mega

A keypad can be used for providing user input for various applications, like entering passwords, navigating menus, or controlling devices. A keypad can be interfaced with an Arduino Mega board by connecting the keypad's rows and columns to the Mega's digital pins. The keypresses can be managed by using the Keypad library in the Arduino sketch.

Let us consider a 4 x 4 keypad interfacing to implement a password verification system. The user is allowed to input the four-digit password from the keypad and the keypad input is read using the Keypad library by including the header file 'Keypad.h'. The hardware connections from the keypad are labelled as R1 to R4 indicating the rows and C1 to C4 indicating the columns as defined in Fig. 4.27.

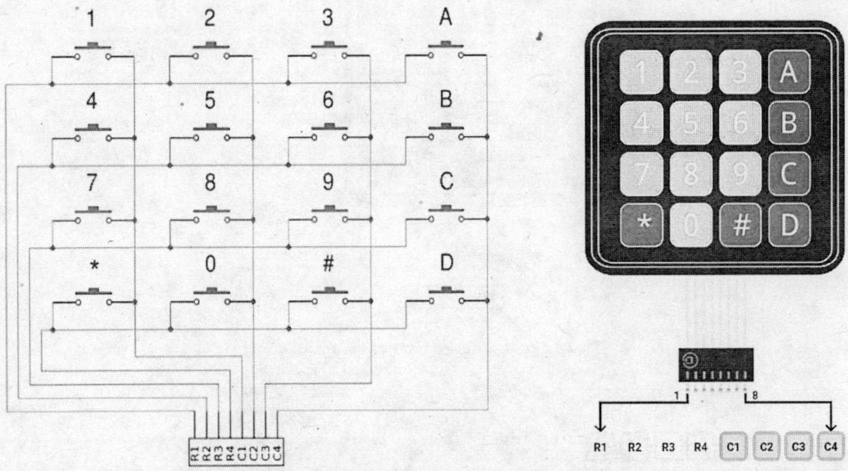

Fig. 4.27 Row and Column connections for a 4 x 4 keypad interface

To interface the 4 x 4 keypad with the Arduino Mega, the row and column pins are mapped to the digital pins of the Arduino Mega board as listed in Table 4.11 and Fig. 4.27.

Table 4.11: Hardware Connection for Interfacing Keypad with Arduino Mega

Arduino Digital Pin	Keypad pins
3	R1 (pin 1)
4	R2 (pin 2)

5	R3 (pin 3)
6	R4 (pin 4)
10	C1 (pin 5)
9	C2 (pin 6)
8	C3 (pin 7)
7	C4 (pin 8)

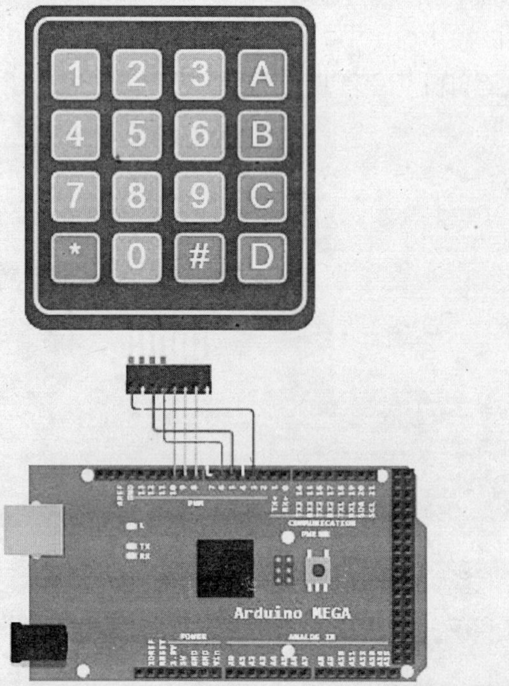

Fig. 4.28 Schematic for Interfacing Keypad with Arduino Mega for Password Verification

Arduino Code - Keypad Interfacing for Password Verification system

It makes use of the Keypad library to manage keypad inputs and defines the keypad layout and connections as a two-dimensional array of rows and columns. ***(keymap)***

```
#include <Keypad.h>
String numpad;
const byte Rows = 4;
```

```
const byte Cols = 4;
String pwd = "4321";
char keypressed='*'; //* denotes delete or start from first
char keymap[Rows][Cols] =
{
  {'1', '2', '3', 'A'},
  {'4', '5', '6', 'B'},
  {'7', '8', '9', 'C'},
  {'*', '0', '#', 'D'}
};
byte Pins_row[Rows] = {3, 4, 5, 6};
byte Pins_col[Cols] = {10, 9, 8, 7};
Keypad pattern = Keypad(makeKeymap(keymap), Pins_row, Pins_col, Rows,
Cols); //mapping keypad
void setup() {
  Serial.begin(9600);
}
void loop() {
  if (keypressed == '#') { // check if end of password typing (#
denotes enter)
    if (numpad == pwd) {
      Serial.println("Access Granted");
    } else {
      Serial.println("Access Denied");
    }
    keypressed = '*';
    delay(500);
  }
  else {
    readKeypad();
}
  if (keypressed == '*') {
    numpad = "";
    Serial.flush();
  }
}
void readKeypad() {
  keypressed = pattern.getKey();
  if (keypressed != '#') {
    String konv = String(keypressed);
    numpad += konv;
  }
  if (keypressed!='\0'){
    Serial.println(numpad);
  }
}
```

In the above Arduino code, the user inputs are taken from the keypad until the # (hash) key is pressed. Once the # key is pressed, the entered password is verified against a predefined one. If the password entered is correct, it prints *"Password correct"*; otherwise, it indicates an incorrect password. The readKeypad() function handles reading input from the keypad and appends the entered characters to the numpad string, which is printed to the serial monitor as shown in Fig. 4.30. The hardware interfacing of the 4 x 4 keypad with the Arduino Mega is shown in Fig. 4.29.

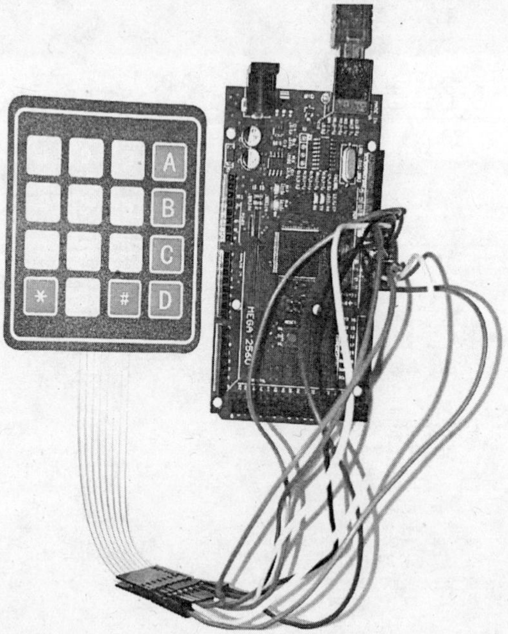

Fig. 4.29 Interfacing Keypad with Arduino Mega

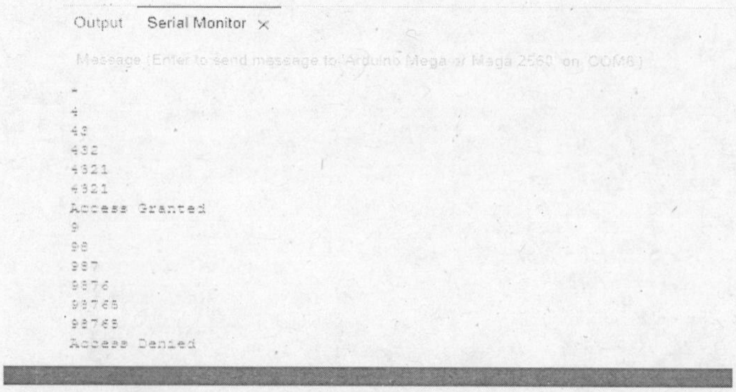

Fig. 4.30 Output of Password Verification System - Keypad Interfacing

4.2.5 Interfacing LDR and Relay

Light sensing is enabling devices to detect and respond to varying light levels in their environment. Light sensors such as photodiodes, phototransistors and Light Dependent Resistors (LDRs) are components that change their electrical characteristics in response to light intensity.

In a Light Dependent Resistor (LDR), the resistance varies based on the light intensity falling on it. Resistance decreases when the resistor is exposed to light and increases when it is in darkness. LDRs are commonly used in light-sensing and control circuits, such as automatic streetlights and light meters. They find use in a wide range of applications from outdoor solar devices to robotics and smart home technologies.

Let us use a LDR to connect a bulb which switches on automatically when the light intensity goes below a specific threshold. The hardware connections between the LDR, relay and the bulb are given as shown in Table 4.12 and Fig. 4.31 The output from the LDR is connected to the Analog Input (A0).

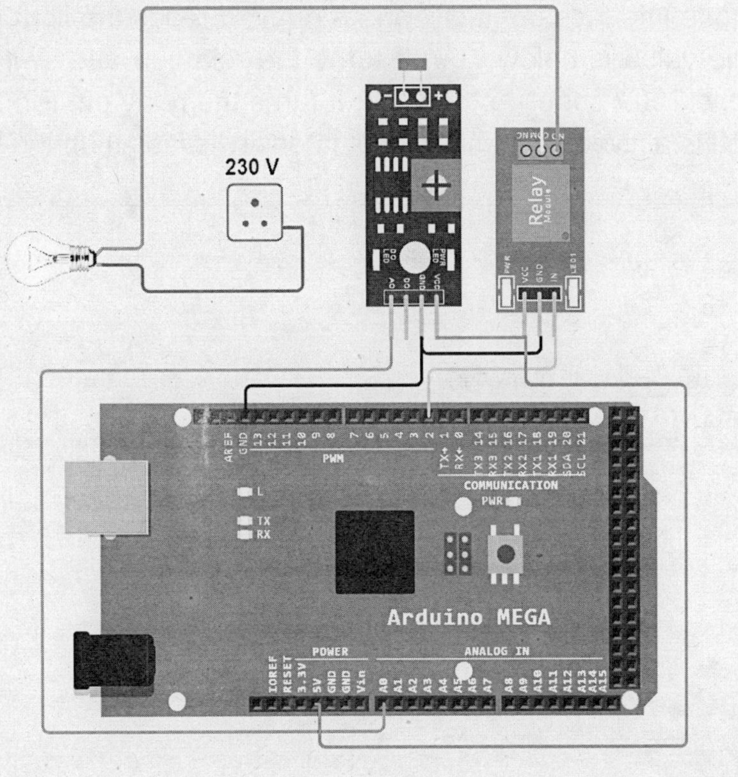

Fig. 4.31 Schematic for Interfacing LDR, Relay and bulb with Arduino Mega

Table 4.12: Hardware connection between LDR, Relay and Arduino Mega

LDR	Relay	Arduino pin
Vcc	Vcc	5 V
Gnd	Gnd	Gnd
Out	-	A0
-	IN	2
-	Common to 230V Neutral	-
-	NO to Bulb & Bulb to 230V phase	-

Arduino Code - LDR and Relay Interfacing with Arduino Mega

The Arduino code interfaces an LDR and a relay. It reads the light intensity from the LDR, and if the value is below 700, it turns the relay on and switches on the bulb connected to the 230V supply, otherwise, it turns the relay off. Pin 2 is connected to the relay, which is activated when the light intensity is less than the threshold.

```
int LDR_Pin = A0;    // input pin for LDR is A0
int LDR_Value = 0;   // Sensor data storage variable
int relay_pin = 2;   // Pin connected to the relay
void setup() {
  pinMode(relay_pin , OUTPUT);
  Serial.begin(9600); //start serial communication
}
void loop() {
  // read the value of the LDR
  LDR_Value = analogRead(LDR_Pin);
  //print sensor values
  if (LDR_Value < 700) //set the threshold value
  {
  Serial.println(LDRValue);
  digitalWrite(relay_pin,HIGH); //turn ON the relay
  delay(500);
  }
```

```
else if(LDR_Value > 700)
  {
  Serial.println(LDRValue);
  digitalWrite(relay_pin,LOW); //turn OFF the relay
  delay(500);
  }
}
```

Fig. 4.32 shows the hardware connections between the Arduino Mega, LDR, relay and the bulb. The 'LDRvalue' quantifies the light intensity in the surroundings. When the light intensity is high, the relay is switched OFF, thereby not providing a connection to the bulb connected to the 230V through the relay.

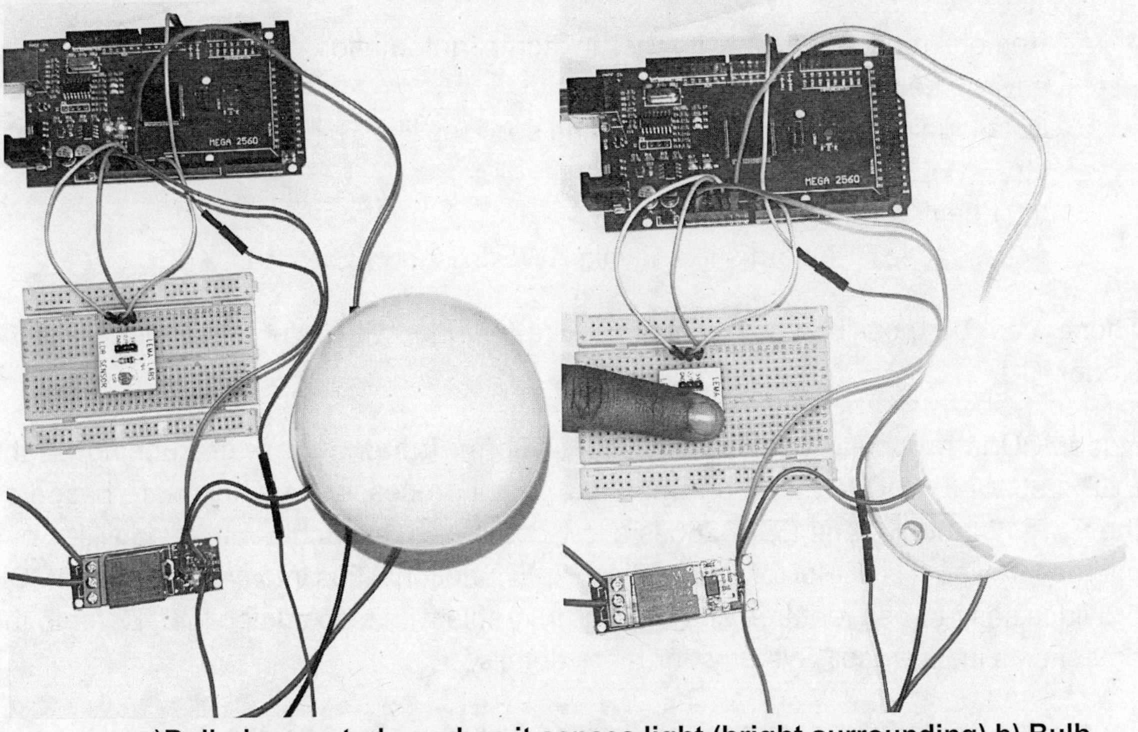

a)Bulb does not glow when it senses light (bright surrounding) b) Bulb switches ON when the LDR is blocked (dark surrounding)

Fig. 4.32 Hardware Interfacing of LDR, Relay and bulb with Arduino Mega

4.2.6 Wi-Fi using NodeMCU

Wi-Fi, or Wireless Fidelity, allows a device to connect to the internet. Wi-Fi wireless communication is established using radio waves, enabling various devices to share data and resources without the need for physical cables. In embedded systems and microcontroller projects, Wi-Fi allows devices to communicate with each other and with cloud services, making it a crucial element for Internet of Things (IoT) applications.

The Arduino Mega 2560, despite its power and versatility, does not have built-in Wi-Fi capabilities. Adding Wi-Fi to Arduino projects expands the range of potential applications such as

a. Remote monitoring and control in home automation, security systems, and environmental monitoring.
b. Data logging and cloud storage using services like Thingspeak, Google sheets, etc.
c. Inter device communication
d. Access to IoT Platforms like Blynk, AWS IoT and Azure IoT

These can be possible using options like pairing with Wi-Fi modules like the NodeMCU.

NodeMCU is a popular open-source IoT platform. It has a firmware running on the ESP8266 Wi-Fi SoC (System on Chip) and 32-bit processor as a hardware based on the ESP-12 module. The ESP8266 is a low-cost Wi-Fi microchip with capabilities of a microcontroller. It is useful for embedding Wi-Fi functionalities into projects. NodeMCU provides easy-to-use features and is programmable with the Arduino IDE. Refer to the datasheets in Espressif Systems for more details.

Data may be serially communicated from Arduino Mega to the NodeMCU. The NodeMCU then transmits this data to a cloud service like ThingSpeak for real-time monitoring and analysis. Here is a sample code to program the NodeMCU to transmit DHT sensor data to the cloud. It is left as an exercise to the learners to apply the serial communication between the NodeMCU and Mega to integrate the Wi-Fi. Refer to Section 4.1.1 for serial interfacing.

Know more

The DHT sensor is frequently used to measure temperature and humidity. The DHT11 model measures temperatures ranging from 0 to 50°C with an accuracy of ±2°C and humidity levels from 20 to 80% with an accuracy of ±5%. It provides a digital output via a single data wire, which can be easily read by microcontrollers such as Arduino or NodeMCU. The sensor has three pins: VCC, GND, and Data Pin.

Firstly, the DHT sensor is connected with nodeMCU. The VCC, GND and Data pin of the sensor are connected to Vin, Gnd and Pin 0 (GPIO3) of the NodeMCU respectively. The NodeMCU pinout details are available in the component datasheet.

Next, setting up a ThingSpeak account is simple and can be done using any email account. Set up a ThingSpeak channel and note down the Write API key to be used in the sketch. An example is shown in Fig. 4.33.

In order to program the NodeMCU,

- Open the Arduino IDE.
- Go to File > Preferences.
- In the "Additional Boards Manager URLs" field, add: http://arduino.esp8266.com/stable/package_esp8266com_index.json.
- Go to Tools > Board > Boards Manager and install ESP8266.
- Select the ESP8266 board from Tools > Board as shown in Fig. 4.34. The example illustrates ESP 12-E Module. Also select the respective COM port in the Tools menu, before uploading the sketch.

Fig. 4.33 Setting up ThingSpeak Channel

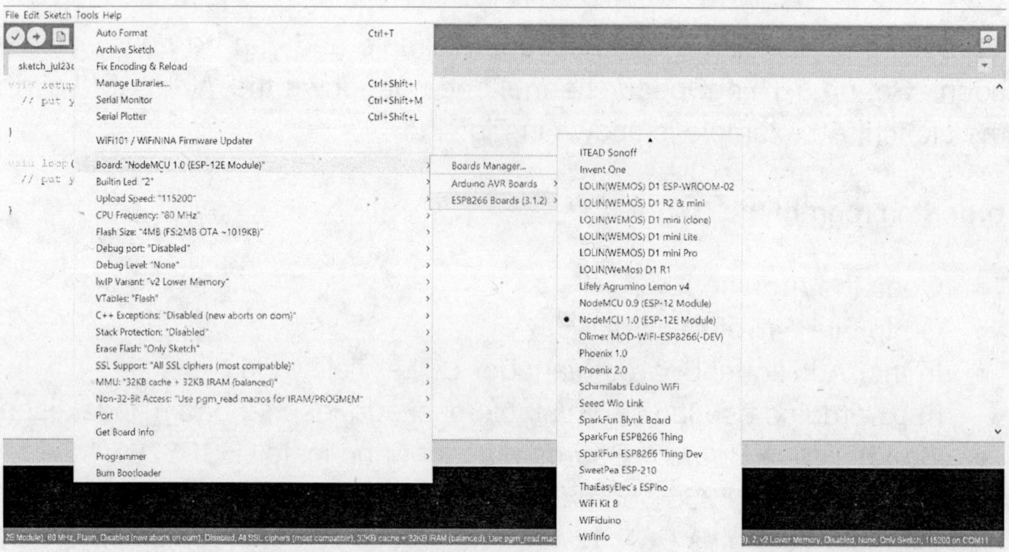

Fig. 4.34 Configuring Arduino IDE for NodeMCU - ESP 12 E

Arduino Code - NodeMCU interfacing with DHT sensor and data logging

```
#include <ESP8266WiFi.h> //header for the NodeMCU Module
#include <DHT.h>   //library for utilizing dht read functions
// Pin 0 (Digital pin D3 of NodeMCU connected to the DHT data pin
DHT sensor(0, DHT11); //DHT sensor (type DHT 11)
// Wi-Fi Network credentials
```

```
const char* ssid = "Redmi8";//Wi-Fi name
const char* pwd = "01234567";//password
// ThingSpeak settings
const char* server = "api.thingspeak.com";
const char* apiKey = "PL9UNJT9M6AYSP8K";  //API key for the channel
void setup()
{ Serial.begin(9600);
  sensor.begin();
  delay(100);
  // Connect to Wi-Fi
  Serial.println();
  Serial.print("Connecting to wifi named ");
  Serial.println(ssid);
  WiFi.begin(ssid, pwd);
  //wait for connection establishment
  while (WiFi.status() != WL_CONNECTED)
   {delay(500);
    Serial.print(".");
   }
  //print connection status
  Serial.println();
  Serial.println("WiFi connected");
  Serial.println("IP address: ");
  Serial.println(WiFi.localIP());
}
void loop() {
  // Read temperature or humidity from dht sensor
  float h = sensor.readHumidity();
  float t = sensor.readTemperature();
  // Check sensor
  if (isnan(h) || isnan(t)) {
    Serial.println("DHT sensor reading failed!");
    return;
  }
```

```
// Print to Serial Monitor
Serial.print("Temperature: ");
Serial.print(t);
Serial.print(" oC ");
Serial.print("Humidity: ");
Serial.print(h);

Serial.println(" %");
// Connect to ThingSpeak and send data
if (WiFi.status() == WL_CONNECTED)
 {
  WiFiClient client;
  if (client.connect(server, 80)) {
    //HTTP POST request header and body
    //postStr is needed to send data to the ThingSpeak server
    String postStr = apiKey;
    postStr += "&field1=";
    postStr += String(t);
    postStr += "&field2=";
    postStr += String(h);
    postStr += "\r\n\r\n";// end of header
    //http request body
    String httpRequest = "POST /update HTTP/1.1\n"
                         "Host: " + String(server) + "\n"
                         "Connection: close\n"
                       "X-THINGSPEAKAPIKEY: " + String(apiKey) + "\n
                  "Content-Type: application/x-www-form-urlencoded\n
               "Content-Length: " + String(postStr.length()) + "\n\n
                          + postStr;
    //send http protocol request
    client.print(httpRequest);
    delay(10);
    // Check for a successful connection with ThingSpeak
    if (client.connected()) {
```

```
      Serial.print("Connected to ThingSpeak\n");
      }
    client.stop();
   }
  }
  // Wait for 10 secs before sending the next data
  delay(10000);
}
```

Fig. 4.35 shows the output as shown on the Serial Monitor window. Fig. 4.36 shows the interfacing of the Wi-Fi module with the DHT sensor, and the data is logged in the ThingSpeak platform as shown in Fig. 4.37.

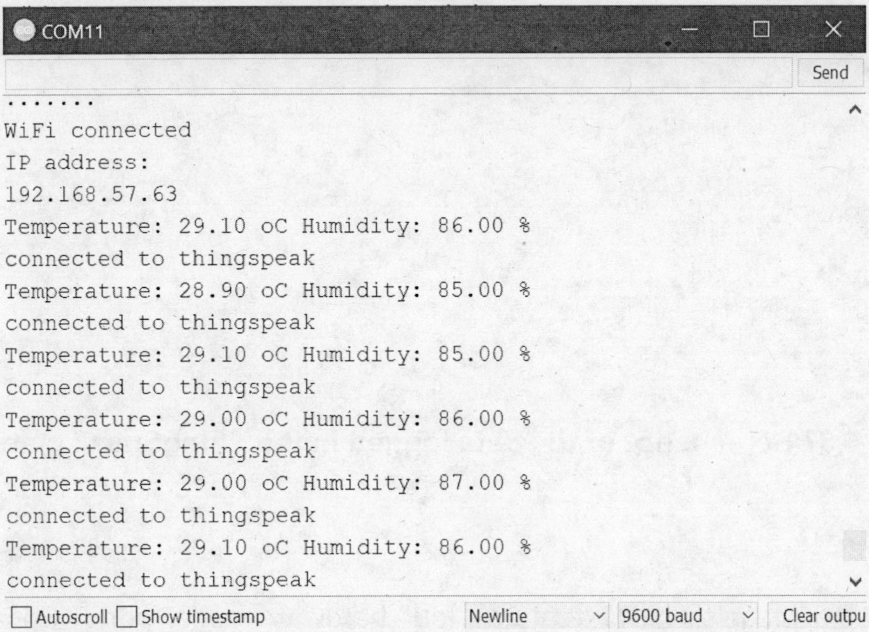

Fig. 4.35 Serial Monitor output for establishment of Wi-Fi connection, DHT sensor data displayed in serial monitor and sent to the cloud

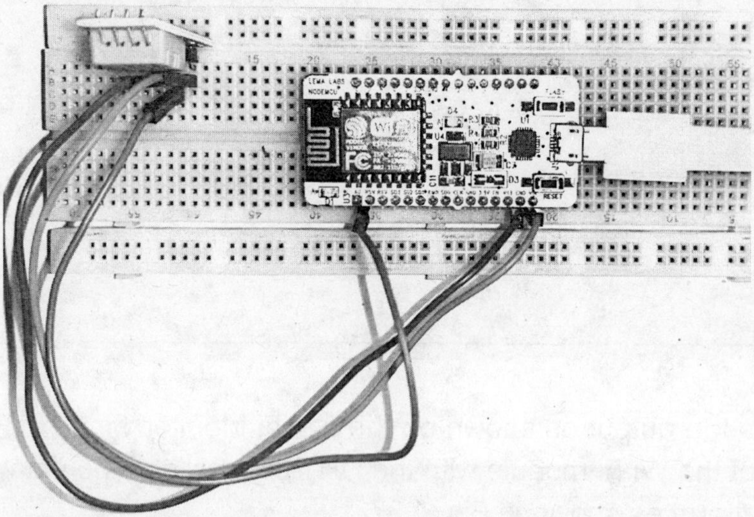

Fig. 4.36 Wi-Fi Module Interfacing with DHT Sensor

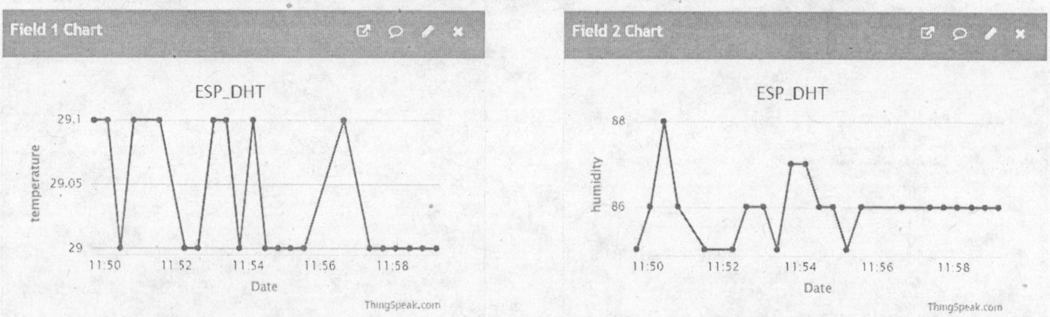

Fig. 4.37 Screenshot of the data logged in the ThingSpeak platform

Unit Recap

- Arduino Mega's **UART** features four hardware serial ports (Serial, Serial1, Serial2, Serial3), enabling multiple simultaneous serial communications.
- **SPI** uses four pins (MOSI, MISO, SCK, and SS) for high-speed communication with devices such as SD cards and sensors.
- **I2C** uses only signals (SDA - data and SCL - clock) to communicate with several devices using just two wires. I2C is frequently used for connecting sensors, displays, and EEPROMs.

- **Bluetooth** with Arduino facilitates wireless communication between Arduino and other Bluetooth-enabled devices, allowing for remote control and data exchange.
- **Motors** are actuators that transform electrical energy into mechanical motion, enabling movement and control in various applications like robotics, automation, and vehicles.
- A **keypad** is a grid of buttons designed for user input, allowing the Arduino to detect and process key presses for various applications like password verification.
- An **LDR** measures light intensities to control a relay, which can switch devices on or off based on light conditions.
- **Wi-Fi** using **NodeMCU** allows for easy wireless connectivity and communication between the NodeMCU and the internet.

Mind map - Communication Modules

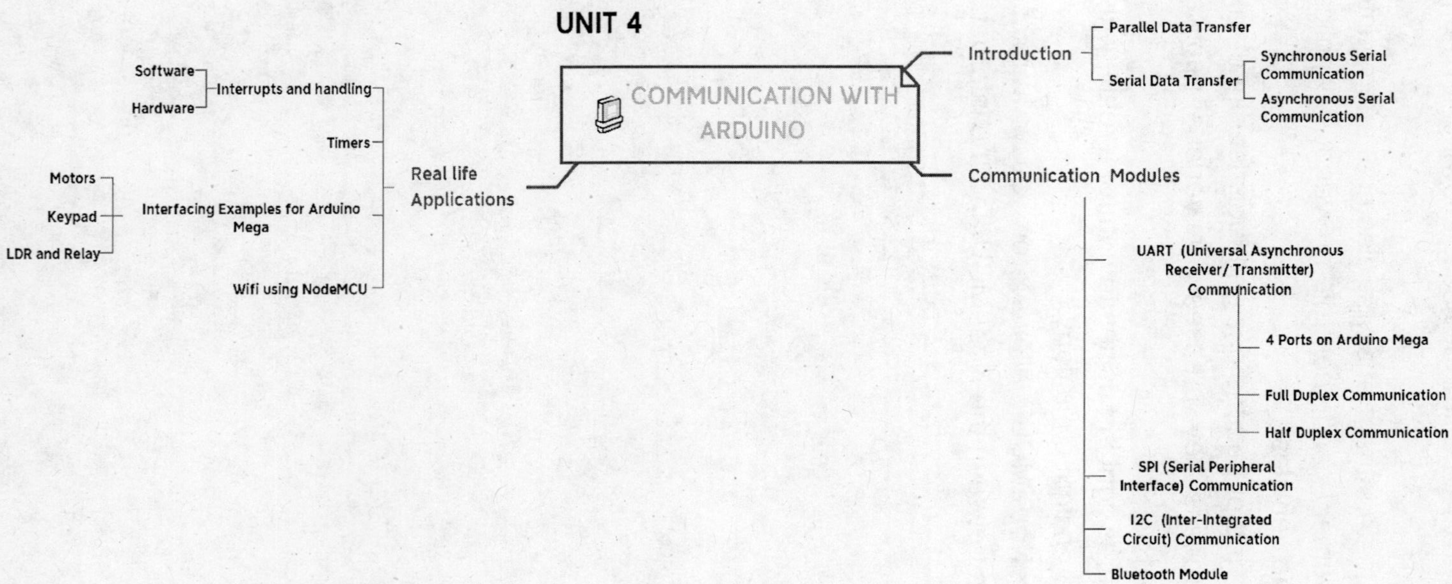

Multiple Choice Questions

1. _______________ is not a type of serial communication in Arduino.
   a. I2C
   b. SPI
   c. Digital I/Os
   d. UART
2. Which is not a standard baud rate for serial communication in Arduino?
   a. 9600
   b. 115200
   c. 57600
   d. 56700
3. UART is a slow wire, _________________________ serial communication in Arduino Mega.
   a. half duplex, synchronous
   b. full duplex, synchronous
   c. full duplex, asynchronous
   d. half duplex, asynchronous
4. Virtual ports can be configured through ____________ in an Arduino board.
   a. Digital I/O pins
   b. SoftwareSerial.h library
   c. Serial1.available
   d. Analog I/O pins
5. How many UART ports are available in Arduino Mega?
   a. 2
   b. 6
   c. 4
   d. 1
6. Which of the following statements accurately describes the difference between full duplex and half duplex communication?
   a. Full duplex permits simultaneous two-way communication, whereas half duplex permits only one-way communication at a time.
   b. Full duplex permits only one-way communication at a time, whereas half duplex permits simultaneous two-way communication.

    c. Full duplex permits communication only in one direction, whereas half duplex permits communication in both directions but not at the same time.
    d. Full duplex and half duplex are essentially the same and allow communication in both directions simultaneously.
7. Is I2C (Inter-Integrated Circuit) communication synchronous or asynchronous?
    a. Synchronous
    b. Asynchronous
    c. Neither
    d. Both
8. In a master-slave configuration, which of the following statements is true?
    a. The master device controls the communication and can initiate data transfers with one or more slave devices.
    b. The slave devices control the communication and can initiate data transfers with the master device.
    c. All devices in the master-slave configuration have equal authority to initiate communication.
    d. A one-to-one configuration is always established between the master and slave.
9. Which of the following describes the operating range and frequency of Bluetooth?
    a. Bluetooth operates at 2.4 GHz frequency range and has an effective range of up to 100 meters.
    b. Bluetooth operates at 2.4 GHz frequency range and has an effective range of up to 10 meters.
    c. Bluetooth operates at 1.8 GHz frequency range and has an effective range of up to 100 meters.
    d. Bluetooth operates at 2.0 GHz frequency range and has an effective range of up to 10 meters.
10. What does a digital potentiometer do?
    a. It stores digital data.
    b. It adjusts resistance electronically.
    c. It amplifies audio signals.
    d. It measures temperature.

11. Relay is a ______________ device.
    a. Electrically controlled switch
    b. Mechanical switch
    c. Magnetically controlled switch
    d. Electromagnetic switch
12. Number of interrupts in Arduino Mega is _________________.
    a. 13
    b. 7
    c. 6
    d. 2
13. Interrupt is recognized in both leading and trailing edge when, mode in the function attachInterrupt(digitalPinToInterrupt(pin), ISR, mode) is ________.
    a. Low to High
    b. High to Low
    c. Change
    d. None
14. Number of timers in Arduino Mega is ______________.
    a. 2
    b. 10
    c. 5
    d. 6
15. delay() is generated by ______________.
    a. Timer0
    b. Timer1
    c. Timer2
    d. Timer3

Programming Questions

1. Generate a triangular waveform using the Analog output pins.
2. Interface an LCD to display the ambient temperature.
3. Get a single digit input from the keypad and add the data until a * is pressed and displays the sum output of all the digits on seven segment LED displays.
4. Interface a sound sensor and a buzzer to alert the user if a loud noise is detected.
5. Write an Embedded C code to control a fan using a mobile phone.

Know More

QR code for all the Arduino codes used in Unit 4.

References

1. George, K., Davis, B., & Prasanna, S. R. M. (2013). *Arduino Projects For Dummies* (For Dummies Series). Wiley. ISBN: 978-1118551479
2. Nussey, J. (2013). *Arduino For Dummies*. Wiley.
3. Adafruit. (n.d.). *Learn Arduino*. Adafruit. https://learn.adafruit.com/category/learn-arduino
4. Spoken Tutorial: https://spoken-tutorial.org/tutorial-search/?search_foss=Arduino&search_language=English
5. ESP8266EX Datasheet Version 4.3 Espressif Systems IOT Team http://bbs.espressif.com/

References

Book References

1. George, K., Davis, B., & Prasanna, S. R. M. (2013). *Arduino Projects For Dummies* (For Dummies Series). Wiley. ISBN: 978-1118551479
2. Banzi, M., & Shiloh, M. (2014). *Make: Getting Started with Arduino - The Open Source Electronics Prototyping Platform* (3rd ed.). Shroff/Maker Media. ISBN: 978-9351109075
3. Nussey, J. (2013). *Arduino For Dummies*. Wiley.
4. Norris, T. (2018). *Beginning Arduino 4th Edition: A Complete Introduction to Arduino Programming*.
5. Pajankar, A. (2018). *Arduino made simple with interactive projects*. BPB Publications.
6. Schmidt, M. (2015). *Arduino: A quick-start guide* (2nd ed., illustrated). Pragmatic Bookshelf. ISBN: 1941222242, 9781941222249
7. Hughes, J. M. (2016). *Arduino: A technical reference*. O'Reilly Media, Inc. ISBN: 9781491934494
8. Wolf, W. (2008). *Computers as components: Principles of embedded computing system design*. Morgan Kaufmann Publishers.

Online Resource References

9. Arduino. (n.d.). *Arduino Mega 2560 Rev3.*, from https://docs.arduino.cc/hardware/mega-2560/
10. Sinha, B. P., & Chakrabarty, K. (2020). *Introduction to Arduino and its applications*. National Programme on Technology Enhanced Learning (NPTEL). Retrieved from https://nptel.ac.in/courses/108/108/108108124/
11. Kumar, B. V. (2019). *Microcontrollers and applications*. National Programme on Technology Enhanced Learning (NPTEL). Retrieved from https://nptel.ac.in/courses/108/108/108108098/
12. Evans, B. (2011). *Beginning Arduino programming* [eBook]. Apress. https://doi.org/10.1007/978-1-4302-3778-5

13. Adafruit. (n.d.). *Learn Arduino*. Adafruit. https://learn.adafruit.com/category/learn-arduino
14. Spoken Tutorial: https://spoken-tutorial.org/tutorial-search/?search_foss=Arduino&search_language=English
15. ESP8266EX Datasheet Version 4.3 Espressif Systems IOT Team http://bbs.espressif.com/

Other Articles for Reference

16. Deepa, M., Susithra, N., Santhanamari, G., & Reba, P. (2024). Leveraging Agile Framework for a Project Based Learning Environment in Embedded Systems Design Course. *Journal of Engineering Education Transformations*, *37*.
17. Deepa, M., Reba, P., Santhanamari, G., & Susithra, N. (2020). Enriched blended learning through virtual experience in microprocessors and microcontrollers course. *Journal of Engineering Education Transformations*, *34*(Special Issue).
18. Susithra, N., Deepa, M., Reba, P., & Santhanamari, G. (2023). Coalescing Mind Maps as a Learning Aid cum Formative Assessment Tool for Effective Teaching and Learning of Computer Architecture and Organization Course. *Journal of Engineering Education Transformations*, *36*(Special Issue 2).

Project Inspirations

The authors present a collection of problem statements for readers, whose solutions can be prototyped using Arduino and its related peripherals. These can serve as DIY (Do It Yourself) project ideas.

- **GPS Tracker:** Use an Arduino and a 'Global Positioning System' module to track a vehicle or person on maps in real time.
- **Flight Controller for Quadcopter**: Use an Arduino and sensors like accelerometer and gyroscope to change direction and speed of a quadcopter. Use additional sensors to maintain the altitude.
- **Heart rate monitor**: Use a finger pulse rate recording module to detect the pulse based on plethysmography principle.
- **Home automation:** Manage home appliances (Wi-Fi-enabled devices) wirelessly using relays and resistors.
- **Obstacle avoiding robot**: Design a robot to change its path or move away when it senses obstacles using a distance sensor driver.
- **Parking Management System:** Use proximity sensors to monitor and control parking area availability in real-time and update the same on a cloud.
- **Hall Effect Sensor (Gauss meter):** Measure magnetic fields using a Hall effect sensor and display it on an LCD screen.
- **Music Player**: Create a simple MP3 player and generate sounds using components like piezo buzzer and a resistive network based on the principle of a voltage divider circuit.
- **Brainwave-Controlled Prosthetic Arm:** Create a prosthetic arm controlled by brainwaves using a Mindwave Mobile headset to control the arm based on user thoughts to combat disability.
- **Digital Clock:** Build a digital clock using the DS1307 real-time clock chip to provide accurate time related information and print it on an LCD display screen.
- **Digital Combination Lock:** Use an Arduino and a hex keypad to control a door lock based on a numeric code.
- **Automated Gardening System:** Develop a "Garduino", an automatic gardening system to monitor the soil moisture content and atmospheric humidity with sensors and adjust watering accordingly to maintain optimal growing conditions.

The diverse range of project ideas presented demonstrates the immense potential of Arduino boards in real-time embedded systems applications. From simple home automation systems to complex robotics and real-time data monitoring, Arduino's versatility, user-friendliness, and robust forum support make it a perfect platform to experiment with and prototype a wide variety of electronic and automation projects.

Other commonly used boards for creating prototypes include:

- **Raspberry Pi:** It is an affordable single-board computer with ARM-based CPU and an operating system.
- **ESP8266/ESP32:** These boards offer built-in Wi-Fi and Bluetooth capabilities, making them suitable for IoT applications and wireless communication projects.
- **STM32:** Known for its high performance and extensive peripheral options, it is great for advanced embedded system projects.
- **BeagleBone:** Provides more processing power and expansion options, suitable for industrial and advanced computing applications.
- **PIC Microcontrollers:** Known for their reliability and extensive range of built-in peripherals, including timers, ADCs (Analog-to-Digital Converters), it is used particularly in industrial and automotive sectors, and PIC programming uses an IDE called MPLAB.
- **TI CC3200:** Texas Instruments SimpleLink CC3200 wireless microcontroller (MCU) combines a high-performance ARM Cortex-M4 core with a built-in Wi-Fi network processor. It also helps in the creation of applications based on IoT (Internet of Things).

These boards, along with Arduino, provide a varied range of capabilities for developing innovative and practical solutions for embedded systems.

Troubleshooting Q&A

1. **All the connections are done, compilation and uploading are also done. But there is no output. Why?**
   - Ensure that all connecting wires and jumper wires are securely and correctly connected. Loose or incorrect connections can cause the circuit to malfunction. Double-check each wire against the circuit diagram to confirm proper connections.
   - Check all the connecting wires/Jumper wires before using them. Faulty wires with connectivity issues/ tampered wires must be replaced. Use a multimeter to test for continuity in each wire.
   - Test each hardware component individually to ensure they are functioning correctly. For example, verify that the LED lights up when connected directly to a power source, or that the sensor produces expected readings when tested separately.
   - Display debug messages using the Serial Monitor to verify that the program runs as intended.

2. **Error "timeout communicating with programmer" or "Failed uploading: no upload port provided".**
   - Open the Device Manager, find the COM port to which the Arduino Mega is connected, and select the corresponding port in the Tools menu before uploading the sketch.

```
Sketch uses 1536 bytes (0%) of program storage space. Maximum is 253952 bytes.
Global variables use 9 bytes (0%) of dynamic memory, leaving 8183 bytes for local variables. Maximum is 8192 bytes.
Failed uploading: no upload port provided
```

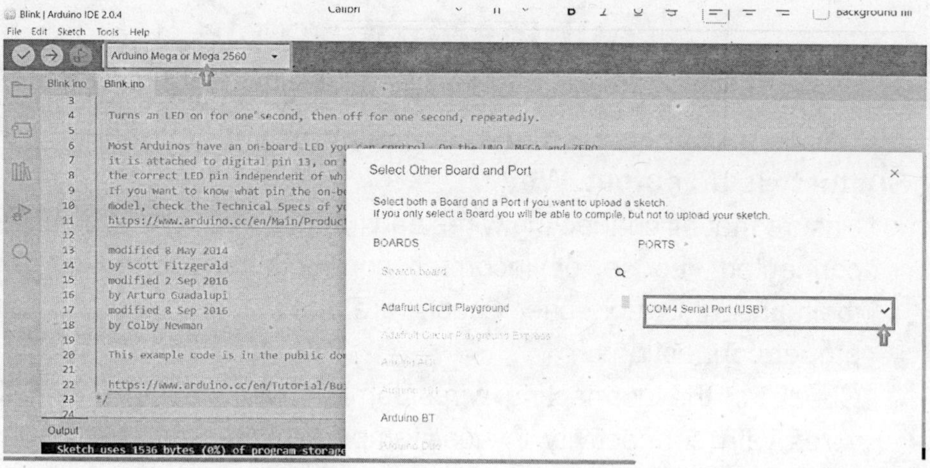

3. **Serial monitor is used to print a message. The Arduino sketch is verified and uploaded in the IDE, but the intended message is not visible on the serial monitor.**
   - Check for logical errors in placing the serial print statements. Check if the statements are executed or skipped due to any logical conditions.
   - Next, check that the same baud rate mentioned in the code in Serial.begin(xxxx) should be set in the serial monitor. Drop box to change the baud rate is available in the right corner of the serial monitor.

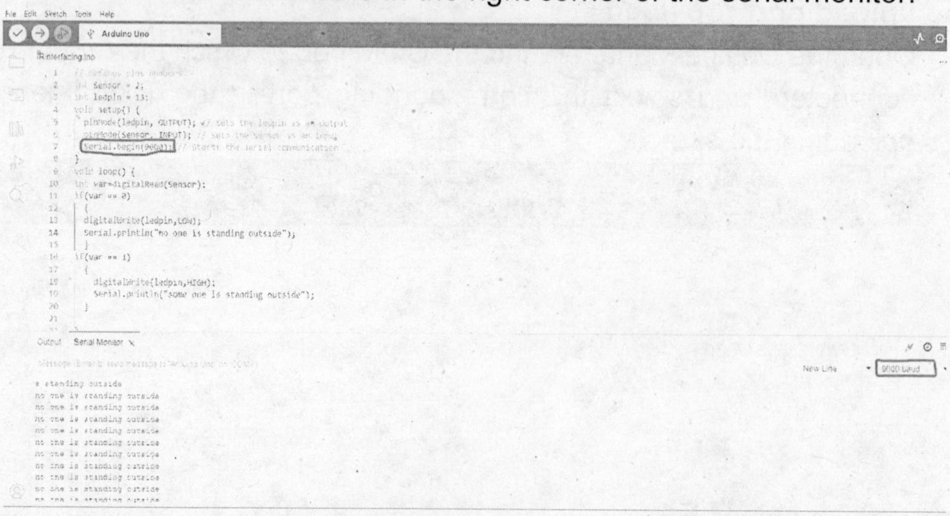

4. **The code to vary the brightness of the LED to understand the PWM operation was run. Though the LED glows, the brightness is not varied.**

The sketch is verified and uploaded in the IDE and the correct PWM pin was also used in code.

- Write the value in the LED pin as analogWrite(LED, i). If digitalWrite(LED, i), the variations cannot be seen.

5. **The seven segment LED is interfaced with Arduino Mega board, but the LED did not glow. The sketch is verified and uploaded in the IDE.**
   - Seven segment LEDs are of two different types. Common Cathode (CC) and Common Anode (CA). So, check with the data sheet and accordingly connect the common point from the seven segment LED to Vcc (CA display) or Ground (CC display) of the board.
6. **UART 0 is used for serial transmission or reception with another device/peripheral. The Personal Computer (PC) where Arduino code was run in IDE, gets hanged during execution. Why?**
   - Since UART 0 is dedicated for serial monitors to speak with PCs, that cannot be used for serial communication with another device. So virtual port (UART 1) can be configured by using #include <SoftwareSerial.h> library. Moreover, Arduino mega has 4 UART ports available for serial communication. So, any port other than UART 0 can be used for applications involving UART serial communication with devices other than the PC Monitor.
7. **UART is used for serial transmission or reception using the serial monitor. Arduino sketch is verified and uploaded in the IDE. But transmitted or received messages are not available in the serial monitor.**
   - Include delay() functions with required amount of time units, according to the baud rate used for communication to balance transmission/reception of characters between the Arduino board and the serial monitor.
8. **Timer0 is used in code for an application and causes build errors.**
   - By default, timer0 is used to execute the delay() function, which cannot be used in other applications. So other available timers can be used.
9. **When using OLED, the code is compiled and uploaded in IDE. But OLED displays just the horizontal bar lines in the display instead of given characters.**
   - The OLED supports both SSD1306 and SH1106 libraries. The correct library corresponding to the type of OLED (I2C or SPI or commercially

available) being used, should be installed from the internet sources. OLED specifications can be noted from the data sheet.

10. **When interfacing Arduino mega with IR sensor, the sketch is verified and uploaded in the IDE, but proximity is not sensed.**
    - Adjust the potentiometer on the sensor module to set the correct sensitivity. This adjustment ensures that the sensor can accurately detect proximity and provide the output as specified in the code.
11. **When a matrix keypad (4 x 4) is interfaced with Arduino mega, numbers are displayed in the serial monitor randomly, instead of row/column order.**
    - Check the keypad row and column pinouts against the datasheet or manual of the component. Pinouts may vary due to individual manufacturing defects. Verify and ensure the correct pinouts through trial and error.
12. **Sensors or other hardware components may get damaged, produce a popping sound, or burn out during testing.**
    - Check the connections and power supply before powering the circuit. Ensure that all components are properly connected and that the power supply voltage is within the recommended range for each component to prevent damage. Sometimes, careless interchange of supply and ground connections may cause irreparable damage to the board or components.

Appendices

Appendix A: List of Laboratory Experiments

S.No	Laboratory Experiment	Reference
1	Complement the state of the built-in LED whenever a push button position is changed	Refer Section 2.3.1.2
2	Built-in LED blinking by toggling states based on a) A delay function b) Output of a binary operation	Refer Section 2.2.1.2
3	Control the state of the Built-in LED using Serial Monitor interface	Refer Section 2.3.1.2 and 2.2.2.2
4	Create an interactive sketch to perform a) Boolean and bitwise operation b) Compounded operation using a serial communication	Refer Section 1.6.2.2, 1.6.2.3 and 1.6.2.4 for operations and 2.2.2.2 for interactive interface
5	Use loop to check and print the state of a push button on the serial monitor	Refer Section 2.3.1.2
6	Control multiple LEDs using a loop and an array	Refer Section 1.6.1.1 and 2.2.1.2
7	Use an analog output PWM pin to decrease the brightness of an LED	Refer Section 3.4.2.2.2
8	Use a potentiometer to control the brightness of an LED	Refer Section 3.4.2.1.2
9	Implement a simple counter to increment the count when a push button is pressed and decrement when another push button is pressed. Display the number using a 7-segment display.	Refer Section 3.4.1.2.3
10	Interface DC motor and rotate it at high speed in forward direction and low speed in reverse direction using PWM	Refer Section 4.2.3
11	Interface temperature sensor and display its reading on the serial monitor	Refer Section 4.2.5
12	Interface a 4x4 keypad and display the pressed key on the serial monitor	Refer Section 4.2.4
13	Interface an OLED using I2C protocol and display a message based on the input received from user	Refer Section 4.1.3.1

Appendix B: Answers for MCQs

Unit 1	
1	d) Open-source electronics platform
2	c) Editor->Compiler->Preprocessor
3	c) No cost limit
4	c) Serial Monitor
5	a) Removing the line *"Serial.println ("Welcome home");"* from the void setup and transferring it to the void loop.
6	d) 2 (bytes)
7	b) Loop
8	d) Sketch
9	b) Programmer
10	a) Peripherals
Unit 2	
1	a) Avoid repetition of code
2	a) for (initialization; condition; increment) { statements }
3	b) do-while loop
4	b) Help Help Help
5	a) The case that is executed when none of the other cases match the switch expression.
6	a) The else block executes only if the condition in the if block is false.
7	d) All the cases below the selected case, including the default case will be executed
8	b) Prints the data and then goes to the next line

9	d) 5 4 3 2 1
10	c) LED is switched OFF
Unit 3	
1	d) 5 V
2	d) 4
3	b) 54, 16, 15
4	c) 16 MHz
5	b) Port F
6	c) Floating
7	a) 0 to 1023
8	c) ICSP
9	b) analogWrite
10	c) (0.1n)s
11	d) 34cm
12	a) cm.The value of x is:4
13	c) Trimpot
14	b) A-H, B-F, C-G, D-E
Unit 4	
1	c) Digital I/Os
2	d) 56700
3	c) full duplex, asynchronous
4	b) SoftwareSerial.h library

5	c) 4
6	a) Full duplex permits simultaneous two-way communication, whereas half duplex permits only one-way communication at a time.
7	a) Synchronous
8	a) The master device controls the communication and can initiate data transfers with one or more slave devices.
9	a) Bluetooth operates at 2.4 GHz frequency range and has an effective range of up to 100 meters.
10	b) It adjusts resistance electronically.
11	d) Electromagnetic switch
12	c) 6
13	c) Change
14	d) 6
15	a) Timer0

Appendix C: Arduino® Mega 2560 Rev3 Data sheet

Arduino® Mega 2560 Rev3

Product Reference Manual
SKU: A000067

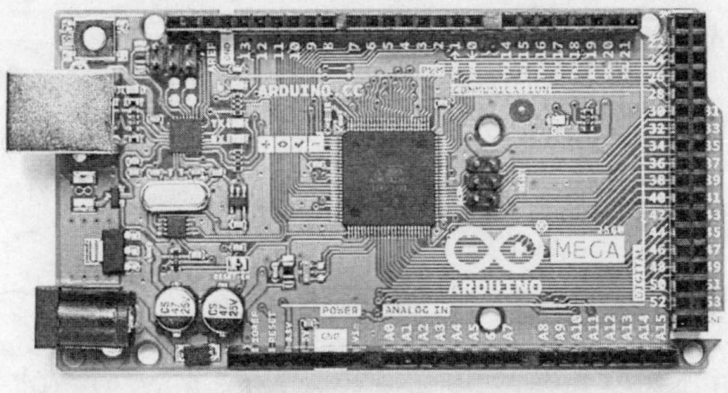

Description

Arduino® Mega 2560 Rev3 is an exemplary development board dedicated for building extensive applications as compared to other maker boards by Arduino. The board accommodates the ATmega2560 microcontroller, which operates at a frequency of 16 MHz. The board contains 54 digital input/output pins, 16 analog inputs, 4 UARTs (hardware serial ports), a USB connection, a power jack, an ICSP header, and a reset button.

Target Areas

3D Printing, Robotics, Maker

Features

a. **ATmega2560 Processor**
- Up to 16 MIPS Throughput at 16MHz
- 256k bytes (of which 8k is used for the bootloader)
- 4k bytes EEPROM
- 8k bytes Internal SRAM
- 32 × 8 General Purpose Working Registers
- Real Time Counter with Separate Oscillator
- Four 8-bit PWM Channels
- Four Programmable Serial USART
- Controller/Peripheral SPI Serial Interface

b. **ATmega16U2**
- Up to 16 MIPS Throughput at 16 MHz
- 16k bytes ISP Flash Memory
- 512 bytes EEPROM
- 512 bytes SRAM
- USART with SPI master only mode and hardware flow control (RTS/CTS) Master/Slave SPI Serial Interface

c. **Sleep Modes**
- Idle
- ADC Noise Reduction
- Power-save
- Power-down
- Standby
- Extended Standby

d. **Power**
- USB Connection
- External AC/DC Adapter

e. **IO**
- 54 Digital
- 16 Analog
- 15 PWM Output

1 The Board

Mega 2560 Rev3 is a successor board of Arduino Mega, it is dedicated to applications and projects that require large number of input output pins and the use cases which need high processing power. The Mega 2560 Rev3 comes with a much larger set of IOs when we compare it with the traditional Arduino® UNO board considering the form factor of both the boards.

1.1 Application Examples

- **Robotics**: Featuring the high processing capacity, the Mega 2560 Rev3 can handle the extensive robotic applications. It is compatible with the motor controller shield that enables it to control multiple motors at an instance, thus making it perfect of robotic applications. The large number of I/O pins can accommodate many robotic sensors as well.
- **3D Printing**: Algorithms play a significant role in implementation of 3D printers. Mega 2560 Rev3 has the power to process these complex algorithms required for 3D printing. Additionally, the slight changes to the code is easily possible with the Arduino IDE and thus 3D printing programs can be customized according to user requirements.
- **Wi-Fi**: Integrating wireless functionality enhances the utility of the applications. Mega 2560 Rev3 is compatible with Wi-Fi® shields hence allowing the wireless features for the applications in 3D printing and Robotics.

1.2 Related Products

- Arduino® UNO R3
- Arduino® Nano
- Arduino® Due without headers

2 Ratings

2.1 Recommended Operating Conditions

U{ o dqn	Fguetkrvkqp	Okp	V{r	Ocz	Wpkv
VIN	Input voltage from VIN pad / DC Jack	7	7.0	12	V
VUSB	Input voltage from USB connector	4.8	5.0	5.5	V
TOP	Operating Temperature	-40	25	85	°C

3 Functional Overview

3.1 Block Diagram

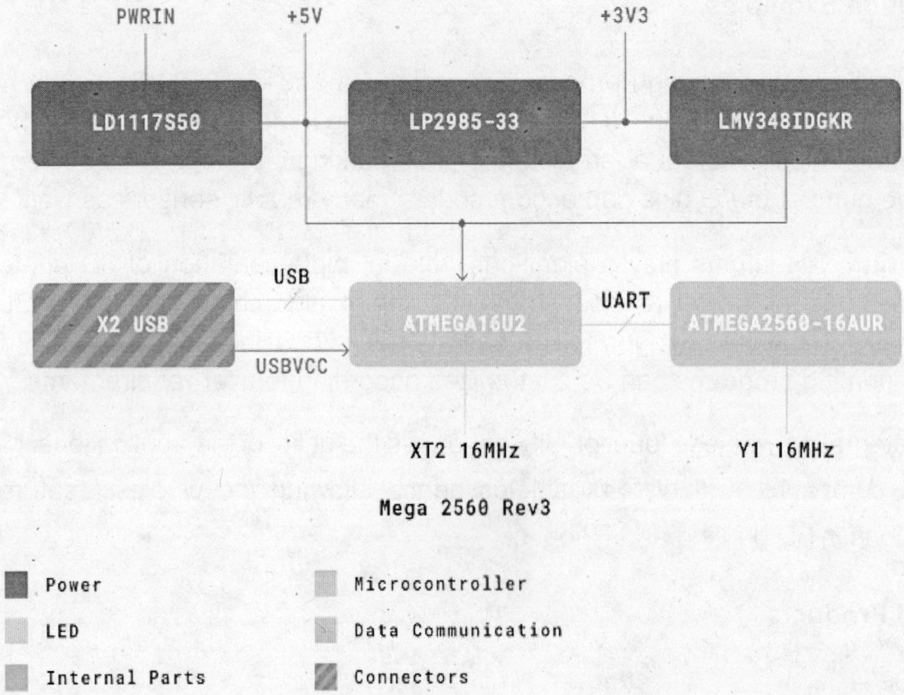

Arduino Mega 2560 Rev3 Block Diagram

3.2 Board Topology

Front View

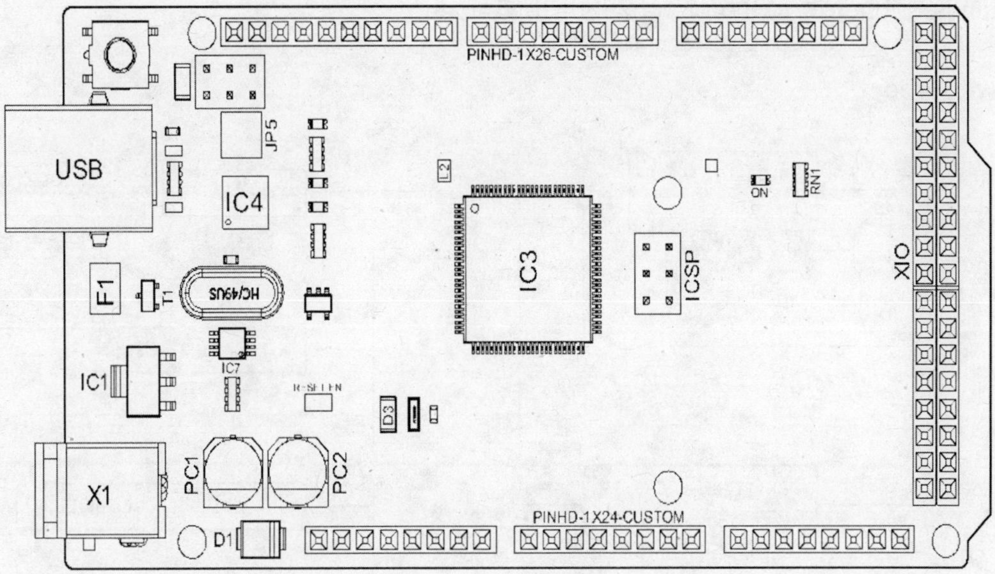

Arduino Mega 2560 Rev3 Top View

Ref.	Description	Ref.	Description
USB	USB B Connector	F1	Chip Capacitor
IC1	5V Linear Regulator	X1	Power Jack Connector
JP5	Plated Holes	IC4	ATmega16U2 chip
PC1	Electrolytic Alumninum Capacitor	PC2	Electrolytic Alumninum Capacitor
D1	General Purpose Rectifier	D3	General Purpose Diode
L2	Fixed Inductor	IC3	ATmega2560 chip
ICSP	Connector Header	ON	Green LED
RN1	Resistor Array	XIO	Connector

3.3 Processor

Primary processor of Mega 2560 Rev3 board is ATmega2560 chip which operates at a frequency of 16 MHz. It accommodates a large number of input and output lines which gives the provision of interfacing many external devices. At the same time the operations and processing are not slowed due to its significantly larger RAM than the other processors. The board also features a USB serial processor ATmega16U2 which acts an interface between the USB input signals and the main processor. This increases the flexibility of interfacing and connecting peripherals to the Mega 2560 Rev3 board.

3.4 Power Tree

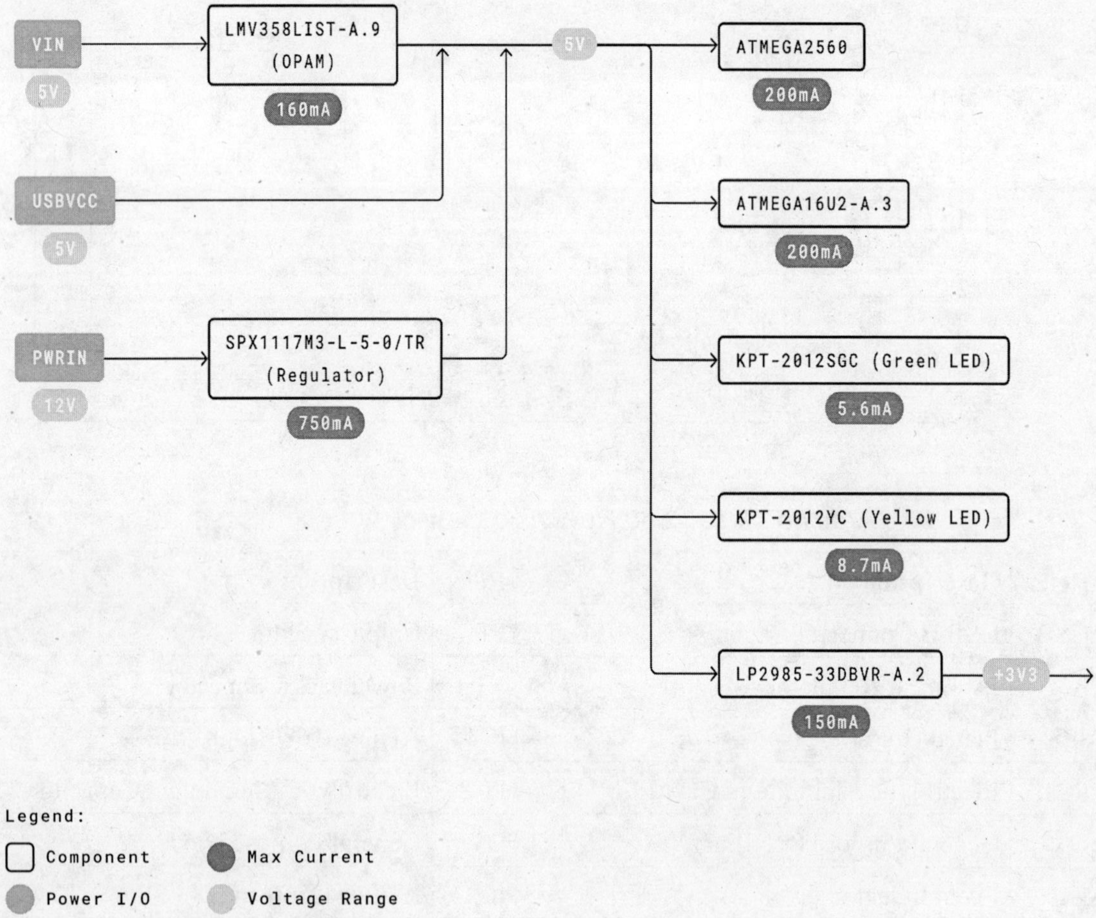

Power Tree

4 Board Operation

4.1 Getting Started - IDE

If you want to program your Mega 2560 Rev3 while offline you need to install the Arduino Desktop IDE. To connect the Mega 2560 Rev3 to your computer, you'll need a Type-B USB cable. This also provides power to the board, as indicated by the LED.

4.2 Getting Started - Arduino Cloud Editor

All Arduino boards, including this one, work out-of-the-box on the Arduino Cloud Editor, by just installing a simple plugin.
The Arduino Cloud Editor is hosted online; therefore, it will always be up-to-date with the latest features and support for all boards. To start coding on the browser and upload your sketches onto your board.

4.3 Sample Sketches

Sample sketches for the Mega 2560 Rev3 can be found either in the "Examples" menu in the Arduino IDE or under the "Documentation" menu on the Arduino website.

4.4 Online Resources

Now that you have gone through the basics of what you can do with the board you can explore the endless possibilities it provides by checking exciting projects on Arduino Project Hub, the Arduino Library Reference and the online store where you will be able to complement your board with sensors, actuators and more.

5 Connector Pinouts

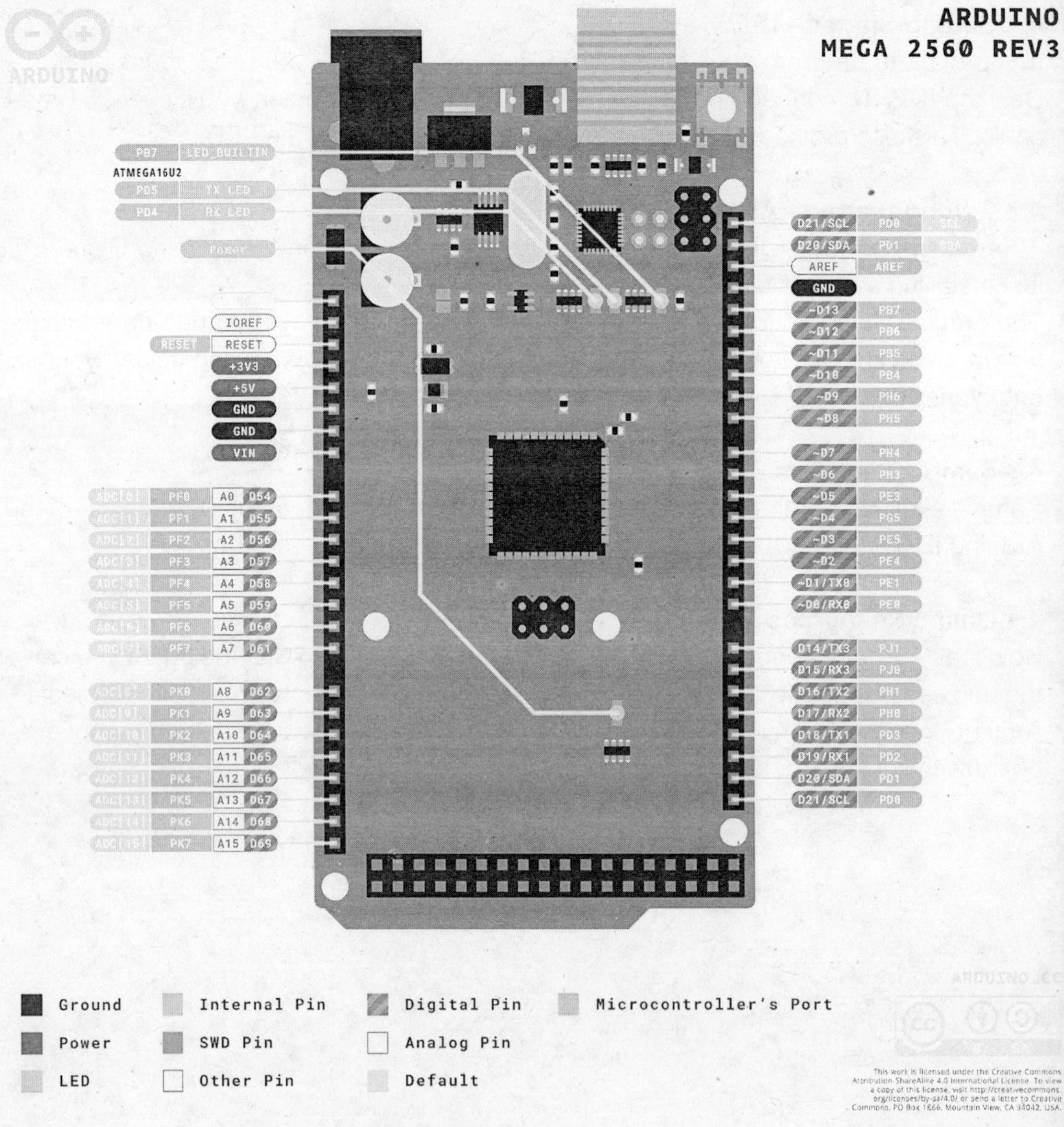

Arduino Mega 2560 Rev3 Pinout

5.1 Analog

Pin	Function	Type	Description
1	NC	NC	Not Connected
2	IOREF	IOREF	Reference for digital logic V - connected to 5V
3	Reset	Reset	Reset
4	+3V3	Power	+3V3 Power Rail
5	+5V	Power	+5V Power Rail
6	GND	Power	Ground
7	GND	Power	Ground
8	VIN	Power	Voltage Input
9	A0	Analog	Analog input 0 /GPIO
10	A1	Analog	Analog input 1 /GPIO
11	A2	Analog	Analog input 2 /GPIO
12	A3	Analog	Analog input 3 /GPIO
13	A4	Analog	Analog input 4 /GPIO
14	A5	Analog	Analog input 5 /GPIO
15	A6	Analog	Analog input 6 /GPIO
16	A7	Analog	Analog input 7 /GPIO
17	A8	Analog	Analog input 8 /GPIO
18	A9	Analog	Analog input 9 /GPIO
19	A10	Analog	Analog input 10 /GPIO
20	A11	Analog	Analog input 11 /GPIO
21	A12	Analog	Analog input 12 /GPIO
22	A13	Analog	Analog input 13 /GPIO
23	A14	Analog	Analog input 14 /GPIO
24	A15	Analog	Analog input 15 /GPIO

5.2 Digital

Pin	Function	Type	Description
1	D21/SCL	Digital Input/I2C	Digital input 21/I2C Dataline
2	D20/SDA	Digital Input/I2C	Digital input 20/I2C Dataline
3	AREF	Digital	Analog Reference Voltage
4	GND	Power	Ground
5	D13	Digital/GPIO	Digital input 13/GPIO
6	D12	Digital/GPIO	Digital input 12/GPIO
7	D11	Digital/GPIO	Digital input 11/GPIO
8	D10	Digital/GPIO	Digital input 10/GPIO
9	D9	Digital/GPIO	Digital input 9/GPIO
10	D8	Digital/GPIO	Digital input 8/GPIO
11	D7	Digital/GPIO	Digital input 7/GPIO
12	D6	Digital/GPIO	Digital input 6/GPIO
13	D5	Digital/GPIO	Digital input 5/GPIO
14	D4	Digital/GPIO	Digital input 4/GPIO
15	D3	Digital/GPIO	Digital input 3/GPIO
16	D2	Digital/GPIO	Digital input 2/GPIO
17	D1/TX0	Digital/GPIO	Digital input 1 /GPIO
18	D0/Tx1	Digital/GPIO	Digital input 0 /GPIO
19	D14	Digital/GPIO	Digital input 14 /GPIO
20	D15	Digital/GPIO	Digital input 15 /GPIO
21	D16	Digital/GPIO	Digital input 16 /GPIO
22	D17	Digital/GPIO	Digital input 17 /GPIO
23	D18	Digital/GPIO	Digital input 18 /GPIO
24	D19	Digital/GPIO	Digital input 19 /GPIO
25	D20	Digital/GPIO	Digital input 20 /GPIO
26	D21	Digital/GPIO	Digital input 21 /GPIO

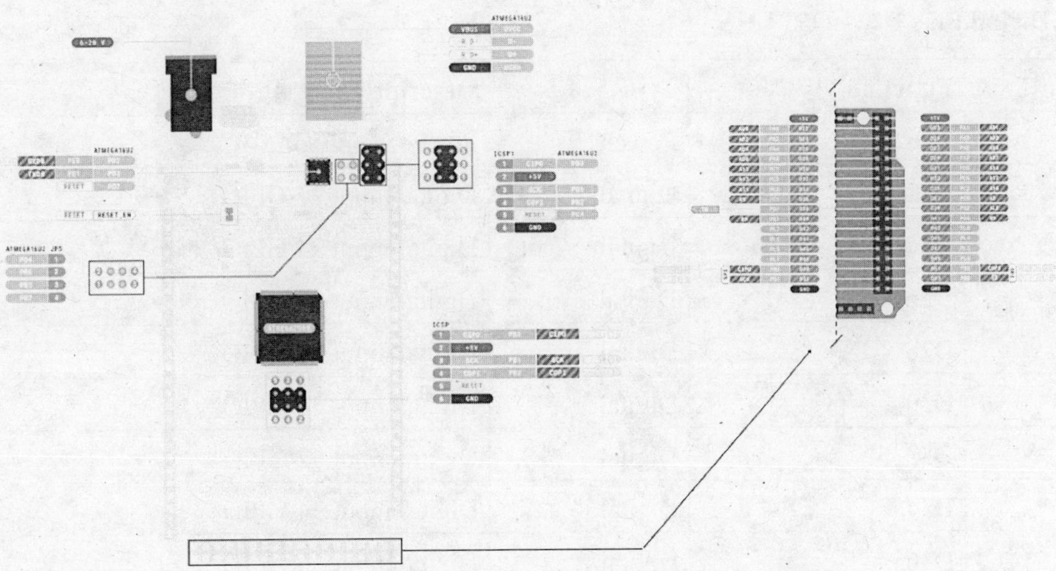

Arduino Mega 2560 Rev3 Pinout

5.3 ATMEGA16U2 JP5

Pin	Function	Type	Description
1	PB4	Internal	Serial Wire Debug
2	PB6	Internal	Serial Wire Debug
3	PB5	Internal	Serial Wire Debug
4	PB7	Internal	Serial Wire Debug

5.4 ATMEGA16U2 ICSP1

Pin	Function	Type	Description
1	CIPO	Internal	Controller In Peripheral Out
2	+5V	Internal	Power Supply of 5V
3	SCK	Internal	Serial Clock
4	COPI	Internal	Controller Out Peripheral In
5	RESET	Internal	Reset
6	GND	Internal	Ground

5.5 Digital Pins D22 - D53 LHS

Pin	Function	Type	Description
1	+5V	Power	Power Supply of 5V
2	D22	Digital	Digital input 22/GPIO
3	D24	Digital	Digital input 24/GPIO
4	D26	Digital	Digital input 26/GPIO
5	D28	Digital	Digital input 28/GPIO
6	D30	Digital	Digital input 30/GPIO
7	D32	Digital	Digital input 32/GPIO
8	D34	Digital	Digital input 34/GPIO
9	D36	Digital	Digital input 36/GPIO
10	D38	Digital	Digital input 38/GPIO
11	D40	Digital	Digital input 40/GPIO
12	D42	Digital	Digital input 42/GPIO
13	D44	Digital	Digital input 44/GPIO
14	D46	Digital	Digital input 46/GPIO
15	D48	Digital	Digital input 48/GPIO
16	D50	Digital	Digital input 50/GPIO
17	D52	Digital	Digital input 52/GPIO
18	GND	Power	Ground

5.6 Digital Pins D22 - D53 RHS

Rkp	Hwpevkqp	V{r g	F guetkr vkqp
1	+5V	Power	Power Supply of 5V
2	D23	Digital	Digital input 23/GPIO
3	D25	Digital	Digital input 25/GPIO
4	D27	Digital	Digital input 27/GPIO
5	D29	Digital	Digital input 29/GPIO
6	D31	Digital	Digital input 31/GPIO
7	D33	Digital	Digital input 33GPIO
8	D35	Digital	Digital input 35/GPIO
9	D37	Digital	Digital input 37/GPIO
10	D39	Digital	Digital input 39/GPIO
11	D41	Digital	Digital input 41/GPIO
12	D43	Digital	Digital input 43/GPIO
13	D45	Digital	Digital input 45/GPIO
14	D47	Digital	Digital input 47/GPIO
15	D49	Digital	Digital input 49/GPIO
16	D51	Digital	Digital input 51/GPIO
17	D53	Digital	Digital input 53/GPIO
18	GND	Power	Ground

CO and PO Attainment Table

Course outcomes (COs) for this course can be mapped with the programme outcomes (POs) after the completion of the course and a correlation can be made for the attainment of POs to analyze the gap. After proper analysis of the gap in the attainment of POs necessary measures can be taken to overcome the gaps.

Table for CO and PO attainment

Course Outcomes	**Attainment of Programme Outcomes** *(1- Weak Correlation; 2- Medium correlation; 3- Strong Correlation)*						
	PO-1	**PO-2**	**PO-3**	**PO-4**	**PO-5**	**PO-6**	**PO-7**
CO-1							
CO-2							
CO-3							
CO-4							
CO-5							

Index